A VISION

W. B. YEATS, 1907

From an etching by Augustus John, R. A.

A Vision

W. B. YEATS

A REISSUE WITH THE AUTHOR'S

FINAL REVISIONS

COLLIER BOOKS

NEW YORK

CONTENTS

CONTENTS

ILLUSTRATIONS

A PACKET FOR EZRA POUND

RAPALLO

I

MOUNTAINS that shelter the bay from all but the south wind, bare brown branches of low vines and of tall trees blurring their outline as though ,with a soft mist; houses mirrored in an almost motionless sea; a verandahed gable a couple of miles away bringing to mind some Chinese painting. Rapallo's thin line of broken mother-of-pearl along the water's edge. The little town described in the *Ode on a Grecian Urn*. In what better place could I, forbidden Dublin winters and all excited crowded places, spend what winters yet remain? On the broad pavement by the sea pass Italian peasants or working people, people out of the little shops, a famous German dramatist, the barber's brother looking like an Oxford don, a British retired skipper, an Italian prince descended from Charlemagne and no richer than the rest of us, a few tourists seeking tranquillity. As there is no great harbour full of yachts, no great yellow strand, no great ballroom, no great casino, the rich carry elsewhere their strenuous lives.

II

I shall not lack conversation. Ezra Pound, whose art is the opposite of mine, whose criticism commends what I most condemn, a man with whom I should quarrel more than with anyone else if we were not united by affection, has for years lived in rooms open-

ing on to a flat roof by the sea. For the last hour we
have sat upon the roof which is also a garden, discussing
that immense poem of which but seven and twenty
cantos are already published.[1] I have often found there
brightly printed kings, queens, knaves, but have never
discovered why all the suits could not be dealt out in
some quite different order. Now at last he explains that
it will, when the hundredth canto is finished, display a
structure like that of a Bach Fugue. There will be no
plot, no chronicle of events, no logic of discourse, but two
themes, the Descent into Hades from Homer, a Metamorphosis from Ovid, and, mixed with these, mediaeval or modern historical characters. He has tried to
produce that picture Porteous commended to Nicholas
Poussin in *Le chef d'œuvre inconnu* where everything
rounds or thrusts itself without edges, without con-
tours—conventions of the intellect—from a splash of
tints and shades; to achieve a work as characteristic
of the art[2] of our time as the paintings of Cézanne,
avowedly suggested by Porteous, as *Ulysses* and its
dream association of words and images, a poem in which
there is nothing that can be taken out and reasoned
over, nothing that is not a part of the poem itself. He

---

[1] There are now forty-nine.
[2] Mr. Wyndham Lewis, whose criticism sounds true to a man of
my generation, attacks this art in *Time and Western Man*. If we reject, he argues, the forms and categories of the intellect there is
nothing left but sensation, "eternal flux". Yet all such rejections
stop at the conscious mind, for as Dean Swift says in a meditation
on a woman who paints a dying face,

> Matter as wise logicians say
> Cannot without a form subsist;
> And form, say I as well as they,
> Must fail, if matter brings no grist.

has scribbled on the back of an envelope certain sets of letters that represent emotions or archetypal events—I cannot find any adequate definition—A B C D and then J K L M, and then each set of letters repeated, and then A B C D inverted and this repeated, and then a new element X Y Z, then certain letters that never recur, and then all sorts of combinations of X Y Z and J K L M and A B C D and D C B A, and all set whirling together. He has shown me upon the wall a photograph of a Cosimo Tura decoration in three compartments, in the upper the Triumph of Love and the Triumph of Chastity, in the middle Zodiacal signs, and in the lower certain events in Cosimo Tura's day. The Descent and the Metamorphosis—A B C D and J K L M—his fixed elements, took the place of the Zodiac, the archetypal persons—X Y Z—that of the Triumphs, and certain modern events—his letters that do not recur—that of those events in Cosimo Tura's day.

I may, now that I have recovered leisure, find that the mathematical structure, when taken up into imagination, is more than mathematical, that seemingly irrelevant details fit together into a single theme, that here is no botch of tone and colour, all Hodos Chameliontos, except for some odd corner where one discovers beautiful detail like that finely modelled foot in Porteous' disastrous picture.

III

Sometimes about ten o'clock at night I accompany him to a street where there are hotels upon one side, upon the other palm-trees and the sea, and there, taking out of his pocket bones and pieces of meat, he begins to call the cats. He knows all their histories—the brindled cat looked like a skeleton until he began to feed it; that fat grey cat is an hotel proprietor's favourite, it never begs from the guests' tables and it turns cats that do not belong to the hotel out of the garden; this black cat and that grey cat over there fought on the roof of a four-storied house some weeks ago, fell off, a whirling ball of claws and fur, and now avoid each other. Yet now that I recall the scene I think that he has no affection for cats—"some of them so ungrateful", a friend says—he never nurses the café cat, I cannot imagine him with a cat of his own. Cats are oppressed, dogs terrify them, landladies starve them, boys stone them, everybody speaks of them with contempt. If they were human beings we could talk of their oppressors with a studied violence, add our strength to theirs, even organise the oppressed and like good politicians sell our charity for power. I examine his criticism in this new light, his praise of writers pursued by ill-luck, left maimed or bedridden by the War; and thereupon recall a person as unlike him as possible, the only friend who remains to me from late boyhood, grown gaunt in the injustice of what seems her blind nobility of pity: "I will fight until I die", she wrote to me once, "against the cruelty of small ambitions". Was this pity a characteristic of his generation that has survived the Romantic Move-ment, and of mine and hers that saw it die—I too a revolutionist—some drop of hysteria still at the bottom of the cup?

IV

I have been wondering if I shall go to church and seek the company of the English in the villas. At Ox-ford I went constantly to All Souls Chapel, though never at service time, and parts of *A Vision* were thought out there. In Dublin I went to Saint Patrick's and sat there, but it was far off; and once I remember saying to a friend as we came out of Sant' Ambrogio at Milan, "That is my tradition and I will let no priest rob me". I have sometimes wondered if it was but a timidity come from long disuse that keeps me from the service, and yesterday as I was wondering for the hundredth time, seated in a café by the sea, I heard an English voice say: "Our new Devil-dodger is not so bad. I have been practising with his choir all afternoon. We sang hymns and then God Save the King, more hymns and He's a Jolly Good Fellow. We were at the hotel at the end of the esplanade where they have the best beer." I am too anaemic for so British a faith; I shall haunt empty churches and be satisfied with Ezra Pound's society and that of his travelling Americans.

V

All that is laborious or mechanical in my book is finished; what remains can be added as a momentary rest from writing verse. It must be this thought of a burden dropped that made me think of attending church, if it is not that these mountains under their brilliant light fill me with an emotion that is like gratitude. Descartes went on pilgrimage to some shrine of the Virgin when he made his first philosophical discovery, and the mountain road from Rapallo to Zoagli seems like something in my own mind, something that I have discovered.

March and October 1928

INTRODUCTION TO "A VISION"

> "This way of publishing introductions to books, that are God knows when to come out, is either wholly new, or so long in practice that my small reading cannot trace it."—SWIFT.

I

THE other day Lady Gregory said to me: "You are a much better educated man than you were ten years ago and much more powerful in argument". And I put *The Tower* and *The Winding Stair* into evidence to show that my poetry has gained in self-possession and power. I owe this change to an incredible experience.

II

On the afternoon of October 24th 1917, four days after my marriage, my wife surprised me by attempting automatic writing. What came in disjointed sentences, in almost illegible writing, was so exciting, sometimes so profound, that I persuaded her to give an hour or two day after day to the unknown writer, and after some half-dozen such hours offered to spend what remained of life explaining and piecing together those scattered sentences. "No," was the answer, "we have come to give you metaphors for poetry." The unknown writer took his theme at first from my just published *Per Amica Silentia Lunae*. I had made a distinction between the perfection that is from a man's combat with himself and that which is from a combat with circumstance, and upon this simple distinction he built up an

8

elaborate classification of men according to their more or less complete expression of one type or the other. He supported his classification by a series of geometrical symbols and put these symbols in an order that answered the question in my essay as to whether some prophet could not prick upon the calendar the birth of a Napoleon or a Christ. A system of symbolism, strange to my wife and to myself, certainly awaited expression, and when I asked how long that would take I was told years. Sometimes when my mind strays back to those first days I remember that Browning's Paracelsus did not obtain the secret until he had written his spiritual history at the bidding of his Byzantine teacher, that before initiation Wilhelm Meister read his own history written by another, and I compare my *Per Amica* to those histories.

III

When the automatic writing began we were in a hotel on the edge of Ashdown Forest, but soon returned to Ireland and spent much of 1918 at Glendalough, at Rosses Point, at Coole Park, at a house near it, at Thoor Ballylee, always more or less solitary, my wife bored and fatigued by her almost daily task and I thinking and talking of little else. Early in 1919 the communicator of the moment—they were constantly changed—said they would soon change the method from the written to the spoken word as that would fatigue her less, but the change did not come for some months. I was on a lecturing tour in America to earn a roof for Thoor Ballylee when it came. We had one of those little sleeping compartments in a train, with two berths, and were somewhere in Southern California. My wife, who

had been asleep for some minutes, began to talk in her
sleep, and from that on almost all communications
came in that way. My teachers did not seem to speak
out of her sleep but as if from above it, as though it
were a tide upon which they floated. A chance word
spoken before she fell asleep would sometimes start a
dream that broke in upon the communications, as if
from below, to trouble or overwhelm, as when she
dreamed she was a cat lapping milk or a cat curled up
asleep and therefore dumb. The cat returned night after
night, and once when I tried to drive it away by making
the sound one makes when playing at being a dog
to amuse a child, she awoke trembling, and the shock
was so violent that I never dared repeat it. It was
plain therefore that, though the communicators' critical
powers were awake, hers slept, or that she was aware
of the idea the sound suggested but not of the sound.

IV

Whenever I received a certain signal (I will explain
what it was later), I would get pencil and paper ready.
After they had entranced my wife suddenly when sitting in a chair, I suggested that she must always be
lying down before they put her to sleep. They seemed
ignorant of our surroundings and might have done so
at some inconvenient time or place; once when they
had given their signal in a restaurant they explained
that because we had spoken of a garden they had
thought we were in it. Except at the start of a new topic,
when they would speak or write a dozen sentences un-
questioned, I had always to question, and every question
to rise out of a previous answer and to deal with their

chosen topic. My questions must be accurately worded, and, because they said their thought was swifter than ours, asked without delay or hesitation. I was constantly reproved for vague or confused questions, yet I could do no better, because, though it was plain from the first that their exposition was based upon a single geometrical conception, they kept me from mastering that conception. They shifted ground whenever my interest was at its height, whenever it seemed that the next day must reveal what, as I soon discovered, they were determined to withhold until all was upon paper. November 1917 had been given to an exposition of the twenty-eight typical incarnations or phases and to the movements of their *Four Faculties*, and then on December 6th a cone or gyre had been drawn and related to the soul's judgment after death; and then just as I was about to discover that incarnations and judgment alike implied cones or gyres, one within the other, turning in opposite directions, two such cones were drawn and related neither to judgment nor to incarnations but to European history. They drew their first symbolical map of that history, and marked upon it the principal years of crisis, early in July 1918, some days before the publication of the first German edition of Spengler's *Decline of the West*, which, though founded upon a different philosophy, gives the same years of crisis and draws the same general conclusions, and then returned to the soul's judgment. I believe that they so changed their theme because, had I grasped their central idea, I would have lacked the patience and the curiosity to follow their application of it, preferring some hasty application of my own. They once told me not to speak of any part of the system, except of the incarnations which were almost fully expounded, because if I did the people I talked to would talk to other people, and the communicators would mistake that misunderstanding for their own thought.

V

For the same reason they asked me not to read philosophy until their exposition was complete, and this increased my difficulties. Apart from two or three of the principal Platonic Dialogues I knew no philosophy. Arguments with my father, whose convictions had been formed by John Stuart Mill's attack upon Sir William Hamilton, had destroyed my confidence and driven me from speculation to the direct experience of the Mystics. I had once known Blake as thoroughly as his unfinished confused Prophetic Books permitted, and I had read Swedenborg and Boehme, and my initiation into the "Hermetic Students" had filled my head with Cabbalistic imagery, but there was nothing in Blake, Swedenborg, Boehme or the Cabbala to help me now. They encouraged me, however, to read history in relation to their historical logic, and biography in relation to their twenty-eight typical incarnations, that I might give concrete expression to their abstract thought. I read with an excitement I had not known since I was a boy with all knowledge before me, and made continual discoveries, and if my mind returned too soon to their unmixed abstraction they would say, "We are starved".

VI

Because they must, as they explained, soon finish, others whom they named Frustrators attempted to confuse us or waste time. Who these Frustrators were or why they acted so was never adequately explained, nor will be unless I can finish "The Soul in Judgment" (Book III of this work), but they were always ingenious and sometimes cruel. The automatic script would deteriorate, grow sentimental or confused, and when I pointed this out the communicator would say, "From such and such an hour, on such and such a day, all is frustration". I would spread out the script and he would cross all out back to the answer that began it, but had I not divined frustration he would have said nothing. Was he constrained by a drama which was part of conditions that made communication possible, was that drama itself part of the communication, had my question to be asked before his mind cleared? Only once did he break the rule and without waiting for a question declare some three or four days' work frustration. A predecessor of his had described the geometrical symbolism as created for my assistance and had seemed to dislike it, another had complained that I used it to make their thought mechanical, and a Frustrator doubtless played upon my weakness when he described a geometrical model of the soul's state after death which could be turned upon a lathe. The sudden indignant interruption suggested a mind under a dream constraint which it could throw off if desire were strong enough, as we can sometimes throw off a nightmare. It was part of their purpose to affirm that all the gains of man come from conflict with the opposite of his true being. Was communication itself such a conflict? One said, as though it rested with me to decide what part I should play in their dream, "Remember we will deceive you if we can". Upon the

other hand they seem like living men, are interested in
all that interests living men, as when at Oxford, where
we spent our winters, one asked upon hearing an owl
hoot in the garden, if he might be silent for a while.
"Sounds like that", he said, "give us great pleasure."
But some frustrations found us helpless. Some six
months before the communications came to an end, a
communicator announced that he was about to explain
a new branch of the philosophy and seemed to add, "But
please do not write anything down, for when all is
finished I will dictate a summary". He spoke almost
nightly for I think three months, and at last I said, "Let
me make notes, I cannot keep it all in my head". He
was disturbed to find that I had written nothing down,
and when I told him of the voice, said it was frustration and that he could not summarise. I had already
noticed that if their thought was interrupted they had
to find some appropriate moment before they could
take it up again, and that though they could sometimes foretell physical events they could not foretell
those moments. Later still a frustration, if the communicator did not dream what he said, took, as will be
seen, a more cruel form.

VII

The automatic writing and the speech during sleep
were illustrated or accompanied by strange phenomena.
While we were staying at a village near Oxford we met
two or three nights in succession what seemed a sudden
warm breath coming up from the ground at the same
corner of the road One night when I was about to tell
my wife some story of a Russian mystic, without re-

membering that it might make her misunderstand an
event in her own life, a sudden flash of light fell between us and a chair or table was violently struck. Then
too there was much whistling, generally as a warning
that some communicator would come when my wife
was asleep. At first I was inclined to think that these
whistlings were made by my wife without her knowing
it, and once, when I heard the whistle and she did not,
she felt a breath passing through her lips as though she
had whistled. I had to give up this explanation when
servants at the other end of the house were disturbed
by a "whistling ghost", and so much so that I asked
the communicators to choose some other sign. Sweet
smells were the most constant phenomena, now that of
incense, now that of violets or roses or some other
flower, and as perceptible to some half-dozen of our
friends as to ourselves, though upon one occasion when
my wife smelt hyacinth a friend smelt eau-de-cologne.
A smell of roses filled the whole house when my son
was born and was perceived there by the doctor and my
wife and myself, and I have no doubt, though I did not
question them, by the nurse and servants. Such smells
came most often to my wife and myself when we passed
through a door or were in some small enclosed place,
but sometimes would form themselves in my pocket or
even in the palms of my hands. When I took my hands
out of my pocket on our way to Glastonbury they were
strongly scented, and when I held them out for my wife
to smell she said, "May-flower, the Glastonbury thorn
perhaps". I seldom knew why such smells came, nor
why one sort rather than another, but sometimes they
approved something said. When I spoke of a Chinese
poem in which some old official described his coming

retirement to a village inhabited by old men devoted to
the classics, the air filled suddenly with the smell of
violets, and that night some communicator explained
that in such a place a man could escape those "knots" of
passion that prevent Unity of Being and must be expiated
between lives or in another life. (Have I not found just
such a village here in Rapallo? for, though Ezra Pound
is not old, we discuss Guido Cavalcanti and only quarrel
a little.)

Sometimes if I had been ill some astringent smell
like that of resinous wood filled the room, and sometimes, though rarely, a bad smell. These were often
warnings: a smell of cat's excrement announced some
being that had to be expelled, the smell of an extinguished candle that the communicators were "starved".
A little after my son's birth I came home to confront
my wife with the statement "Michael is ill". A smell of
burnt feathers had announced what she and the doctor
had hidden. When regular communication was near its
end and my work of study and arrangement begun, I
was told that henceforth the Frustrators would attack
my health and that of my children, and one afternoon,
knowing from the smell of burnt feathers that one of
my children would be ill within three hours, I felt
before I could recover self-control the mediaeval helpless horror at witchcraft. I can discover no apparent
difference between a natural and a supernatural smell,
except that the natural smell comes and goes gradually
while the other is suddenly there and then as suddenly
gone. But there were other phenomena. Sometimes they
commented on my thoughts by the ringing of a little
bell heard by my wife alone, and once my wife and I
heard at the same hour in the afternoon, she at Ballylee

and I at Coole, the sound of a little pipe, three or four notes, and once I heard a burst of music in the middle of the night; and when regular communications through script and sleep had come to an end, the communicators occasionally spoke—sometimes a word, sometimes a whole sentence. I was dictating to my wife, perhaps, and a voice would object to a sentence, and I could no more say where the voice came from than I could of the whistling, though confident that it came through my wife's personality. Once a Japanese who had dined with my wife and myself talked of Tolstoi's philosophy, which fascinates so many educated Japanese, and I put my objections vehemently. "It is madness for the East", I said, "which must face the West in arms", and much more of the same sort, and was, after he had gone, accusing myself of exaggerated and fantastic speech when I heard these words in a loud clear voice: "You have said what we wanted to have said". My wife, who was writing a letter at the other end of the room, had heard nothing, but found she had written those words in the letter, where they had no meaning. Sometimes my wife saw apparitions: before the birth of our son a great black bird, persons in clothes of the late sixteenth century and of the late seventeenth. There were still stranger phenomena that I prefer to remain silent about for the present because they seemed so incredible that they need a long story and much discussion.

VIII

Exposition in sleep came to an end in 1920, and I began an exhaustive study of some fifty copy-books of automatic script, and of a much smaller number of books recording what had come in sleep. Probably as many words had been spoken in sleep as had been written, but I could only summarise and much had been lost through frustration. I had already a small concordance in a large manuscript book, but now made a much larger, arranged like a card index. And then, though I had mastered nothing but the twenty-eight Phases and the historical scheme, I was told that I must write, that I must seize the moment between ripe and rotten—there was a metaphor of apples about to fall and just fallen. They showed when I began that they assisted or approved, for they sent sign after sign. Sometimes if I stopped writing and drew one hand over another my hands smelt of violets or roses, sometimes the truth I sought would come to me in a dream, or I would feel myself stopped—but this has occurred to me since boyhood—when forming some sentence, whether in my mind or upon paper. When in 1926 the English translation of Spengler's book came out, some weeks after *A Vision*,[1] I found that not only were dates that I had been given the same as his but whole metaphors and symbols that had seemed my work alone. Both he and I had symbolised a difference between Greek and Roman thought by comparing the blank or painted eyes of Greek statues with the pierced eyeballs of the Roman statues, both had described as an illustration of Roman character the naturalistic portrait heads screwed on to stock bodies, both had found the same meaning in the round bird-like eyes of Byzantine sculpture, though he or his translator had preferred "staring at infinity" to my "staring at miracle". I knew of no

[1] Published by Werner Laurie in 1925.

common source, no link between him and me, unless through

> The elemental things that go
> About my table to and fro.

IX

The first version of this book, *A Vision*, except the section on the twenty-eight Phases, and that called "Dove or Swan" which I repeat without change, fills me with shame. I had misinterpreted the geometry, and in my ignorance of philosophy failed to understand distinctions upon which the coherence of the whole depended, and as my wife was unwilling that her share should be known, and I to seem sole author, I had invented an unnatural story of an Arabian traveller which I must amend and find a place for some day because I was fool enough to write half a dozen poems that are unintelligible without it.[1]

X

When the proof sheets came I felt myself relieved from my promise not to read philosophy and began with Berkeley because a young revolutionary soldier who was living a very dangerous life said, "All the philosophy a man needs is in Berkeley", and because Lennox Robinson, hearing me quote that sentence, bought me an old copy of Berkeley's works upon the Dublin quays. Then I took down from my wife a list of what she had read, two or three volumes of Wundt, part of Hegel's *Logic*, all Thomas Taylor's *Plotinus*, a Latin

[1] *Michael Robartes and his Friends* is the amended version.

work of Pico della Mirandola, and a great deal of mediaeval mysticism. I had to ignore Pico, for I had forgotten
my school Latin and my wife had burnt her translation when she married me, "to reduce her luggage". I
did not expect to find that the communicators echoed
what she had read, for I had proof they were not dependent on her memory or mine, but did expect to find
somewhere something from which their symbolic geometry had been elaborated, something used as they had
used *Per Amica Silentia Lunae*. I read all MacKenna's
incomparable translation of Plotinus, some of it several
times, and went from Plotinus to his predecessors and
successors whether upon her list or not. And for four
years now I have read nothing else except now and then
some story of theft and murder to clear my head at
night. Although the more I read the better did I understand what I had been taught, I found neither the
geometrical symbolism nor anything that could have
inspired it except the vortex of Empedocles.

XI

I might have gone on reading for some two or three
years more but for something that happened at Cannes.
I was ill after pneumonia and general nervous break-
down, had partly recovered but fallen ill again, and
spent most of the days on my back considering a slowly
narrowing circle. Two months ago I had walked to the
harbour at Algeciras, two miles; a month ago to the
harbour at Cannes, a mile; and now thought two hundred
yards enough. It had begun to widen again, and I had
returned from my walk at a quarter to five one afternoon when I heard my wife locking her room door.

Then walking in her sleep, as I could see by her fixed
look, she came through the connecting door and lay
down upon a sofa. The communicator had scarcely
spoken before I heard somebody trying to get into her
room and remembered that the nurse brought our
daughter there every afternoon at five. My wife heard
and, being but half awakened, fell in trying to get on to
her feet, and though able to hide her disturbance from
the nurse and from our daughter, suffered from the
shock. The communicator came next day, but later, and
only to say over and over in different words, "It cannot
happen again, for at this hour nobody comes", and then
day after day to discuss what I had written. My wife's
interests are musical, literary, practical, she seldom
comments upon what I dictate except upon the turn of
a phrase; she can no more correct it than she could her
automatic script at a time when a slight error brought
her new fatigue. But the communicator, as independent
of her ignorance as of her knowledge, had no tolerance
for error. He had no more than tolerated my philosophical study and was enraged by the intrusion, not
so much into what I had written as into the questions
I put, of a terminology not his. This led to one of
those quarrels which I have noticed almost always precede the clearest statements, and seem to arise from an
independence excited to injustice because kept with
difficulty. "I am always afraid", he said in apology, "that
when not at our best we may accept from you false
reasoning." I had half forgotten—there had been no
communication longer than a sentence or two for four
years—how completely master they could be down to
its least detail of what I could but know in outline, how
confident and dominating. Sometimes they had seemed

but messengers; they knew nothing but the thought that brought them; or they had forgotten and must refer to those that sent them. But now in a few minutes they drew that distinction between what their terminology calls the *Faculties* and what it calls the *Principles*, between experience and revelation, between understanding and reason, between the higher and lower mind, which has engaged the thought of saints and philosophers from the time of Buddha.

XII

I have heard my wife in the broken speech of some quite ordinary dream use tricks of speech characteristic of the philosophic voices. Sometimes the philosophic voices themselves have become vague and trivial or have in some other way reminded me of dreams. Furthermore their doctrine supports the resemblance, for one said in the first month of communication, "We are often but created forms", and another, that spirits do not tell a man what is true but create such conditions, such a crisis of fate, that the man is compelled to listen to his Daimon. And again and again they have insisted that the whole system is the creation of my wife's Daimon and of mine, and that it is as startling to them as to us. Mere "spirits", my teachers say, are the "objective", a reflection and distortion; reality itself is found by the Daimon in what they call, in commemoration of the Third Person of the Trinity, the Ghostly Self. The blessed spirits must be sought within the self which is common to all.

Much that has happened, much that has been said, suggests that the communicators are the personalities

of a dream shared by my wife, by myself, occasionally
by others—they have, as I must some day prove, spoken
through others without change of knowledge or loss
of power—a dream that can take objective form in
sounds, in hallucinations, in scents, in flashes of light,
in movements of external objects. In partly accepting
and partly rejecting that explanation for reasons I cannot now discuss, in affirming a Communion of the
Living and the Dead, I remember that Swedenborg has
described all those between the celestial state and death
as plastic, fantastic and deceitful, the dramatis personae
of our dreams; that Cornelius Agrippa attributes to
Orpheus these words: "The Gates of Pluto must not
be unlocked, within is a people of dreams". What I
have to say of them is in "The Soul in Judgment",[1] but
because it came when my wife's growing fatigue made
communication difficult and because of defects of my
own, it is the most unfinished of my five books.

XIII

Some, perhaps all, of those readers I most value, those
who have read me many years, will be repelled by what
must seem an arbitrary, harsh, difficult symbolism.
Yet such has almost always accompanied expression
that unites the sleeping and waking mind. One remembers the six wings of Daniel's angels, the Pytha-
gorean numbers, a venerated book of the Cabala where
the beard of God winds in and out among the stars, its
hairs all numbered, those complicated mathematical
tables that Kelly saw in Dr. Dee's black scrying-stone,
the diagrams in Law's *Boehme*, where one lifts a flap

[1] It is now finished, but less detailed than I once hoped.

of paper to discover both the human entrails and the
starry heavens. William Blake thought those diagrams
worthy of Michael Angelo, but remains himself almost
unintelligible because he never drew the like. We can
(those hard symbolic bones under the skin) substitute
for a treatise on logic the *Divine Comedy*, or some little
song about a rose, or be content to live our thought.

XIV

Some will associate the story I have just told with
that popular spiritualism which has not dared to define
itself, to go like all great spiritual movements through
a tragedy of separation and rejection, which instead of
asking whether it is not something almost incredible,
because altogether new or forgotten, clings to all that is
vague and obvious in popular Christianity; and hate me
for that association. But Muses resemble women who
creep out at night and give themselves to unknown
sailors and return to talk of Chinese porcelain—porcelain is best made, a Japanese critic has said, where the
conditions of life are hard—or of the Ninth Symphony
—virginity renews itself like the moon—except that
the Muses sometimes form in those low haunts their
most lasting attachments.

XV

Some will ask whether I believe in the actual existence of my circuits of sun and moon. Those that include,
now all recorded time in one circuit, now what Blake
called "the pulsaters of an artery", are plainly symbolical,
but what of those that fixed, like a butterfly upon a

pin, to our central date, the first day of our Era, divide actual history into periods of equal length? To such a question I can but answer that if sometimes, overwhelmed by miracle as all men must be when in the midst of it, I have taken such periods literally, my reason has soon recovered; and now that the system stands out clearly in my imagination I regard them as stylistic arrangements of experience comparable to the cubes in the drawing of Wyndham Lewis and to the ovoids in the sculpture of Brancusi. They have helped me to hold in a single thought reality and justice.

November 23rd 1928, and later

TO EZRA POUND

I

My dear Ezra,

Do not be elected to the Senate of your country. I think myself, after six years, well out of that of mine. Neither you nor I, nor any other of our excitable profession, can match those old lawyers, old bankers, old business men, who, because all habit and memory, have begun to govern the world. They lean over the chair in front and talk as if to half a dozen of their kind at some board-meeting, and, whether they carry their point or not, retain moral ascendancy. When a politician follows, his thought shaped by newspaper and public meeting, it is as though somebody recited "Eugene Aram" as it used to be recited in my youth. Once when I had called at a Dublin bank, rifle fire began all round the bank, and I was told that nobody could leave for an hour or two and invited to lunch with the Directors. We lunched in a room overlooking the courtyard, and from time to time I got up and looked out of the window at a young soldier who ran from the protection of a wall, fell upon one knee and fired through the gateway. The Republicans were attacking the next building, but was the bank well protected? How many such young soldiers stood or crouched about us? The bankers talked their ordinary affairs, not one went to the window or asked whether a particular shot was fired by the young soldier or at him; they had to raise their voices a little as we do when we have selected by accident a restaurant where there is an orchestra.

Should you permit yourself to enter the Senate, that irascible mind of yours will discover something of the utmost importance, and the group you belong to will invite you to one of those private meetings where the real work of legislation is done, and the ten minutes they can grant you, after discussing the next Bill upon the agenda for two hours with unperturbed lucidity, will outlast your self-confidence. No, Ezra, those generalities that make all men politicians and some few eloquent are not as true as they were. You and I, those impressive and convinced politicians, that young man reciting "Eugene Aram", are as much out of place as would be the first composers of sea-shanties in an age of steam. Whenever I stood up to speak, no matter how long I had pondered my words, unless I spoke of something that concerned the arts, or upon something that depended not upon precise knowledge but upon public opinion—we writers are public opinion's children though we defy our mother—I was ashamed until shame turned at last, even if I spoke but a few words —my body being somewhat battered by time—into physical pain.

II

I send you the introduction of a book which will, when finished, proclaim a new divinity. Oedipus lay upon the earth at the middle point between four sacred objects, was there washed as the dead are washed, and thereupon passed with Theseus to the wood's heart until amidst the sound of thunder earth opened, "riven by love", and he sank down soul and body into the earth. I would have him balance Christ who, crucified standing up, went into the abstract sky soul and body, and I see him altogether separated from Plato's Athens, from all that talk of the Good and the One, from all that cabinet of perfection, an image from Homer's age. When it was already certain that he must bring himself under his own curse did he not still question, and when answered as the Sphinx had been answered, stricken with the horror that is in *Gulliver* and in the *Fleurs du Mal*, did he not tear out his own eyes? He raged against his sons, and this rage was noble, not from some general idea, some sense of public law upheld, but because it seemed to contain all life, and the daughter who served him as did Cordelia Lear—he too a man of Homer's kind—seemed less attendant upon an old railing rambler than upon genius itself. He knew nothing but his mind, and yet because he spoke that mind fate possessed it and kingdoms changed according to his blessing and his cursing. Delphi, that rock at earth's navel, spoke through him, and though men shuddered and drove him away they spoke of ancient poetry, praising the boughs overhead, the grass under foot, Colonus and its horses. I think that he lacked compassion, seeing that it must be compassion for himself, and yet stood nearer to the poor than saint or apostle, and I mutter to myself stories of Cruachan, or of Crickmaa, or of the road-side bush withered by Raftery's curse.[1] What if Christ and

---

[1] Was Oedipus familiar to Theban "wren boys"? One of those Lives "collected out of good authors" at the end of North's *Plutarch* describes a meeting between Epaminondas and what I would like to consider some propitiation of his shade. "Even as they were marching away out of Thebes, divers of the souldiers thought they had had many unluckie signes. For as they were going out of the gates, Epaminondas met on his way a Herald, that following an auncient ceremonie and custome of theirs, brought an old blind man as if he had bene run away; and the Herald crying out aloud, Bring him

Oedipus or, to shift the names, Saint Catherine of
Genoa and Michael Angelo, are the two scales of a
balance, the two butt-ends of a seesaw? What if every
two thousand and odd years something happens in the
world to make one sacred, the other secular; one wise,
the other foolish; one fair, the other foul; one divine, the
other devilish? What if there is an arithmetic or geometry that can exactly measure the slope of a balance, the
dip of a scale, and so date the coming of that something?
   You will hate these generalities, Ezra, which are
themselves, it may be, of the past—the abstract sky—
yet you have written "The Return", and though you but
announce in it some change of style, perhaps, in book
and picture it gives me better words than my own.

> See, they return; ah, see the tentative
> Movements, and the slow feet,
> The trouble in the pace and the uncertain
> Wavering!
>
> See, they return, one, and by one.
> With fear, as half-awakened;
> As if the snow should hesitate
> And murmur in the wind,
>   and half turn back;
> These were the "Wing'd-with-Awe",
>   Inviolable.
>
> Gods of the winged shoe!
> With them the silver hounds
>   sniffing the trace of air!

not out of Thebes nor put him not to death, but carie him backe
againe, and save his life." The accepted explanation is that he was
a runaway slave welcomed back with some traditional ceremony because he returned of his own will; but imagination boggles at a runaway, old blind slave.

Haie! Haie!
    These were the swift to harry;
These the keen-scented;
These were the souls of blood.

Slow on the leash,
        pallid the leash-men!

STORIES OF MICHAEL ROBARTES AND
HIS FRIENDS: AN EXTRACT FROM
A RECORD MADE BY HIS PUPILS

Huddon, Duddon and Daniel O'Leary[1]
Delighted me as a child;
But where that roaring, ranting crew
Danced, laughed, loved, fought through
Their brief lives I never knew.

Huddon, Duddon and Daniel O'Leary
Delighted me as a child.
I put three persons in their place
That despair and keep the pace
And love wench Wisdom's cruel face.

Huddon, Duddon and Daniel O'Leary
Delighted me as a child.
Hard-living men and men of thought
Burn their bodies up for nought,
I mock at all so burning out.

[1] As a child I pronounced the word as though it rhymed to
"dairy".

THREE of us, two young men and a young woman, sat round a fire at eleven o'clock at night on the ground floor of a house in Albert Road, Regent's Park. Presently a third young man came in, drew a chair into the circle and said, "You do not recognise me, but I am the chauffeur: I always am on these occasions, it prevents gossip". Said I, "Where is Mr. Owen Aherne?" "Owen", said he, "is with Michael Robartes making his report." Said I, "Why should there be a report?" Said he, "Oh, there is always a report. Meanwhile I am to tell you my story and to hear yours. There will be plenty of time, for as I left the study Michael Robartes called the universe a great egg that turns inside-out perpetually without breaking its shell, and a thing like that always sets Owen off.

"My name is Daniel O'Leary, my great interest is the speaking of verse, and the establishment some day or other of a small theatre for plays in verse. You will remember that a few years before the Great War the realists drove the last remnants of rhythmical speech out of the theatre. I thought common sense might have returned while I was at war or in the starvation afterwards, and went to *Romeo and Juliet* to find out. I caught those well-known persons Mr. . . . and Miss . . . at their kitchen gabble. Suddenly this thought came into my head: What would happen if I were to take off my boots and fling one at Mr. . . . and one at Miss . . .? Could I give my future life such settled purpose that the act would take its place not among whims but among forms of intensity? I ran through my life from child-hood and decided that I could. 'You have not the courage', said I, speaking aloud but in a low voice. 'I have', said I, and began unlacing my boots. 'You have not', said I, and after several such interchanges I stood up and flung the boots.

"Unfortunately, although I can do whatever I command myself to do, I lack the true courage, which is self-possession in an unforeseen situation. My aim was bad. Had I been throwing a cricket-ball at a wicket, which is a smaller object than an actor or an actress, I would not have failed; but as it was, one boot fell in the stalls and the other struck a musician or the brassy thing in his hand. Then I ran out of a side door and down the stairs. Just as I came to the street door I heard feet behind and thought it must be the orchestra, and that increased my panic. The realists turn our words into gravel, but the musicians and the singers turn them into honey and oil. I have always had the idea that some day a musician would do me an injury. The street door opened on to a narrow lane, and down this lane I ran until I ran straight into the arms of an old gentleman standing at a street corner by the open door of a big covered motor-car. He pulled me into the car, for I was so out of breath that I could not resist, and the car drove off. 'Put on these boots', he said. 'I am afraid they are too large, but I thought it best to be on the safe side, and I have brought you a pair of clean socks.' I was in such a panic, and everything so like a dream, that I did what I was told. He dropped my muddy socks out of the window and said, 'You need not say what you have done, unless you care to tell Robartes. I was told to wait at the corner for a man without boots.' He brought me here. All I need add is that I have lived in this house since that night some six or seven months ago, and that it is a great relief to talk to people of my own generation. You at any rate cannot sympathise with a horrible generation that in childhood sucked Ibsen from Archer's hygienic bottle. You can understand even better than Robartes why that protest must always seem the great event of my life."

"I find my parents detestable", said the young woman, "but I like my grandparents." "How could Mr. Aherne know", said I, "what was going to happen? You only thought of the protest when sitting in the theatre." "Robartes", said O'Leary, "sees what is going to happen, between sleeping and waking at night, or in the morning before they bring him his early cup of tea. Aherne is a pious Catholic, thinks it Pagan or something of the kind and hates it, but he has to do what Robartes tells him, always had to from childhood up. But Robartes says you must not ask me questions, but introduce yourselves and tell your story."

"My name is John Duddon," said I, "and this young woman insists on calling herself Denise de L'Isle Adam, and that tall fair young man is Peter Huddon. He gets everything he wants and I hate him. We were friends until Denise began going about with him." At this point I was interrupted by Denise saying that I had starved until Huddon bought my pictures, that he had bought seven large landscapes, thirty sketches from life, nine portraits of herself, and that I had charged twice their value. Huddon stopped her, said that he would give more could he afford it, for my pictures were his greatest pleasure, and O'Leary begged me to continue my story. "This afternoon", I said, "Huddon came to my studio and I overheard an appointment for dinner at the Café Royal. When I warned her that she would be sorry if she went, she declared that no such conversation had taken place. However, I bought a heavy stick and to-night stood outside the Café Royal waiting till they came out. Presently a man came out. I thought it was Huddon and brought my stick down on his head. He dropped on the pavement and I thought, 'I have knocked down my only patron, and that is a magnificent thing to have done', and I felt like dancing. Then I saw that the man on the pavement was a strange old gentleman. I found the café porter, said the old gentleman had fallen down in a fit, and we carried him a few doors up the street and into a chemist's shop. But I knew the truth would come out when he woke up, so I slipped into the café, found Huddon's table, told him what had happened and asked his advice. He said, 'The right thing is to get the old gentleman not to prosecute'. So we went to the chemist's shop where a small crowd had gathered. The old gentleman was sitting up in a little back room muttering, 'Just like my luck . . . bound to happen sooner or later'. Huddon said, 'It was an accident, sir; you cannot take offence at being knocked down in mistake for me'. 'In mistake for you?' said the old gentleman, staring steadily at Huddon. 'An upstanding man, a fine upstanding man—no offence.' And then as though he had suddenly thought of something, 'I will not say a word to the police on the condition that you and this young man and this young woman meet a friend of mine and drink a little wine'."

II

Presently Aherne came in with a big old man. Aherne, now that I saw him in a good light, was stout and sedentary-looking, bearded and dull of eye, but this other was lank, brown, muscular, clean-shaven, with an alert, ironical eye. "This is Michael Robartes", said Aherne, and took a plate of sandwiches, glasses and a bottle of champagne out of a cupboard and laid them upon a small table, and found chairs for himself and Robartes. Robartes asked which was which, for he already knew our names, and said, "I want the right sort of young men and women for pupils. Aherne acts as my messenger. What shall we talk about? Art?" Denise is shy with old men, and Huddon calls old men "sir" and makes them shy, so for the sake of saying something, I said, "No. That is my profession." "War?" said Robartes, and Huddon said, "That is my profession, sir, and I am tired of it". "Love?" said Robartes, and Denise, whose struggles with shyness always drive her into audacity, said, "Oh, no. That is my profession. Tell me the story of your life." "Aherne, the book", said Robartes. Aherne unlocked a bookcase and brought out a bit of goatskin and out of this an old battered book. "I have brought you here", said Robartes, "to tell you where I found that book, what followed from the finding of it, what is still to follow. I had founded a small Cabalistic society in Ireland; but, finding time and place were against me, dissolved it and left the country. I went to Rome and there fell violently in love with a ballet-dancer who had not an idea in her head. All might have been well had I been content to

take what came; had I understood that her coldness and
cruelty became in the transfiguration of the body an inhuman majesty; that I adored in body what I hated in
will; that judgment is a Judith and drives the steel into
what has stirred its flesh; that those my judgment
approves seem to me, owing to an infliction of my
moon, insipid. The more I tried to change her character
the more did I uncover mutual enmity. A quarrel, the
last of many, parted us at Vienna where her troupe was
dancing, and to make the quarrel as complete as possible
I cohabited with an ignorant girl of the people and
hired rooms ostentatious in their sordidness. One night
I was thrown out of bed and saw when I lit my candle
that the bed, which had fallen at one end, had been
propped up by a broken chair and an old book with a
pig-skin cover. In the morning I found that the book
was called *Speculum Angelorum et Hominum*, had been
written by a certain Giraldus, had been printed at
Cracow in 1594, a good many years before the cele-
brated Cracow publications. It was very dilapidated,
all the middle pages had been torn out; but there still
remained a series of allegorical pictures, a man torn in
two by an eagle and some sort of wild beast, a man
whipping his shadow, a man between a hunchback and
a fool in cap and bells, and so on to the number of eight
and twenty, a portrait of Giraldus, a unicorn several
times repeated, a large diagram in the shape of a wheel
where the phases of the moon were mixed up with an
apple, an acorn, a cup, and what looked like a sceptre
or wand. My mistress had found it in a wall cupboard
where it had been left by the last tenant, an unfrocked
priest who had joined a troupe of gypsies and disappeared, and she had torn out the middle pages to light

Portrait of Giraldus
from the *Speculum Angelorum et Hominum*

our fire. Though little remained of the Latin text, I
spent a couple of weeks comparing one passage with
another and all with the unintelligible diagrams. One
day I returned from a library, where I had made a fruit-
less attempt to identify my Giraldus with Giraldus of
Bologna, and found my mistress gone, whether in mere
disgust at my preoccupation or, as I hope, to some
more attentive man. I had nothing now to distract my
thoughts that ran through my past loves, neither
numerous nor happy, back to the platonic love of boyhood, the most impassioned of all, and was plunged
into hopeless misery. I have always known that love
should be changeless and yet my loves drank their oil
and died—there has been no ever-burning lamp." He
sank his head upon his breast and we sat in silence,
until Denise said, "I do not think we should blame ourselves as long as we remain unmarried. I have always
believed that neither Church nor State should grant
divorce under any circumstances. It is necessary to keep
in existence the symbol of eternal love." Robartes did
not seem to have heard, for he took up his theme where
he had left it. "Love contains all Kant's antinomies, but
it is the first that poisons our lives. Thesis, there is no
beginning; antithesis, there is a beginning; or, as I
prefer: thesis, there is an end; antithesis, there is no
end. Exhausted by the cry that it can never end, my
love ends; without that cry it were not love but desire,
desire does not end. The anguish of birth and that
of death cry out in the same instant. Life is no series
of emanations from divine reason such as the Cabalists imagine, but an irrational bitterness, no orderly
descent from level to level, no waterfall but a whirlpool, a gyre.

"One night, between three and four in the morning, as I lay sleepless, it came into my head to go pray at the Holy Sepulchre. I went, prayed, grew somewhat calmer, until I said to myself, 'Jesus Christ does not understand my despair, He belongs to order and reason'. The day after, an old Arab walked unannounced into my room. He said that he had been sent, stood where the *Speculum* lay open at the wheel marked with the phases of the moon, described it as the doctrine of his tribe, drew two whorls working one against the other, the narrow end of one in the broad end of the other, showed that my single wheel and his two whorls had the same meaning. He belonged to a tribe of Arabs who called themselves Judwalis or Diagrammatists because their children are taught dances which leave upon the sand traces full of symbolical meaning. I joined that tribe, accepted its dress, customs, morality, politics, that I might win its trust and its knowledge. I have fought in its wars and risen to authority. Your young Colonel Lawrence never suspected the nationality of the old Arab fighting at his side. I have completed my life, balanced every pleasure with a danger lest my bones might soften."

III

Three months later, Huddon, Denise, O'Leary and I sat in silence round the same fire. For the last few days we had slept and eaten in the house that Robartes might teach us without interruption. Robartes came in carrying a little chest of carved ivory and sat down, the chest upon his knees. Denise, who had been in a state of suppressed excitement all day, said, "Nobody knows

why I call myself Denise de L'Isle Adam, but I have
decided to tell my story". "You told that story", said
Huddon, "half a dozen times at the Café Royal and
should be satisfied."

At that moment, to my great relief, Aherne ushered
in a pale slight woman of thirty-five and a spectacled
man who seemed somewhat older. When Aherne had
found them chairs, Robartes said: "This is John Bond
and this is Mary Bell. Aherne has brought John Bond
from Ireland that you may hear what he has to say, and
Mary Bell because I think her a suitable guardian for
what I carry in this box. Before John Bond tells his story,
I must insist upon Denise telling hers; from what I know
of her, I feel certain that it will be a full and admirable
introduction."

Denise began: "I was reading *Axel* in bed. It was between twelve and one on the 2nd June last year. A
date that I will never forget, because on that night I
met the one man I shall always love. I was turning the
pages of the Act where the lovers are in the vault under
the castle. Axel and Sarah decide to die rather than
possess one another. He talks of her hair as full of the
odour of dead rose leaves—a pretty phrase—a phrase I
would like somebody to say to me; and then comes
the famous sentence: 'As for living, our servants will do
that for us'. I was wondering what made them do anything so absurd, when the candle went out. I said,
'Duddon, I heard you open the window, creep over the
floor on your toes, but I never guessed that you would
blow the candle out'. 'Denise,' he said, 'I am a great
coward. I am afraid of unfamiliar women in pyjamas.' I
said: 'No, my dear, you are not a coward, you were just
shy, but why should you call me unfamiliar? I thought I

had put everything right when I told you that I slept on the ground floor, that there was nobody else on that floor, and that I left the window open.' Five minutes later I said: 'Duddon, you are impotent, stop trembling; go over there and sit by the fire. I will give you some wine.' When he had drunk half a tumbler of claret, he said: 'No, I am not really impotent, I am a coward, that is all. When Huddon tires of a girl, I make love to her, and there is no difficulty at all. He has always talked about her, but if he had not, it would not make much difference. He is my greatest friend, and when she and he have been in the same bed, it is as though she belonged to the house. Twice I have found somebody on my own account, and been a failure, just as I have to-night. I had not indeed much hope when I climbed through the window but I had a little, because you had made it plain that I would be welcome.' I said: 'Oh, my dear, how delightful; now I know all about Axel. He was just shy. If he had not killed the Commander in the Second Act—and it would have been much more dramatic at the end of the play—he could have sent for him and all would have come right. The Commander was not a friend, of course; Axel hated him; but he was a relation, and afterwards Axel could have thought of Sarah as a member of the family. I love you because you would not be shy if you had not so great respect for me. You feel about me what I feel about a Bishop in a surplice. I would not give you up now for anything.' Duddon said, wringing his hands: 'Oh, what am I to do'. I said: 'Fetch the Commander'. He said, getting cheerful at once: 'I am to bring Huddon?'

"A fortnight later Duddon and I were in Florence.

We had plenty of money, for Huddon had just bought a large picture, and were delighted with each other. I said: 'I am going to send Huddon this little cigarette-case'. It was one of those pretty malachite things they sell in Florence. I had had it engraved with the words: 'In memory of the 2nd June'. He said: 'Why put into it only one cigarette?' I said: 'Oh, he will understand'.

"And now you know," said Denise, "why I have named myself after the author of *Axel*." I said: "You wish always to remember that upon that night I introduced you to Huddon". She said: "What a fool you are. It is you that I love, and shall always love." I said: "But you are Huddon's mistress?" She said: "When a man gives me a cigarette, and I like the brand, I want a hundred, but the box is almost empty"

"Now", said Robartes, "the time has come for John Bond." John Bond, after fixing a bewildered eye, first upon Denise and then upon me, began. He had evidently prepared his words beforehand. "Some fifteen years ago this lady married an excellent man, much older than herself, who lived in a large house on the more peaceable side of the Shannon. Her marriage was childless but happy and might have continued so had she not in its ninth year been told to winter abroad. She went alone to the South of France, for her husband had scientific and philanthropic work that he could not leave. I was resting at Cannes after completing the manuscript of a work on the migratory birds, and at Cannes we met and fell in love at first sight. Brought up in the strictest principles of the Church of Ireland, we were horror-struck and hid our feelings from one another. I fled from Cannes to find her at Monaco, from Monaco to find her at Antibes, from Antibes to find her at Cannes, until chancing upon the same hotel we so far accepted fate that we dined at the same table, and after parting for ever in the garden accepted fate completely. In a little while she was with child. She was the first woman that had come into my life, and had I not remembered an episode in the life of Voltaire I had been helpless. We were penniless; for the child's sake and her own she must return to her husband at once.

"As Mary Bell left my letters unanswered I concluded that she meant me to drop out of her life. I read of our child's birth, heard nothing more for five years. I accepted a post in the Dublin Museum, specialised in the subject of the Irish migratory birds, and at four o'clock one afternoon an attendant brought her into my office. I was greatly moved, but she spoke as if to a stranger. I was 'Mr. Bond', she was 'sorry to intrude upon my time' but I was 'the only person in Ireland who could give her certain information'. I took the hint and became the courteous Curator, I was there 'to help the student'. She wished to study the nests of certain migratory birds, thought the only exact method was to make their nests with her own hands. She had found and copied nests in her own neighbourhood, but as progress, entirely dependent on personal observation, was slow, wanted to know what had been published on the subject. Every species preferred some special materials, twigs, lichens, grasses, mosses, bunches of hair and so on, and had a special architecture. I told her what I knew, sent her books, proceedings of learned societies, and passages translated from foreign tongues. Some months later she brought me swift's, swallow's, corncrake's, and reed-warbler's nests made by her own hands and so well that, when I compared them with the natural nests in the cases of stuffed birds, I could see no difference. Her manner had changed; it was embarrassed, almost mysterious, as though she were keeping something back. She wanted to make a nest for a bird of a certain size and shape. She could not or would not name its species but named its genus. She wanted information about the nesting habits of that genus, borrowed a couple of books, and saying that she had a train to catch, went away. A month later a telegram called me to her country house. I found her waiting at the little station. Her husband was dying, and wished to consult with me about a scientific work he had carried on for many years; he did not know that we knew each other but was acquainted with my work. When I asked what his scientific work was, she said that he would explain, and began to speak of the house and its surroundings. The deplorable semi-gothic gateway we had passed a moment before was the work of her husband's father, but I must notice the great sycamores and lucombe oaks and the clump of cedars, and there were great plantations behind the house. There had been a house there in the seventeenth century, but the present house was made in the eighteenth century, when most of the trees were planted. Arthur Young had described their planting and spoken of the great change it would make in the neighbourhood. She thought a man who planted trees, knowing that no descendant nearer than his great-grandson could stand under their shade, had a noble and generous confidence. She thought there was something terrible about it, for it was terrible standing under great trees to say 'Am I worthy of that confidence?'

"The doors were opened by an elderly maid who met us with the smile of the country servant. As she brought me to my room and as I mounted the stairs I noticed walls covered with photographs and engravings, Grillion Club portraits, photographs signed by celebrities of the sixties and seventies of the last century. I knew that Mr. Bell's father had been a man of considerable culture, that Mr. Bell himself had been in the Foreign Office as a young man, but here was evidence that one or other had known most of the famous writers, artists and politicians of his time. I returned to the ground floor to find Mary Bell at the tea-table with a little boy. I had begun to discover in his face characteristics of my family when she said, 'Everybody thinks he is so like his great-uncle, the famous Chancery lawyer, the friend of Goldsmith and of Burke, but you can judge for yourself, that is his great-uncle's portrait by Gainsborough'. Then she sent the little boy away but told him not to make a noise because of his father's illness. I stood at a window which opened on to the garden, noticed a number of square boxes much too large to be beehives, and asked their purpose. She said, 'They are connected with Mr. Bell's work', but seemed disinclined to say more. I wandered about the room studying family portraits; a Peter Lely; mezzotints, framed letters from Chatham and Horace Walpole, duelling swords and pistols arranged upon the walls by generations who did not care how incongruous the mixture that called up their own past history. Presently an hospital nurse came to say, 'Mr. Bell has been asking for Mr. Bond. He is very weak; very near his end; but when he has spoken what is on his mind will die happier. He wants to see Mr. Bond alone.' I followed her upstairs and found the old man in a great four-poster, in a room hung with copies of paintings by Murillo and his contemporaries brought from Italy in the days of the Grand Tour, and one modern picture, a portrait of Mary in her early twenties, painted by Sargent.

"The old man, who must have been animated and genial once, smiled and tried to rise from his pillow but fell back with a sigh. The nurse arranged the pillows, told me to call her when he had finished, and went into a dressing-room. He said: 'When I left the Foreign Office because I wanted to serve God I was a very young man. I wanted to make men better but not to leave this estate, and here nobody did wrong except as children do. Providence had surrounded me with such goodness that to think of altering it seemed blasphemy. I married, and it seemed wrong to give nothing in return for so much happiness. I thought a great deal and remembered that birds and beasts, dumb brutes of all kinds, were robbing and killing one another. There at any rate I could alter without blasphemy. I have never taken Genesis literally. The passions of Adam, torn out of his breast, became the birds and beasts of Eden. Partakers in original sin, they can be partakers in salvation. I knew that the longest life could do but little, and wishing especially to benefit those who lacked what I possessed, I decided to devote my life to the cuckoos. I put cuckoos in cages, and have now so many cages that they stand side by side along the whole southern wall of the garden. My great object was of course to persuade them to make nests; but for a long time they were so obstinate, so unteachable, that I almost despaired. But the birth of a son renewed my resolution and a year ago I persuaded some of the oldest and cleverest birds to make circles with matches, twigs and fragments of moss, but though the numbers who can do this are increasing, even the cleverest birds make no attempt to weave them into a structure. I am dying, but you have far greater knowledge than I and I ask you to continue my work.' At that moment I heard Mary Bell's voice behind me: 'It is unnecessary, a cuckoo has made a nest. Your long illness made the gardeners careless. I only found it by chance a moment ago, a beautiful nest, finished to the last layer of down.' She had crept unnoticed into the room and stood at my elbow holding out a large nest. The old man tried to take it but was too weak. 'Now let Thy servant depart in peace', he murmured. She laid the nest upon the pillow and he turned over, closing his eyes. Calling the nurse we crept out, and shutting the door stood side by side. Neither of us spoke for almost a minute, then Mary flung herself into my arms and said amid her sobs, 'We have given him great happiness'.

"Next morning when I came down to breakfast I learnt that Mr. Bell had died in his sleep a little before daybreak. Mary did not come down, and when I saw her some hours later she spoke of nothing but the boy. 'We must devote our whole lives to him. You must think of his education. We must not think of ourselves.'

"At the funeral Mary noticed an old, unknown man among the neighbours and dependents, and when the funeral was over he introduced himself as Mr. Owen Aherne. He told us of scenes that had risen before Mr. Robartes' eyes on several successive mornings as he awaited his early tea. These scenes being part of our intimate lives, our first meeting in the South of France, our first meeting in the museum, the four-poster with the nest on the pillow, so startled us that we set out for London that very evening. All afternoon we have talked with Mr. Robartes, that inspired man, and Mary Bell has at his bidding undertaken a certain task. I return to Ireland to-morrow to take charge until her return of the estate and of her son."

IV

Said Robartes, "I have now two questions to ask, and four of you must answer. Mary Bell and John Bond need not, for I have taught them nothing. Their task in life is settled." Then he turned towards O'Leary, Denise, Huddon and myself, and said, "Have I proved by practical demonstrations that the soul survives the body?" He looked at me and I said, "Yes"; and after me the others, speaking in turn, said, "Yes". He went on: "We have read Swift's essay upon the dissensions of the Greeks and Romans; you have heard my comments, corrections, amplifications. Have I proved that civilisations come to an end when they have given all their light like burned-out wicks, that ours is near its end?" "Or transformation", Aherne corrected. I said, speaking in the name of all, "You have proved that civilisations burn out and that ours is near its end". "Or transformation", Aherne corrected once more. "If you had answered differently ', said Robartes, "I would have sent you away, for we are here to consider the terror that is to come."

Mary Bell then opened the ivory box and took from

it an egg the size of a swan's egg, and standing between us and the dark window-curtains, lifted it up that we might all see its colour. "Hyacinthine blue, according to the Greek lyric poet", said Robartes. "I bought it from an old man in a green turban at Teheran; it had come down from eldest son to eldest son for many generations." "No", said Aherne, "you never were in Teheran." "Perhaps Aherne is right", said Robartes. "Sometimes my dreams discover facts, and sometimes lose them, but it does not matter. I bought this egg from an old man in a green turban in Arabia, or Persia, or India. He told me its history, partly handed down by word of mouth, partly as he had discovered it in ancient manuscripts. It was for a time in the treasury of Harun Al-Rashid and had come there from Byzantium, as ransom for a prince of the imperial house. Its history before that is unimportant for some centuries. During the reign of the Antonines tourists saw it hanging by a golden chain from the roof of a Spartan temple. Those of you who are learned in the classics will have recognised the lost egg of Leda, its miraculous life still unquenched. I return to the desert in a few days with Owen Aherne and this lady chosen by divine wisdom for its guardian and bearer. When I have found the appointed place, Owen Aherne and I will dig a shallow hole where she must lay it and leave it to be hatched by the sun's heat." He then spoke of the two eggs already hatched, how Castor and Clytaemnestra broke the one shell, Helen and Pollux the other, of the tragedy that followed, wondered what would break the third shell. Then came a long discourse founded upon the philosophy of the Judwalis and of Giraldus, sometimes eloquent, often obscure. I set down a few passages without attempting to recall their context or to arrange them in consecutive order.

"I found myself upon the third antinomy of Immanuel Kant, thesis: freedom; antithesis: necessity; but I restate it. Every action of man declares the soul's ultimate, particular freedom, and the soul's disappearance in God; declares that reality is a congeries of beings and a single being; nor is this antinomy an appearance imposed upon us by the form of thought but life itself which turns, now here, now there, a whirling and a bitterness."

"After an age of necessity, truth, goodness, mechanism, science, democracy, abstraction, peace, comes an age of freedom, fiction, evil, kindred, art, aristocracy, particularity, war. Has our age burned to the socket?"

"Death cannot solve the antinomy: death and life are its expression. We come at birth into a multitude and after death would perish into the One did not a witch of Endor call us back, nor would she repent did we shriek with Samuel: 'Why hast thou disquieted me?' instead of slumbering upon that breast."

"The marriage bed is the symbol of the solved antinomy, and were more than symbol could a man there lose and keep his identity, but he falls asleep. That sleep is the same as the sleep of death."

"Dear predatory birds, prepare for war, prepare your children and all that you can reach, for how can a nation or a kindred without war become that 'bright particular star' of Shakespeare, that lit the roads in boyhood? Test art, morality, custom, thought, by Thermopylae; make rich and poor act so to one another that they can stand together there. Love war because of its horror, that belief may be changed, civilisation re-

newed. We desire belief and lack it. Belief comes from
shock and is not desired. When a kindred discovers
through apparition and horror that the perfect cannot
perish nor even the imperfect long be interrupted, who
can withstand that kindred? Belief is renewed continu-
ally in the ordeal of death."

Aherne said:

"Even if the next divine influx be to kindreds why
should war be necessary? Cannot they develop their
characteristics in some other way?" He said something
more which I did not hear, for I was watching Mary
Bell standing motionless with ecstatic eyes. Denise
whispered: "She has done very well, but Robartes
should have asked me to hold it, for I am taller, and
my training as a model would have helped".

Robartes put the egg in its box again, and said good-
bye to us one after the other.

JOHN DUDDON

DEAR MR. YEATS,

I have access to records of Robartes' thought and
action. There are diaries kept by my brother Owen
during their tramps in Ireland in 1919, 1922 and 1923.
Should I live, and my brother consent, I may publish
some part of these, for they found themselves, as always,
where life is at tension, and met, amidst Free State
soldiers, irregulars, country gentlemen, tramps and
robbers, events that suggest, set down as they are without context or explanation, recent paintings by Mr.
Jack Yeats where one guesses at the forms from a few
exciting blotches of colour. There is a record made
by Robartes' pupils in London that contains his diagrams and their explanations, and John Duddon's long

narrative. You have sent me three poems founded upon "hearsay" as you put it, "The Phases of the Moon", "The Double Vision", and "The Gift of Harun Al-Rashid". The first two compared with what I find in the diaries are sufficiently accurate. One has to allow of course for some condensation and heightening. "The Gift of Harun Al-Rashid" seems to have got the dates wrong, for according to the story Robartes told my brother, the Founder of the Judwali Sect, Kusta ben Luka, was a young or youngish man when Harun Al-Rashid died. However, poetic licence may still exist.

I have compared what you sent of your unpublished book with the diagrams and explanations recorded by his pupils, and find no essential difference. That you should have found what was lost in the *Speculum* or survives in the inaccessible encampments of the Judwalis, interests me but does not astonish. I recall what Plato said of memory, and suggest that your automatic script, or whatever it was, may well have been but a process of remembering. I think that Plato symbolised by the word "memory" a relation to the timeless, but Duddon is more literal and discovers a resemblance between your face and that of Giraldus in the *Speculum*. I enclose a photograph of the woodcut.

You ask if Robartes and my brother are as hot as ever about that old quarrel and exactly what is the quarrel. This is what I found after questioning various people. Some thirty years ago you made "Rosa Alchemica", "The Tables of the Law" and "The Adoration of the Magi", out of "a slight incident". Robartes, then a young man, had founded a society, with the unwilling help of my brother Owen, for the study of the *Kabbala Denudata* and similar books, invented some kind of ritual and hired an old shed on Howth Pier for its meetings. A foolish rumour got out among the herring or mackerel sorters, and some girls (from Glasgow, my brother says, for they come from all parts) broke the window. You hatched out of this the murder of Robartes and his friends, and though my brother incorporated Christ in the ritual, described a sort of orgy in honour of the pagan gods. My brother is very bitter about the pagan gods, but is so, according to Robartes, to prove himself an orthodox man. Robartes makes no complaint about your description of his death and says nobody would have thought the Aherne and Robartes of such fantastic stories real men but for Owen's outcry. He is, however (and this I confirm from my own knowledge), bitter about your style in those stories and says that you substituted sound for sense and ornament for thought. What happened immediately before his separation from Europe must stand out with an unnatural distinction. I wrote once to remonstrate. I said that you wrote in those tales as many good writers wrote at the time over half Europe, that such prose was the equivalent of what somebody had called "absolute poetry" and somebody else "pure poetry"; that though it lacked speed and variety, it would have acquired both, as Elizabethan prose did after the *Arcadia*, but for the surrender everywhere to the sensational and the topical; that romance driven to its last ditch had a right to swagger. He answered that when the candle was burnt out an honest man did not pretend that grease was flame.

JOHN AHERNE

THE PHASES OF THE MOON

THE PHASES OF THE MOON

An old man cocked his ear upon a bridge;
He and his friend, their faces to the South,
Had trod the uneven road. Their boots were soiled,
Their Connemara cloth worn out of shape;
They had kept a steady pace as though their beds,
Despite a dwindling and late-risen moon,
Were distant still. An old man cocked his ear.

AHERNE

What made that sound?

ROBARTES

　　　　A rat or water-hen
Splashed, or an otter slid into the stream.
We are on the bridge; that shadow is the tower,
And the light proves that he is reading still.
He has found, after the manner of his kind,
Mere images; chosen this place to live in
Because, it may be, of the candle-light
From the far tower where Milton's Platonist
Sat late, or Shelley's visionary prince:
The lonely light that Samuel Palmer engraved,
An image of mysterious wisdom won by toil;
And now he seeks in book or manuscript
What he shall never find.

AHERNE

　　　　Why should not you
Who know it all ring at his door, and speak
Just truth enough to show that his whole life
Will scarcely find for him a broken crust
Of all those truths that are your daily bread;
And when you have spoken take the roads again?

ROBARTES

He wrote of me in that extravagant style
He had learned from Pater, and to round his tale
Said I was dead; and dead I choose to be.

AHERNE

Sing me the changes of the moon once more;
True song, though speech: "mine author sung it me".

ROBARTES

Twenty-and-eight the phases of the moon,
The full and the moon's dark and all the crescents,
Twenty-and-eight, and yet but six-and-twenty
The cradles that a man must needs be rocked in;
For there's no human life at the full or the dark.
From the first crescent to the half, the dream
But summons to adventure, and the man
Is always happy like a bird or a beast;
But while the moon is rounding towards the full
He follows whatever whim's most difficult
Among whims not impossible, and though scarred,
As with the cat-o'-nine-tails of the mind,
His body moulded from within his body
Grows comelier. Eleven pass, and then
Athena takes Achilles by the hair,
Hector is in the dust, Nietzsche is born,
Because the hero's crescent is the twelfth.
And yet, twice born, twice buried, grow he must,
Before the full moon, helpless as a worm.
The thirteenth moon but sets the soul at war
In its own being, and when that war's begun
There is no muscle in the arm; and after,
Under the frenzy of the fourteenth moon,
The soul begins to tremble into stillness,
To die into the labyrinth of itself!

AHERNE

Sing out the song; sing to the end, and sing
The strange reward of all that discipline.

ROBARTES

All thought becomes an image and the soul
Becomes a body: that body and that soul
Too perfect at the full to lie in a cradle,
Too lonely for the traffic of the world:
Body and soul cast out and cast away
Beyond the visible world.

AHERNE

All dreams of the soul
End in a beautiful man's or woman's body.

ROBARTES

Have you not always known it?

AHERNE

The song will have it
That those that we have loved got their long fingers
From death, and wounds, or on Sinai's top,
Or from some bloody whip in their own hands.
They ran from cradle to cradle till at last
Their beauty dropped out of the loneliness
Of body and soul.

ROBARTES

The lover's heart knows that.

AHERNE

It must be that the terror in their eyes
Is memory or foreknowledge of the hour
When all is fed with light and heaven is bare.

ROBARTES

When the moon's full those creatures of the full
Are met on the waste hills by country men
Who shudder and hurry by: body and soul
Estranged amid the strangeness of themselves,
Caught up in contemplation, the mind's eye
Fixed upon images that once were thought,
For separate, perfect, and immovable
Images can break the solitude
Of lovely, satisfied, indifferent eyes.

And thereupon with aged, high-pitched voice
Aherne laughed, thinking of the man within,
His sleepless candle and laborious pen.

ROBARTES

And after that the crumbling of the moon:
The soul remembering its loneliness
Shudders in many cradles; all is changed.
It would be the world's servant, and as it serves,
Choosing whatever task's most difficult
Among tasks not impossible, it takes
Upon the body and upon the soul
The coarseness of the drudge.

AHERNE

Before the full
It sought itself and afterwards the world.

ROBARTES

Because you are forgotten, half out of life,
And never wrote a book, your thought is clear.
Reformer, merchant, statesman, learned man,
Dutiful husband, honest wife by turn,
Cradle upon cradle, and all in flight and all

Deformed, because there is no deformity
But saves us from a dream.

AHERNE

And what of those
That the last servile crescent has set free?

ROBARTES

Because all dark, like those that are all light,
They are cast beyond the verge, and in a cloud,
Crying to one another like the bats;
But having no desire they cannot tell
What's good or bad, or what it is to triumph
At the perfection of one's own obedience;
And yet they speak what's blown into the mind;
Deformed beyond deformity, unformed,
Insipid as the dough before it is baked,
They change their bodies at a word.

AHERNE

And then?

ROBARTES

When all the dough has been so kneaded up
That it can take what form cook Nature fancies,
The first thin crescent is wheeled round once more.

AHERNE

But the escape; the song's not finished yet.

ROBARTES

Hunchback and Saint and Fool are the last crescents.
The burning bow that once could shoot an arrow
Out of the up and down, the wagon-wheel

Of beauty's cruelty and wisdom's chatter—
Out of that raving tide—is drawn betwixt
Deformity of body and of mind.

AHERNE

Were not our beds far off I'd ring the bell,
Stand under the rough roof-timbers of the hall
Beside the castle door, where all is stark
Austerity, a place set out for wisdom
That he will never find; I'd play a part;
He would never know me after all these years
But take me for some drunken country man;
I'd stand and mutter there until he caught
"Hunchback and Saint and Fool", and that they came
Under the three last crescents of the moon,
And then I'd stagger out. He'd crack his wits
Day after day, yet never find the meaning.

And then he laughed to think that what seemed hard
Should be so simple—a bat rose from the hazels
And circled round him with its squeaky cry,
The light in the tower window was put out.

THE GREAT WHEEL

The Great Wheel

from the *Speculum Angelorum et Hominum*

BOOK I: THE GREAT WHEEL

Part I: THE PRINCIPAL SYMBOL

I

"When Discord", writes Empedocles, "has fallen into the lowest depths of the vortex"—the extreme bound, not the centre, Burnet points out—"Concord has reached the centre, into it do all things come together so as to be only one, not all at once but gradually from different quarters, and as they come Discord retires to the extreme boundary . . . in proportion as it runs out Concord in a soft immortal boundless stream runs in." And again: "Never will boundless time be emptied of that pair; and they prevail in turn as that circle comes round, and pass away before one another and increase in their appointed turn". It was this Discord or War that Heraclitus called "God of all and Father of all, some it has made gods and some men, some bond and some free", and I recall that Love and War came from the eggs of Leda.

II

According to Simplicius,[1] a late commentator upon Aristotle, the Concord of Empedocles fabricates all things into "an homogeneous sphere", and then Discord separates the elements and so makes the world we inhabit, but even the sphere formed by Concord is not

[1] Quoted by Pierre Duhem in *Le Système du monde*, vol. i, page 75.

the changeless eternity, for Concord or Love but offers us the image of that which is changeless.

If we think of the vortex attributed to Discord as formed by circles diminishing until they are nothing, and of the opposing sphere attributed to Concord as forming from itself an opposing vortex, the apex of each vortex in the middle of the other's base, we have the fundamental symbol of my instructors.

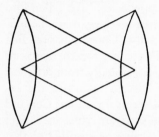 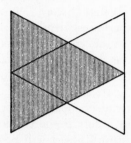

If I call the unshaded cone "Discord" and the other "Concord" and think of each as the bound of a gyre, I see that the gyre of "Concord" diminishes as that of "Discord" increases, and can imagine after that the gyre of "Concord" increasing while that of "Discord" diminishes, and so on, one gyre within the other always. Here the thought of Heraclitus dominates all: "Dying each other's life, living each other's death".

The first gyres clearly described by philosophy are those described in the *Timaeus* which are made by the circuits of "the Other" (creators of all particular things), of the planets as they ascend or descend above or below the equator. They are opposite in nature to that circle of the fixed stars which constitutes "the Same" and confers upon us the knowledge of Universals. Alcemon, a pupil of Pythagoras, thought that men die because they

cannot join their beginning and their end. Their serpent
has not its tail in its mouth. But my friend the poet and
scholar Dr. Sturm sends me an account of gyres in St.
Thomas Aquinas: the circular movement of the angels
which, though it imitates the circle of "the Same",
seems as little connected with the visible heavens as
figures drawn by my instructors, his straight line of the
human intellect and his gyre, the combination of both
movements, made by the ascent and descent [1] of angels
between God and man. He has also found me passages
in Dr. Dee, in Macrobius, in an unknown mediaeval
writer, which describe souls changing from gyre to
sphere and from sphere to gyre. Presently I shall have
much to say of the sphere as the final place of rest.

Gyres are occasionally alluded to, but left unexplored,
in Swedenborg's mystical writings. In the *Principia*, a
vast scientific work written before his mystical life,
he describes the double cone. All physical reality,
the universe as a whole, every solar system, every
atom, is a double cone; where there are "two poles
one opposite to the other, these two poles have the
form of cones".[2] I am not concerned with his explanation of how these cones have evolved from the
point and the sphere, nor with his arguments to
prove that they govern all the movements of the
planets, for I think, as did Swedenborg in his mystical
writings, that the forms of geometry can have but a
symbolic relation to spaceless reality, *Mundus Intelligi-*

[1] In an essay called "The Friends of the People of Faery" in my
Celtic Twilight I describe such an ascent and descent. I found the
same movement in some story I picked up at Kiltartan, and suspected a mediaeval symbolism unknown to me at the time.

[2] Vol. ii, p. 555 of the Swedenborg Society's translation.

bilis. Flaubert is the only writer known to me who has so used the double cone. He talked much of writing a story called "La Spirale". He died before he began it, but something of his talk about it has been collected and published. It would have described a man whose dreams during sleep grew in magnificence as his life grew more and more unlucky, the wreck of some love affair coinciding with his marriage to a dream princess.

III

The double cone or vortex, as used by my instructors, is more complicated than that of Flaubert. A line is a movement without extension, and so symbolical of time —subjectivity—Berkeley's stream of ideas—in Plotinus[1] it is apparently "sensation"—and a plane cutting it at right angles is symbolical of space or objectivity. Line and plane are combined in a gyre which must expand or contract according to whether mind grows in objectivity or subjectivity.

The identification of time[2] with subjectivity is prob-

[1] *Ennead*, vi. i. 8 (MacKenna's translation).

[2] Giovanni Gentile summarises Kant on time and space as follows: "Kant said that space is a form of external sense, time a form of internal sense. He meant that we represent nature, that is what we call the external world and think of as having been in existence before our knowledge and spiritual life began, in space, then we represent the multiplicity of the objects of our internal experience, or what we distinguish as diverse and manifold in the development of our spiritual life, not in space but in time" (*Theory of Mind as Pure Art*, chap. ix, H. Wildon Carr's translation). He thinks these definitions which seem to separate time and space from one another require re-statement. It will be seen, however, when I come to what I have called the *Four Principles*, that my symbols imply his description of time as a spatialising act.

ably as old as philosophy; all that we can touch or handle, and for the moment I mean no other objectivity, has shape or magnitude, whereas our thoughts and emotions have duration and quality, a thought recurs or is habitual, a lecture or a musical composition is measured upon the clock. At the same time pure time

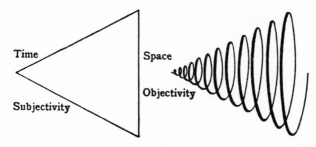

and pure space, pure subjectivity and pure objectivity— the plane at the bottom of the cone and the point at its apex—are abstractions or figments of the mind.

IV

My instructors used this single cone or vortex once or twice but soon changed it for a double cone or vortex, preferring to consider subjectivity and objectivity as intersecting states struggling one against the other. If the musical composition seek to suggest the howling of dogs or of the sea waves it is not altogether in time, it suggests bulk and weight. In what I call the cone of the *Four Faculties* which are what man has made in a past or present life—I shall speak later of what makes man—the subjective cone is called that of the *antithetical tincture* because it is achieved and defended by continual conflict with its opposite; the objective cone is called that of the *primary tincture* because whereas subjectivity—in Empedocles "Discord" as I think—tends to separate man from man, objectivity brings us back to the mass where we begin. I had suggested the word *tincture*, a common word in Boehme, and my instructors took the word *antithetical* from *Per Amica Silentia Lunae.*

I had never read Hegel, but my mind had been full of Blake from boyhood up and I saw the world as a conflict

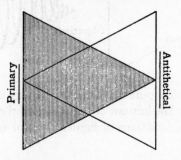

—Spectre and Emanation—and could distinguish between a contrary and a negation. "Contraries are positive", wrote Blake, "a negation is not a contrary", "How great the gulph between simplicity and insipidity", and again, "There is a place at the bottom of the graves where contraries are equally true".

I had never put the conflict in logical form,[1] never thought with Hegel that the two ends of the see-saw

---

[1] Though reality is not logical it becomes so in our minds if we discover logical refutations of the writer or movement that is going out of fashion. There is always error, which has nothing to do with "the conflict" which creates all life. Croce in his study of Hegel identifies error with negation.

are one another's negation, nor that the spring vegetables were refuted when over.

The cones of the *tinctures* mirror reality but are in themselves pursuit and illusion. As will be presently seen, the sphere is reality. By the *antithetical* cone, which is left unshaded in my diagram, we express more and more, as it broadens, our inner world of desire and imagination, whereas by the *primary*, the shaded cone, we express more and more, as it broadens, that objectivity of mind which, in the words of Murray's Dictionary, lays "stress upon that which is external to the mind" or treats "of outward things and events rather than of inward thought" or seeks "to exhibit the actual facts, not coloured by the opinions or feelings". The *antithetical tincture* is emotional and aesthetic whereas the *primary tincture* is reasonable and moral. Within these cones move what are called the *Four Faculties*: *Will* and *Mask*, *Creative Mind* and *Body of Fate*.

It will be enough until I have explained the geometrical diagrams in detail to describe *Will* and *Mask* as the will and its object, or the *Is* and the *Ought* (or that which should be), *Creative Mind* and *Body of Fate* as thought and its object, or the *Knower* and the *Known*, and to say that the first two are lunar or *antithetical* or natural, the second two solar or *primary* or reasonable. A particular man is classified according to the place of *Will*, or choice, in the diagram. At first sight there are only two *Faculties*, because only two of the four, *Will* and *Creative Mind*, are active, but it will be presently seen that the *Faculties* can be represented by two opposing cones so drawn that the *Will* of the one is the *Mask* of the other, the *Creative Mind* of the one the *Body of Fate* of the other. Everything that wills can be desired, resisted or accepted, every creative act can be seen as fact, every *Faculty* is alternately shield and sword.

V

These pairs of opposites whirl in contrary directions, *Will* and *Mask* from right to left, *Creative Mind* and *Body of Fate* like the hands of a clock, from left to right. I will confine myself for the moment to *Will* and *Creative Mind*, will and thought. As *Will* approaches the utmost expansion of its *antithetical* cone it drags *Creative Mind* with it—thought is more and more dominated by will

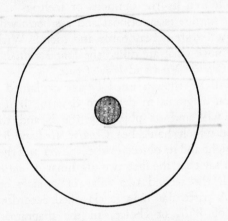

—but *Creative Mind* remains at the same distance from its cone's narrow end that *Will* is from the broad end of the *antithetical* cone. Then, as though satiated by the extreme expansion of its cone, *Will* lets *Creative Mind* dominate, and is dragged by it until *Creative Mind* weakens once more. As *Creative Mind*, let us say, is dragged by *Will* towards the utmost expansion of its *antithetical* cone it is more and more contaminated by *Will*, while *Will* frees itself from contamination. We can, however, represent the two *Faculties* as they approach the full expansion of the *antithetical* cone by the same cross-sections of the cone.

The shaded, or *primary* part, is a contamination of *Will*; the unshaded, or *antithetical* part, a contamination of *Creative Mind*. We can substitute positions in the cones for either symbol: we can represent *Creative Mind* as approaching the extreme expansion of the *antithetical* cone and then as changing into the narrow end of the *primary* cone and expanding once more; the *Will* as approaching the narrow end of the *primary* cone and then, at the same instant when the *Creative Mind* changes cones, passing into the broad end of the *antithetical* cone, and contracting once more. The diagram is sometimes so used by my instructors and gives them a phrase which constantly occurs, "the interchange of the *tinctures*", but it is inconvenient. For this reason they generally represent the *Faculties* as moving always along the outside of the diagram. Just before complete *antithetical* expression they are placed thus:

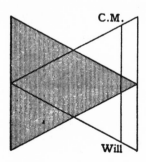

Just after it, thus:

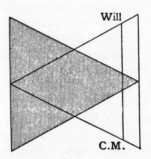

I think of the gyre of *Will* as approaching complete *antithetical* expansion—unshaded cone—along the lower side of the diagram or moving from right to left, and the gyre of *Creative Mind* as approaching it along the upper side, left to right, and then of their passing one another at complete expansion, then of their receding from it, *Will* upon the upper side, *Creative Mind* upon the lower, and always on the outside of the diagram until they pass one another at complete *primary* expansion. These movements are but a convenient pictorial summary of what is more properly a double movement of two gyres. These gyres move not only forward to the *primary* and *antithetical* expansion, but have their own circular movement, the gyre of *Will* from right to left, that of *Creative Mind* from left to right. I shall consider presently the significance of these circlings.

VI

The *Mask* and *Body of Fate* occupy those positions which are most opposite in character to the positions

of *Will* and *Creative Mind.* If *Will* and *Creative Mind* are
approaching complete *antithetical* expansion, *Mask* and
Body of Fate are approaching complete *primary* expansion,
and so on. In the following figure the man is almost
completely *antithetical* in nature.

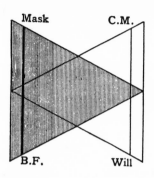

In the following almost completely *primary.*

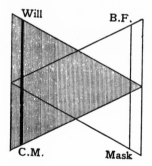

In the following he is completely *primary,* a state which
is like the completely *antithetical* state, as I must show
presently, only a supernatural or ideal existence.

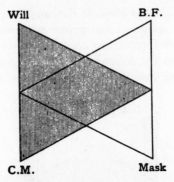

In the following he is midway between *primary* and *antithetical* and moving towards *antithetical* expansion. All four gyres are superimposed.

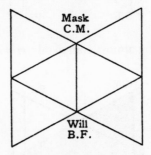

I have now only to set a row of numbers upon the sides to possess a classification, as I will show presently, of every possible movement of thought and of life, and I have been told to make these numbers correspond to the phases of the moon, including among them full moon and the moonless night when the moon is nearest to the sun. The moonless night is called Phase 1, and the full moon is Phase 15. Phase 8 begins the *antithetical* phases, those where the bright part of the moon is greater than the dark, and Phase 22 begins the *primary* phases, where the dark part is greater than the bright. At Phases 15 and 1 respectively, the *antithetical* and *primary tinctures* come to a climax. A man of, say, Phase 13 is a man whose *Will* is at that phase, and the diagram which shows the position of the *Faculties* for a *Will* so placed, describes his character and destiny. The last phase is Phase 28, and the twenty-eight phases constitute a month of which each day and night constitute an incarnation and the discarnate

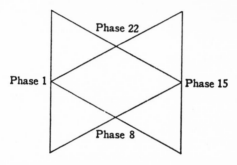

Phase 22

Phase 1   Phase 15

Phase 8

period which follows. I am for the moment only concerned with the incarnation, symbolised by the moon at night.

Phase 1 and Phase 15 are not human incarnations because human life is impossible without strife between the *tinctures*. They belong to an order of existence which we shall consider presently. The figure which I have used to represent *Will* at almost complete subjectivity represents the moon just before its round is complete, and instead of using a black disc with a white dot for *Will* at almost complete objectivity I think of the last crescent.

But it is more convenient to set these figures round a circle thus:

PART II: EXAMINATION OF THE WHEEL

I

DURING the first months of instruction I had the Great Wheel of the lunar phases as printed at the end of this paragraph, but knew nothing of the cones that explain it, and though I had abundant definitions and descriptions of the *Faculties* at their different stations, did not know why they passed one another at certain points, nor why two moved from left to right like the sun's daily course, two from right to left like the moon in the zodiac. Even when I wrote the first edition of this book I thought the geometrical symbolism so difficult, I understood it so little, that I put it off to a later section; and as I had at that time, for a reason I have explained, to use a romantic setting, I described the Great Wheel as danced on the desert sands by mysterious dancers who

left the traces of their feet to puzzle the Caliph of Bagdad
and his learned men. I tried to interest my readers in an
unexplained rule of thumb that somehow explained the
world.

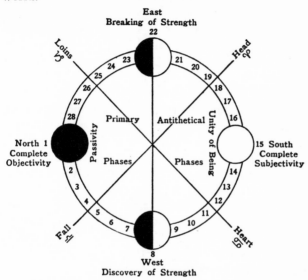

II

This wheel is every completed movement of thought
or life, twenty-eight incarnations, a single incarnation,
a single judgment or act of thought. Man seeks his
opposite or the opposite of his condition, attains his
object so far as it is attainable, at Phase 15 and returns [1]
to Phase 1 again.

[1] A similar circular movement fundamental in the works of Giovanni Gentile is, I read somewhere, the half-conscious foundation of
the political thought of modern Italy. Individuals and classes complete their personality and then sink back to enrich the mass.

Phase 15 is called Sun in Moon because the solar or *primary tincture* is consumed by the lunar, but from another point of view it is *Mask* consumed in *Will*; all is beauty. The *Mask* as it were wills itself as beauty, but because, as Plotinus says, things that are of one kind are unconscious, it is an ideal or supernatural incarnation. Phase 1 is called Moon in Sun because the lunar or *antithetical tincture* is consumed in the *primary* or solar, but from another point of view it is the *Body of Fate* consumed in *Creative Mind*; man is submissive and plastic: unless where supersensual power intervenes, the steel-like plasticity of water where the last ripple has been smoothed away. We shall presently have to consider the *Principles* where pure thought is possible, but in the *Faculties* the sole activity and the sole unity is natural or lunar, and in the *primary* phases that unity is moral. At Phase 1 morality is complete submission. All unity is from the *Mask*, and the *antithetical Mask* is described in the automatic script as a "form created by passion to unite us to ourselves", the self so sought is that Unity of Being compared by Dante in the *Convito* to that of "a perfectly proportioned human body". The *Body of Fate* is the sum, not the unity, of fact, fact as it affects a particular man. Only in the Four *Principles* shall we discover the concord of Empedocles. The *Will* is very much the Will described by Croce.[1] When not affected by

Government must, it is held, because all good things have been created by class war, recognise that class war though it may be regulated must never end. It is the old saying of Heraclitus,"War is God of all, and Father of all, some it has made Gods and some men, some bond and some free", and the converse of Marxian Socialism.

[1] The *Four Faculties* somewhat resemble the four moments to which Croce has dedicated four books; that the resemblance is not closer is because Croce makes little use of antithesis and antinomy.

the other *Faculties* it has neither emotion, morality nor intellectual interest, but knows how things are done, how windows open and shut, how roads are crossed, everything that we call utility. It seeks its own continuance. Only by the pursuit or acceptance of its direct opposite, that object of desire or moral ideal which is of all possible things the most difficult, and by forcing that form upon the *Body of Fate*, can it attain self-knowledge and expression. Phase 8 and Phase 22 are phases of struggle and tragedy, the first a struggle to find personality, the second to lose it. After Phase 22 and before Phase 1 there is a struggle to accept the fate-imposed unity, from Phase 1 to Phase 8 to escape it.

All such abstract statements are, however, misleading, for we are dealing always with a particular man, the man of Phase 13 or Phase 17 let us say. The *Four Faculties* are not the abstract categories of philosophy, being the result of the four memories of the *Daimon* or ultimate self of that man. His *Body of Fate*, the series of events forced upon him from without, is shaped out of the *Daimon's* memory of the events of his past incarnations; his *Mask* or object of desire or idea of the good, out of its memory of the moments of exaltation in his past lives; his *Will* or normal ego out of its memory of all the events of his present life, whether consciously remembered or not; his *Creative Mind* from its memory of ideas—or universals—displayed by actual men in past lives, or their spirits between lives.

III

When I wish for some general idea which will describe the Great Wheel as an individual life I go to the *Com-*

media dell' Arte or improvised drama of Italy. The stage-manager, or *Daimon*, offers his actor an inherited scenario, the *Body of Fate*, and a *Mask* or rôle as unlike as possible to his natural ego or *Will*, and leaves him to improvise through his *Creative Mind* the dialogue and details of the plot. He must discover or reveal a being which only exists with extreme effort, when his muscles are as it were all taut and all his energies active. But this is *antithetical* man. For *primary* man I go to the *Commedia dell' Arte* in its decline. The *Will* is weak and cannot create a rôle, and so, if it transform itself, does so after an accepted pattern, some traditional clown or pantaloon. It has perhaps no object but to move the crowd, and if it "gags" it is that there may be plenty of topical allusions. In the *primary* phases man must cease to desire *Mask* and Image by ceasing from self-expression, and substitute a motive of service for that of self-expression. Instead of the created *Mask* he has an imitative *Mask*; and when he recognises this, his *Mask* may become the historical norm, or an image of mankind. The author of the *Imitation of Christ* was certainly a man of a late *primary* phase. The *antithetical Mask* and *Will* are *free*, and the *primary Mask* and *Will enforced*; and the *free Mask* and *Will* are personality, while the *enforced Mask* and *Will* are code, those limitations which give strength precisely because they are *enforced*. Personality, no matter how habitual, is a constantly renewed choice, varying from an individual charm, in the more *antithetical* phases, to a hard objective dramatisation; but when the *primary* phases begin man is moulded more and more from without.

Antithetical men are, like Landor, violent in themselves because they hate all that impedes their personality, but are in their intellect (*Creative Mind*) gentle, whereas *primary* men whose hatreds are impersonal are violent in their intellect but gentle in themselves, as doubtless Robespierre was gentle.

The *Mask* before Phase 15 is described as a "revelation" because through it the being obtains knowledge of itself, sees itself in personality; while after Phase 15 it is a "concealment", for the being grows incoherent, vague and broken, as its intellect (*Creative Mind*) is more and more concerned with objects that have no relation to its unity but a relation to the unity of society or of material things known through the *Body of Fate*. It adopts a personality which it more and more casts outward, more and more dramatises. It is now a dissolving violent phantom which would grip itself and hold itself together. The being of *antithetical* man is described as full of rage before Phase 12, against all in the world that hinders its expression, after Phase 12, but before Phase 15, the rage is a knife turned against itself. After Phase 15, but before Phase 19, the being is full of phantasy, a continual escape from and yet acknowledgment of all that allures in the world, a continual playing with all that must engulf it. The *primary* is that which serves, the *antithetical* is that which creates.

At Phase 8 is the "Discovery of Strength", its embodiment in sensuality. The imitation that held it to the enforced *Mask*, the norm of the race now a hated convention, has ceased and its own norm has not begun. *Primary* and *antithetical* are equal and fight for mastery; and when this fight is ended through the conviction of weakness and the preparation for rage, the *Mask* becomes once more voluntary. At Phase 22 is the "Breaking of Strength", for here the being makes its last attempt to impose its personality upon the world before the *Mask* becomes enforced once more, character substituted for personality. To these two phases, perhaps to all phases, the being may return up to four times, my instructors say, before it can pass on. It is claimed, however, that four times is the utmost possible. By being is understood that which divides into *Four Faculties*, by individuality the *Will* analysed in relation to itself, by personality the *Will* analysed in relation to the free *Mask*, by character *Will* analysed in relation to the enforced *Mask*. Personality is strongest near Phase 15, individuality near Phase 22 and Phase 8.

In the last phases, Phases 26, 27 and 28, the *Faculties* wear away, grow transparent, and man may see himself as it were arrayed against the supersensual; but of this I shall speak when I consider the *Principles*.

IV

The *Will* looks into a painted picture, the *Creative Mind* looks into a photograph, but both look into something that is the opposite of themselves. The *Creative Mind* contains all the universals in so far as its memory permits their employment, whereas the photograph is heterogeneous. The picture is chosen, the photograph is fated, because by Fate and Necessity—for I need both words—is understood that which comes from without, whereas the *Mask* is predestined, Destiny being that which comes to us from within. We can best explain the heterogeneity of the photograph when we call it the photograph of a crowded street, which the *Creative Mind* when not under the influence of the *Mask* contemplates coldly; while the picture contains but few objects and the contemplating *Will* is impassioned and solitary. When the *Will* predominates the *Mask* or Image is "sensuous"; when *Creative Mind* predominates it is "abstract", when *Mask* predominates it is "idealised", when *Body of Fate* predominates it is "concrete". The automatic script defines "sensuous" in an unexpected way. An object is sensuous if I relate it to myself, "my fire, my chair, my sensation", whereas "a fire, a chair, a sensation", are all concrete or appertain to the *Body of Fate*; while "the fire, the chair, the sensation", because they are looked upon as representative of their kind, are "abstract". To a miser his own money would be "sensuous", another's money "concrete", the money he lacked "idealised", the money economists speak of "abstract".

V

In the Table in section XII the characters of the *Faculties* at all the different phases are described, and the phasal characteristics of a man at any particular phase can be discovered by their means. The descriptions should not be considered as exhaustive but as suggestions to call into imagination the *Four Faculties* at any particular phase.

They were written in the automatic script sometimes two or three, sometimes eight or nine at a time. Even now after years of use I could not re-create them if the Table were lost. I should say they proved a use more prolonged than my own did I not remember that the creators of the script claim a rapidity of thought impossible to our minds. I think of the elaborate pictures one sees between sleeping and waking and often showing powers of design and invention that would have taken hours of an artist's time.

At Phases 11 and 12 occurs what is called the *opening of the tinctures*, at Phase 11 the *antithetical* opens, at Phase 12 the *primary*. A cone is for the moment substituted for the wheel, a gyre encircles the cone, ascending or descending, which completes its journey round the cone, while the larger movement completes a phase. The opening means the reflection inward of the *Four Faculties*: all are as it were mirrored in personality, Unity of Being becomes possible. Hitherto we have been part of something else, but now discover everything within our own nature. Sexual love becomes the most important event in life, for the opposite sex is nature chosen and fated. Personality seeks personality. Every emotion begins to be related to every other as musical notes are related. It is as though we touched a musical string that set other strings vibrating. The *antithetical tincture* (*Will* and *Mask*) opens first because the phases signified by odd numbers are *antithetical*, the *primary tincture* at Phase 12 because those signified by even numbers are *primary*. Though all phases from Phase 8 to Phase 22 are *antithetical*, taken as a whole, and all phases from Phase 22 to Phase 8 *primary*; seen by different analysis the individual phases are alternately *antithetical* and *primary*. At Phase 18 the *primary tincture* closes once more, and at Phase 19 the *antithetical*. At Phases 25 and 26 there is a new opening, and at Phases 4 and 5 a new closing, but this time the *tinctures* open not into personality but into its negation. The whole objectively perceived. One may regard the subjective phases as forming a separate wheel, its Phase 8 between Phases 11 and 12 of larger wheel, its Phase 22 between

Phases 19 and 20; the objective phases as another
separate wheel, its Phase 8 between Phases 25 and 26,
its Phase 22 between Phases 4 and 5. This wheel between its Phases 8 and 22 is not subjective, from the
point of man, but a sharing of or submission to divine
personality experienced as spiritual objectivity, whereas
its three first and three last phases are physical objectivity. During this spiritual objectivity, or spiritual
primary, the *Faculties* "wear thin", the *Principles*, which
are, when evoked from the point of view of the
Faculties, a sphere, shine through. At Phase 15 and
Phase 1 occurs what is called the *interchange of the
tinctures*, those thoughts, emotions, energies, which
were *primary* before Phase 15 or Phase 1 are *antithetical*
after, those that were *antithetical* are *primary*. I was told,
for instance, that before the historical Phase 15 the *antithetical tincture* of the average European was dominated by
reason and desire, the *primary* by race and emotion, and
that after Phase 15 this was reversed, his subjective
nature had been passionate and logical but was now
enthusiastic and sentimental. I have made little use of
this interchange in my account of the twenty-eight
incarnations because when I wrote it I did not understand the relation between the change and Unity of
Being. Every phase is in itself a wheel; the individual
soul is awakened by a violent oscillation (one thinks
of Verlaine oscillating between the church and the
brothel) until it sinks in on that Whole where the
contraries are united, the antinomies resolved.

VI

RULES FOR DISCOVERING TRUE AND FALSE MASKS

When the Will is in antithetical phases the True Mask is the effect of Creative Mind of opposite phase upon that phase; and the False Mask is the effect of Body of Fate of opposite phase upon that phase.

The True *Mask* of Phase 17, for instance, is "Simplification through intensity", derived from Phase 3, modified by the *Creative Mind* of that phase, which is described as "Simplicity" and comes from Phase 27, which is that of the Saint.

The False *Mask* of Phase 17 is "Dispersal", derived from Phase 3, modified by the *Body of Fate* of the Phase which comes from Phase 13 and is described as "Interest". It will be found that this word describes with great accuracy the kind of "Dispersal" which weakens men of Phase 17 when they try to live in the *primary tincture*.

When the Will is in primary phases the True Mask is the effect of Body of Fate of opposite phase upon that phase; and the False Mask is the effect of Creative Mind of opposite phase upon that phase.

The True *Mask* of Phase 3 is "Innocence", derived from Phase 17, modified by the *Body of Fate* of the Phase which is described as "Loss" and comes from Phase 27, which is that of the Saint.

The False *Mask* of Phase 3 is "Folly" derived from Phase 17, modified by the *Creative Mind* of that phase which is described as "Creative imagination through *antithetical* emotion" and comes from Phase 13. The *primary* Phase 3, when it attempts to live *antithetically*, gives itself up to inconsequence because it cannot be creative in the *Mask*. On the other hand, when it lives according to the *primary*, and is true to phase, it takes from its opposite phase delight in passing things, sees "a world in a grain of sand, a Heaven in a wild flower" and becomes a child playing, knows nothing of consequence and purpose. "Loss" affects Phase 17 itself as an enforced withdrawal of *primary* desire, for the *Body of Fate* is inimical to *antithetical* natures.

Only long familiarity with the system can make the whole Table of *Masks, Creative Minds*, etc.—see Sec. XII —intelligible; it should be studied by the help of these two following rules:

In an antithetical phase the being seeks by the help of the Creative Mind to deliver the Mask from Body of Fate.

In a primary phase the being seeks by the help of the Body of Fate to deliver the Creative Mind from the Mask.

VII

RULES FOR FINDING THE TRUE AND FALSE CREATIVE MIND

When the Will is in antithetical phases the True Creative Mind is derived from the Creative Mind phase, modified by the Creative Mind of that phase; while the False Creative Mind is derived from the Creative Mind phase, modified by the Body of Fate of that phase.

For instance, the True *Creative Mind* of Phase 17, "Creative Imagination through *antithetical* Emotion", is derived from Phase 13 as that phase is modified by its *Creative Mind*, which is described as "Subjective truth" and comes from Phase 17.

The False *Creative Mind* of Phase 17, "Enforced self-realization", is derived from Phase 13 as that phase is modified by its *Body of Fate*, "Enforced love", "enforced love of another" derived from Phase 3.

When the Will is in primary phases the True Creative Mind is derived from Creative Mind phase, modified by the Body of Fate of that phase; while the False Creative Mind is derived from the Creative Mind phase modified by the False Creative Mind of that phase.

For instance, the True *Creative Mind* of Phase 27 is described as "Supersensual receptivity" and is derived from Phase 3 as that phase is modified by its *Body of Fate* derived from Phase 13, and described as "Interest"; while its False *Creative Mind* is described as "Pride" and is derived from Phase 3, modified by the False *Creative Mind* of that phase which is derived from Phase 27 and described as "Abstraction".

VIII

RULE FOR FINDING BODY OF FATE

The *Body of Fate* of any particular phase is the effect of the whole nature of its *Body of Fate* phase upon that particular phase. As, however, the *Body of Fate* is always *primary* it is in sympathy with the *primary* phase while it opposes the *antithetical* phase; in this it is the reverse of the *Mask*, which is sympathetic to an *antithetical* phase but opposes a *primary*.

IX

SUBDIVISIONS OF THE WHEEL

Excluding the four phases of crisis (Phases 8, 22, 15, 1), each quarter consists of six phases, or of two sets

XI

The Four Perfections and the Four Automatonisms

The Four Perfections can only be understood when their phases are studied in detail; it will be obvious for instance that self-sacrifice must be the typical virtue of phases where instinct or race is predominant, and especially in those three phases that come before reflection. Automatonism in *antithetical* phases arises from the *Mask* and *Creative Mind*, when separated from the *Body of Fate* and *Will*, through refusal of, or rest from conflict; and in *primary* phases from the *Body of Fate* and *Will*, when weary of the struggle for complete *primary* existence or when they refuse that struggle. It does not necessarily mean that the man is not true to phase or, as it is said, out of phase; the most powerful natures are precisely those who most often need Automatonism as a rest. It is perhaps an element in our enjoyment of art and literature, being awakened in our minds by rhythm and by pattern. He is, however, out of phase, if he refuse for anything but need of rest the conflict with the *Body of Fate* which is the source of *antithetical* energy and so falls under imitative or creative Automatonism, or if in *primary* phases he refuse conflict with the *Mask* and so falls under obedient or instinctive Automatonism.

XII

Table of the Four Faculties

Each *Faculty* is placed after the number of the phase where it is formed, not after the phase which it affects.

TABLE OF THE FOUR FACULTIES

WILL	MASK	CREATIVE MIND	BODY OF FATE
1. No	description except	Complete plasticity.	
2. Beginning of energy.	*True.* Illusion. *False.* Delusion.	*True.* Physical activity. *False.* Cunning.	Enforced love of the world.
3. Beginning of ambition.	*True.* Simplification through intensity. *False.* Dispersal.	*True.* Supersensual receptivity. *False.* Pride.	Enforced love of another.
4. Desire for *primary* objects.	*True.* Intensity through emotions. *False.* Curiosity.	*True.* Beginning of the abstract supersensual. *False.* Fascination of sin.	Enforced intellectual action.
5. Separation from innocence.	*True.* Conviction. *False.* Domination.	*True.* Rhetoric. *False.* Spiritual arrogance.	Enforced belief.
6. Artificial individuality.	*True.* Fatalism. *False.* Superstition.	*True.* Constructive emotion. *False.* Authority.	Enforced emotion.
7. Assertion of individuality.	*True.* Self-analysis. *False.* Self-adaptation.	*True.* Creation through pity. *False.* Self-driven desire.	Enforced sensuality.
8. War between individuality and race.	*True.* Self-immolation. *False.* Self-assurance.	*True.* Amalgamation. *False.* Despair.	The beginning of strength.

Table of the Four Faculties—*Continued*

Will	Mask	Creative Mind	Body of Fate
9. Belief takes place of individuality.	*True.* Wisdom. *False.* Self-pity.	*True.* Domination of the intellect. *False.* Distortion.	Adventure that excites the individuality.
10. The image-breaker.	*True.* Self-reliance. *False.* Isolation.	*True.* Dramatisation of Mask. *False.* Self-desecration.	Humanity.
11. The consumer. The pyre-builder.	*True.* Consciousness of self. *False.* Self-consciousness.	*True.* Emotional intellect. *False.* The Unfaithful.	Natural law.
12. The Forerunner.	*True.* Self-realization. *False.* Self-abandonment.	*True.* Emotional philosophy. *False.* Enforced lure.	Search.
13. The sensuous man.	*True.* Renunciation. *False.* Emulation.	*True.* Creative imagination through antithetical emotion. *False.* Enforced self-realization.	Interest.
14. The obsessed man.	*True.* Oblivion. *False.* Malignity.	*True.* Vehemence. *False.* Opinionated will.	None except monotony.
15.	No description except	Complete beauty.	

TABLE OF THE FOUR FACULTIES—*Continued*

WILL	MASK	CREATIVE MIND	BODY OF FATE
16. The positive man.	*True.* Player on Pan's Pipes. *False.* Fury.	*True.* Emotional will. *False.* Terror.	The Fool is his own Body of Fate.
17. The Daimonic man.	*True.* Innocence. *False.* Folly.	*True.* Subjective truth. *False.* Morbidity.	None except impersonal action.
18. The emotional man.	*True.* Passion. *False.* Will.	*True.* Subjective philosophy. *False.* War between two forms of expression.	The Hunchback is his own Body of Fate.
19. The assertive man.	*True.* Excess. *False.* Limitation.	*True.* Moral iconoclasm. *False.* Self-assertion.	Persecution.
20. The concrete man.	*True.* Justice. *False.* Tyranny.	*True.* Domination through emotional constriction. *False.* Reformation.	Objective action.
21. The acquisitive man.	*True.* Altruism. *False.* Efficiency.	*True.* Self-dramatisation. *False.* Anarchy.	Success.

TABLE OF THE FOUR FACULTIES—*Continued*

WILL	MASK	CREATIVE MIND	BODY OF FATE
22. Balance between ambition and contemplation.	*True*. Courage. *False*. Fear.	*True*. Versatility. *False*. Impotence.	Temptation versus strength.
23. The receptive man.	*True*. Facility. *False*. Obscurity.	*True*. Heroic sentiment. *False*. Dogmatic sentimentality.	Enforced triumph of achievement.
24. The end of ambition.	*True*. Organisation. *False*. Inertia.	*True*. Ideality. *False*. Derision.	Enforced success of action.
25. The conditional man.	*True*. Rejection. *False*. Moral indifference.	*True*. Social intellect. *False*. Limitation.	Enforced failure of action.
26. The multiple man also called The Hunchback.	*True*. Self-exaggeration. *False*. Self-abandonment.	*True*. First perception of character. *False*. Mutilation.	Enforced disillusionment.
27. The Saint.	*True*. Self-expression. *False*. Self-absorption.	*True*. Simplicity. *False*. Abstraction.	Enforced loss.
28. The Fool.	*True*. Serenity. *False*. Self-distrust.	*True*. Hope. *False*. Moroseness.	Enforced illusion.

XIII

Characters of Certain Phases

Four Perfections

At P. 2, P. 3, P. 4 . Self-sacrifice
At P. 13 . . Self-knowledge
At P. 16, P. 17, P. 18 Unity of Being
At P. 27 . . Sanctity

Four Types of Wisdom [1]

At P. 4 . . . Wisdom of Desire
At P. 18 . . Wisdom of Heart
At P. 12 . . Wisdom of Intellect
At P. 26 . . Wisdom of Knowledge

Four Contests

At P. 1 . . . Moral
At P. 8 . . . Emotional
At P. 15 . . Physical
At P. 22 . . Spiritual or supersensual

Rage, Fantasy, etc.

From P. 8 to P. 12 . Rage
From P. 12 to P. 15 . Spiritual or supersensual Rage
From P. 15 to P. 19 . Fantasy
From P. 19 to P. 22 . Power

---

[1] I give the Four Types of Wisdom as they were given. I have more than once transposed Heart and Intellect, suspecting a mistake; but have come to the conclusion that my instructors placed them correctly, the nature of the wisdom depending upon the position of the *Creative Mind*.

XIV

General Character of Creative Mind [1]

(1) Affecting 28, 1, 2 from 2, 1, 28. Controlled.
(2) „ 3, 4, 5, 6 from 27, 26, 25, 24. Transformatory.
(3) „ 7, 8, 9 from 23, 22, 21. Mathematical.
(4) „ 10, 11, 12 from 20, 19, 18. Intellectually passionate.
(5) „ 13 from 17. Stillness.
(6) „ 14, 15, 16 from 16, 15, 14. Emotional.
(7) „ 17, 18, 19, 20 from 13, 12, 11, 10. Emotionally passionate.
(8) „ 21, 22, 23 from 9, 8, 7. Rational.
(9) „ 24 from 6. Obedient.
(10) „ 25, 26, 27 from 3, 4, 5. Serenity.

XV

General Character of Body of Fate affecting Certain Phases

(1) Affecting 28, 1, 2 from 16, 15, 14. Joy.
(2) „ 3, 4, 5, 6 from 13, 12, 11, 10. Breathing.
(3) „ 7, 8, 9 from 9, 8, 7. Tumult.
(4) „ 10, 11, 12 from 6, 5, 4. Tension.
(5) „ 13 from 3. Disease.

[1] This and the following Table are divided into ten divisions because they were given me in this form, and I have not sufficient confidence in my knowledge to turn them into the more convenient twelvefold divisions. At first my instructors divided the Great Year also into ten divisions.

(6) Affecting 14, 15, 16 from 2, 1, 28. The world.
(7)   ,,   17, 18, 19, 20 from 27, 26, 25, 24.
              Sorrow.
(8)   ,,   21, 22, 23 from 23, 22, 21. Ambition.
(9)   ,,   24 from 20. Success.
(10)   ,,   25, 26, 27 from 19, 18, 17. Absorption.

XVI

TABLE OF THE QUARTERS

THE FOUR CONTESTS OF THE ANTITHETICAL WITHIN ITSELF

First quarter. With body. ⎫ In the first quarter body
Second   ,,   With heart. ⎬ should win, in second
Third   ,,   With mind. ⎭ heart, etc.
Fourth   ,,   With soul.

FOUR AUTOMATONISMS

First quarter. Instinctive.
Second   ,,   Imitative.
Third   ,,   Creative.
Fourth   ,,   Obedient.

FOUR CONDITIONS OF THE WILL

First quarter. Instinctive.
Second   ,,   Emotional.
Third   ,,   Intellectual.
Fourth   ,,   Moral.

FOUR CONDITIONS OF THE MASK

First quarter. Intensity (affecting third quarter).
Second   ,,   Tolerance (affecting fourth quarter).

Third quarter. Convention or systematization (affecting first quarter).

Fourth   ,,   Self-analysis (affecting second quarter).

DEFECTS OF FALSE CREATIVE MIND WHICH BRING THE FALSE MASK

First quarter. Sentimentality.
Second   ,,   Brutality (desire for root facts of life).
Third   ,,   Hatred.
Fourth   ,,   Insensitiveness.

Note.—In *primary* phases these defects separate *Mask* from *Body of Fate*, in *antithetical*, *Creative Mind* from *Body of Fate*.

ELEMENTAL ATTRIBUTIONS

Earth . . .	First quarter
Water . . .	Second quarter
Air . . .	Third quarter
Fire . . .	Fourth quarter

XVII

UNCLASSIFIED ATTRIBUTES

Mask worn—moral and emotional.
Mask carried—emotional.

ABSTRACTION

Strong at 6, 7, 8.
Strongest at 22, 23, 24, 25.
Begins at 19, less at 20, increases again at 21.

THREE ENERGIES

Images from self give emotion.

Images from world give passion.
Images from the supersensual give will.

ENFORCED AND FREE FACULTIES

In *primary* phases the *Mask* and *Will* are enforced, the
  Creative Mind and *Body of Fate* free.
In *antithetical* phases the *Creative Mind* and *Body of Fate*
  are enforced and the *Mask* and *Will* free.

THE TWO CONDITIONS

Primary means democratic.
Antithetical means aristocratic.

THE TWO DIRECTIONS

Phase 1 to Phase 15 is towards Nature.
Phase 15 to Phase 1 is towards God.

RELATIONS

Those between *Will* and *Mask*, *Creative Mind* and *Body of
  Fate* are oppositions, or contrasts.
Those between *Will* and *Creative Mind*, *Mask* and *Body
  of Fate* discords.

OBJECTIVITIES

From Phase 23 to Phase 25 is Physical Objectivity.
From Phase 26 to Phase 28 is Spiritual Objectivity.

CONSCIOUSNESS

From Phase 8 to Phase 22 is *Will*.
From Phase 28 to Phase 8 is *Creative Mind*.

Part III: THE TWENTY-EIGHT INCARNATIONS

Phase One and the Interchange of the Tinctures

As will be seen, when late phases are described, every achievement of a being, after Phase 22, is an elimination of the individual intellect and a discovery of the moral life. When the individual intellect lingers on, it is arrogance, self-assertion, a sterile abstraction, for the being is forced by the growing *primary tincture* to accept first the service of, and later on absorption in, the *primary* Whole, a sensual or supersensual objectivity.

When the old *antithetical* becomes the new *primary*, moral feeling is changed into an organisation of experience which must in its turn seek a unity, the whole of experience. When the old *primary* becomes the new *antithetical*, the old realisation of an objective moral law is changed into a subconscious turbulent instinct. The world of rigid custom and law is broken up by "the uncontrollable mystery upon the bestial floor".

Phase 1 not being human can better be described after Phase 28. None of those phases where the *tinctures* open into the Whole, except Phase 27, produce character of sufficient distinctiveness to become historical.

Phase Two

Will—Beginning of Energy.

Mask (from Phase 16). *True*—Player on Pan's Pipes. *False*—Fury.

Creative Mind (from Phase 28). *True*—Hope. *False*—Moroseness.

Body of Fate (from Phase 14)—"None except monotony".

When the man lives out of phase and desires the *Mask*, and so permits it to dominate the *Creative Mind*, he copies the emotional explosion of Phase 16 in so far as difference of phase permits. He gives himself to a violent animal assertion and can only destroy; strike right and left. Incapable of sharing the spiritual absorption of Phase 28, his *Creative Mind* fills him with ignorance and gloom.

> But when they find the frowning Babe,
> Terror strikes through the region wide:
> They cry "The babe! the babe is born!"
> And flee away on every side.

But if he live according to phase, he uses the *Body of Fate* to clear the intellect of the influence of the *Mask*. He frees himself from emotion; and the *Body of Fate*, derived from Phase 14, pushes back the mind into its own supersensual impulse, until it grows obedient to all that recurs; and the *Mask*, now entirely *enforced*, is a rhythmical impulse. He gives himself up to Nature as the Fool (Phase 28) gave himself to God. He is neither immoral nor violent but innocent; is as it were the breath stirring on the face of the deep; the smile on the face of a but half-awakened child. Nobody of our age has, it may be, met him, certainly no record of such meeting exists, but, were such meeting possible, he would be remembered as a form of joy, for he would seem more entirely living than all other men, a personification or summing up of all natural life. He would decide on this or that by no balance of the reason but by an infallible joy, and if born amid a rigid mechanical order, he would make for himself a place, as a dog will scratch a hole for itself in loose earth.

Here, as at Phase 16, the ordinary condition is sometimes reversed, and instead of ugliness, otherwise characteristic of this as of all *primary* phases, there is beauty. The new *antithetical tincture* (the old *primary* reborn) is violent. A new birth, when the product of an extreme contrast in the past life of the individual, is sometimes so violent that lacking foreign admixture it forestalls its ultimate physical destiny. It forces upon the *primary* and upon itself a beautiful form. It has the muscular balance and force of an animal good-humour with all appropriate comeliness as in the Dancing Faun. If this rare accident does not occur, the body is coarse, not deformed, but coarse from lack of sensitiveness, and is most fitted for rough physical labour.

Seen by those lyrical poets who draw their *Masks* from early phases, the man of Phase 2 is transfigured. Weary of an energy that defines and judges, weary of intellectual self-expression, they desire some "concealment", some transcendent intoxication. The bodily instincts, subjectively perceived, become the cup wreathed with ivy. Perhaps even a *Body of Fate* from any early phase may suffice to create this Image, but when it affects Phase 13 and Phase 14 the Image will be more sensuous, more like immediate experience. The Image is a myth, a woman, a landscape, or anything whatsoever that is an external expression of the *Mask*.

> The Kings of Inde their jewelled sceptres vail,
> And from their treasures scatter pearled hail;
> Great Brama from his mystic heaven groans
> And all his priesthood moans;
> Before young Bacchus' eye-wink turning pale.

PHASE THREE

Will—Beginning of Ambition.
Mask (from Phase 17). *True*—Innocence. *False*—Folly.
Creative Mind (from Phase 27). *True*—Simplicity. *False*
—Abstraction.
Body of Fate (from Phase 13)—Interest.

Out of phase and copying the opposite phase he
gives himself up to a kind of clodhopper folly, that
keeps his intellect moving among conventional ideas
with a sort of make-believe. Incapable of consecutive
thought and of moral purpose, he lives miserably seeking to hold together some consistent plan of life,
patching rags upon rags because that is expected of him,
or out of egotism. If on the other hand he uses his
Body of Fate to purify his *Creative Mind* of the *Mask*, if he
is content to permit his senses and his subconscious
nature to dominate his intellect, he takes delight in all
that passes; but because he claims nothing of his own,
chooses nothing, thinks that no one thing is better than
another, he will not endure a pang because all passes.
Almost without intellect, it is a phase of perfect bodily
sanity, for, though the body is still in close contact with
supersensual rhythm, it is no longer absorbed in that
rhythm; eyes and ears are open; one instinct balances
another; every season brings its delight.

> He who bends to himself a joy
> Does the winged life destroy,
> But he who kisses the joy as it flies
> Lives in eternity's sunrise.

Seen by lyrical poets, of whom so many have belonged

to the fantastic Phase 17, the man of this phase becomes an Image where simplicity and intensity are united, he seems to move among yellowing corn or under over-hanging grapes. He gave to Landor his shepherds and hamadryads, to Morris his *Water of the Wondrous Isles*, to Shelley his wandering lovers and sages, and to Theocritus all his flocks and pastures; and of what else did Bembo think when he cried, "Would that I were a shepherd that I might look daily down upon Urbino"? Imagined in some *antithetical* mind, seasonal change and bodily sanity seem images of lasting passion and the body's beauty.

PHASE FOUR

Will—Desire for Exterior World.

Mask (from Phase 18). *True*—Passion. *False*—Will.

Creative Mind (from Phase 26). *True*—First Perception of Character. *False*—Mutilation.

Body of Fate (from Phase 12)—Search.

When out of phase he attempts *antithetical* wisdom (for reflection has begun), separates himself from instinct (hence "mutilation"), and tries to enforce upon him-self and others all kinds of abstract or conventional ideas which are for him, being outside his experience, mere make-believe. Lacking *antithetical* capacity, and *primary* observation, he is aimless and blundering, possesses nothing except the knowledge that there is something known to others that is not mere instinct. True to phase, his interest in everything that happens, in all that excites his instinct ("search"), is so keen that he has no desire to claim anything for his own will; nature still dominates his thought as passion; yet instinct grows reflective. He is full of practical wisdom, a wisdom of saws and proverbs, or founded upon concrete examples. He can see nothing beyond sense, but sense expands and contracts to meet his needs, and the needs of those who trust him. It is as though he woke suddenly out of sleep and thereupon saw more and remembered more than others. He has "the wisdom of instinct", a wisdom perpetually excited by all those hopes and needs which concern his well-being or that of the race (*Creative Mind* from Phase 12 and so acting from whatever in race corresponds to personality unified in thought). The men of the opposite phase, or of the phases nearly opposite, worn out by a wisdom held with labour and uncertainty, see persons of this phase as images of peace. Two passages of Browning come to mind:

> An old hunter, talking with gods
> Or sailing with troops of friends to Tenedos.

> A King lived long ago,
> In the morning of the world,
> When Earth was nigher Heaven than now:
> And the King's locks curled,
> Disparting o'er a forehead full
> As the milk-white space 'twixt horn and horn
> Of some sacrificial bull—
> Only calm as a babe new-born:
> For he was got to a sleepy mood,
> So safe from all decrepitude,
> From age with its bane, so sure gone by,
> (The Gods so loved him while he dreamed)
> That, having lived thus long, there seemed
> No need the King should ever die.

The Opening and Closing of the Tinctures

Since Phase 26 the *primary tincture* has so predominated, man is so sunk in Fate, in life, that there is no reflection, no experience, because that which reflects, that which acquires experience, has been drowned. Man cannot think of himself as separate from that which he sees with the bodily eye or in the mind's eye. He neither loves nor hates though he may be in hatred or in love. Birdalone in *The Water of the Wondrous Isles* (a woman of Phase 3 reflected in an *antithetical* mind) falls in love with her friend's lover and he with her. There is great sorrow but no struggle, her decision to disappear is sudden as if compelled by some power over which she has no control. Has she not perhaps but decided as her unknown fathers and mothers compelled, but conformed to the lineaments of her race? Is she not a child of "Weird", are not all in the most *primary* phases children of "Weird" exercising an unconscious discrimination towards all that before Phase 1 defines their Fate, and after Phase 1 their race? Every achievement of their souls, Phase 1 being passed, springs up out of the body, and their work is to substitute for a life where all is Fate frozen into rule and custom, a life where all is fused by instinct; with them to hunger, to taste, to desire, is to grow wise.

Between Phase 4 and Phase 5 the *tinctures* ceased to be drowned in the One, and reflection begins. Between Phases 25, 26 and Phases 4, 5, there is an approach to absolute surrender of the *Will*, first to God, then, as Phase 1 passes away, to Nature, and the surrender is the most complete form of the freedom of the *Body of Fate* which has been increasing since Phase 22. When

Man identifies himself with his Fate, when he is able
to say "Thy Will is our freedom" or when he is perfectly natural, that is to say, perfectly a portion of his
surroundings, he is free even though all his actions can
be foreseen, even though every action is a logical deduction from all that went before it. He is all Fate but
has no Destiny.

PHASE FIVE

Will—Separation from Innocence.

Mask (from Phase 19). *True*—Excess. *False*—Limitation.

Creative Mind (from Phase 25). *True*—Social Intellect.
False—Limitation.

Body of Fate (from Phase 11)—Natural Law.

Out of phase, and seeking *antithetical* emotion, he is
sterile, passing from one insincere attitude to another,
moving through a round of moral images torn from
their context and so without meaning. He is so proud of
each separation from experience that he becomes a sort
of angry or smiling Punch with a lath between his
wooden arms striking here and there. His *Body of Fate*
is *enforced*, for he has reversed the condition of his
phase and finds himself at conflict with a world which
offers him nothing but temptation and affront. True to
phase, he is the direct opposite of all this. Abstraction
has indeed begun, but it comes to him as a portion of
experience cut off from everything but itself and therefore fitted to be the object of reflection. He no longer
touches, eats, drinks, thinks and feels Nature, but sees
her as something from which he is separating himself,
something that he may dominate, though only for a

moment and by some fragmentary violence of sensation or of thought. Nature may seem half gone, but the laws of Nature have appeared and he can change her rhythms and her seasons by his knowledge. He lives in the moment but with an intensity Phases 2, 3 and 4 have never known, the *Will* approaches its climax, he is no longer like a man but half-awakened. He is a corrupter, disturber, wanderer, a founder of sects and peoples, and works with extravagant energy, and his reward is but to live in its glare.

Seen by a poet of the opposite phase, by a man hiding fading emotion under broken emphasis, he is Byron's Don Juan or his Giaour.

Phase Six

Will—Artificial Individuality.
Mask (from Phase 20). *True*—Justice. *False*—Tyranny.
Creative Mind (from Phase 24). *True*—Ideality. *False*—Derision.
Body of Fate (from Phase 10)—Humanity.
Example: Walt Whitman.

Had Walt Whitman lived out of phase, desire to prove that all his emotions were healthy and intelligible, to set his practical sanity above all not made in his fashion, to cry "Thirty years old and in perfect health!" would have turned him into some kind of jibing demagogue; and to think of him would be to remember that Thoreau, picking up the jaw-bone of a pig with no tooth missing, recorded that there also was perfect health. He would, that he might believe in himself, have compelled others to believe. Not being out of phase, he used his *Body of Fate* (his interest in crowds, in casual loves and affections, in all summary human experience) to clear intellect of *antithetical* emotion (always insincere from Phase 1 to Phase 8), and haunted and hunted by the now involuntary *Mask*, created an Image of vague, half-civilised man, all his thought and impulse a product of democratic bonhomie, of schools, of colleges, of public discussion. Abstraction had been born, but it remained the abstraction of a community, of a tradition, a synthesis starting, not as with Phases 19, 20 and 21 with logical deduction from an observed fact, but from the whole experience or from some experience of the individual or of the community: "I have such and such a feeling. I have such and such a belief. What follows from feeling, what from belief?" While Thomas Aquinas, whose historical epoch was nearly of this phase, summed up in abstract categories all possible experience, not that he might know but that he might feel, Walt Whitman makes catalogues of all that has moved him, or amused his eye, that he may grow more poetical. Experience is all-absorbing, sub-ordinating observed fact, drowning even truth itself, if truth is conceived of as something apart from impulse and instinct and from the *Will*. Impulse or instinct begins to be all in all. In a little while, though not yet, it must, sweeping away catalogue and category, fill the mind with terror.

PHASE SEVEN

Will—Assertion of Individuality.

Mask (from Phase 21). *True*—Altruism. *False*—Efficiency.

Creative Mind (from Phase 23). *True*—Heroic sentiment. *False*—Dogmatic sentimentality.

Body of Fate (from Phase 9)—Adventure that excites
the individuality.

Examples: George Borrow, Alexandre Dumas, Thomas
Carlyle, James Macpherson.

At Phases 2, 3 and 4 the man moved within traditional or seasonable limits, but since Phase 5 limits
have grown indefinite; public codes, all that depend
upon habit, are all but dissolved, even the catalogues
and categories of Phase 6 are no longer sufficient. If out
of phase the man desires to be the man of Phase 21; an
impossible desire, for that man is all but the climax of
intellectual complexity, and all men, from Phase 2 to
Phase 7 inclusive, are intellectually simple. His instincts are all but at their apex of complexity, and he is
bewildered and must soon be helpless. The dissolving
character, out of phase, desires the breaking personality,
and though it cannot possess or even conceive of personality, seeing that its thoughts and emotions are
common to all, it can create a grandiloquent phantom
and by deceiving others deceive itself; and presently we
shall discover Phase 21, out of phase, bragging of an
imaginary naïveté.

Phase 7 when true to phase surrenders to the *Body of
Fate* which, being derived from the phase where personality first shows itself, is excited into forms of character so dissolved in *Will*, in instinct, that they are
hardly distinguishable from personality. These forms of
character, not being self-dependent like personality, are,
however, inseparable from circumstance: a gesture or a
pose born of a situation and forgotten when the situa-

tion has passed; a last act of courage, a defiance of the dogs that must soon tear the man into pieces. Such men have a passion for history, for the scene, for the adventure. They delight in actions, which they cannot consider apart from setting sun or a storm at sea or some great battle, and that are inspired by emotions that move all hearers because such that all understand.

Alexandre Dumas was the phase in its perfection, George Borrow when it halts a little, for Borrow was at moments sufficiently out of phase to know that he was naïve and to brag of imaginary intellectual subjectivity, as when he paraded an unbelievable fit of the horrors, or his mastery of many tongues. Carlyle like Macpherson showed the phase at its worst. He neither could nor should have cared for anything but the personalities of history, but he used them as so many metaphors in a vast popular rhetoric, for the expression of thoughts that seeming his own were the work of preachers and angry ignorant congregations. So noisy, so threatening that rhetoric, so great his own energy, that two generations passed before men noticed that he had written no sentence not of coarse humour that clings to the memory. Sexual impotence had doubtless weakened the *Body of Fate* and so strengthened the False *Mask*, yet one doubts if any mere plaster of ant's eggs could have helped where there was so great insincerity.

Phase Eight

Will—War between Individuality and Race.
Mask (from Phase 22). *True*—Courage. *False*—Fear.
Creative Mind (from Phase 22). *True*—Versatility.
False—Impotence.

Body of Fate (from Phase 8)—The beginning of strength.

Example: The Idiot of Dostoieffsky perhaps.

Out of phase, a condition of terror; when true to phase, of courage unbroken through defeat.

From Phase 1 to Phase 7, there has been a gradual weakening of all that is *primary*. Character (the *Will* analysed in relation to the *enforced Mask*) has become individuality (the *Will* analysed in relation to itself), but now, though individuality persists through another phase, personality (the *Will* analysed in relation to the free *Mask*) must predominate. So long as the *primary tincture* predominated, the *antithetical tincture* accepted its manner of perception; character and individuality were enlarged by those vegetative and sensitive faculties excited by the *Body of Fate*, the nearest a *primary* nature can come to *antithetical* emotion. But now the bottle must be burst. The struggle of idealised or habitual theologised thought with instinct, mind with body, of the waning *primary* with the growing *antithetical*, must be decided, and the vegetative and sensitive faculties must for a while take the sway. Only then can the *Will* be forced to recognise the weakness of the *Creative Mind* when unaided by the *Mask*, and so to permit the *enforced Mask* to change into the free. Every new modification or codification of morality has been its attempt, acting through the *Creative Mind*, to set order upon the instinctive and vegetative faculties, and it must now feel that it can create order no longer. It is the very nature of a struggle, where the soul must lose all form received from the objectively accepted conscience of the world, that it denies us an historical example. One thinks of possible examples only to decide that Hartley Coleridge is not amongst them, that the brother of the Brontës may only seem to be because we know so little about him, but that Dostoieffsky's Idiot is almost certainly an example. But Dostoieffsky's Idiot was too matured a type, he had passed too many times through the twenty-eight phases to help our understanding. Here for the most part are those obscure wastrels who seem powerless to free themselves from some sensual temptation—drink, women, drugs—and who cannot in a life of continual crisis create any lasting thing. The being is often born up to four times at this one phase, it is said, before the *antithetical tincture* attains its mastery. The being clings like a drowning man to every straw, and it is precisely this clinging, this seemingly vain reaching forth for strength, amidst the collapse of all those public thoughts and habits that are the support of *primary* man, that enables it to enter at last upon Phase 9. It has to find its strength by a transformation of that very instinct which has hitherto been its weakness and so to gather up the strewn and broken members. The union of *Creative Mind* and *Mask* in opposition to *Body of Fate* and *Will*, intensifies this struggle by dividing the nature into halves which have no interchange of qualities. The man is inseparable from his fate, he cannot see himself apart, nor can he distinguish between emotion and intellect. He is will-less, dragged hither and thither, and his unemotionalised intellect, gathered up into the mathematical Phase 22, shows him perpetually for object of desire, an emotion that is like a mechanical energy, a thought that is like wheel and piston. He is suspended; he is without bias, and until bias comes, till he has begun groping for strength within his own being, his thought and his emotion bring him to judgment but they cannot help. As those at Phase 22 must dissolve the dramatising *Mask* in abstract mind that they may discover the concrete world, he must dissolve thought into mere impersonal instinct, into mere race, that he may discover the dramatising *Mask*: he chooses himself and not his Fate. Courage is his true *Mask*, and diversity, that has no habitual purpose, his true *Creative Mind*, because these are all that the phase of the greatest possible weakness can take into itself from the phase of the greatest possible strength. When his fingers close upon a straw, that is courage, and his versatility is that any wave may float a straw. At Phase 7, he had tried out of ambition to change his nature, as though a man should make love who had no heart, but now shock can give him back his heart. Only a shock resulting from the greatest possible conflict can make the greatest possible change, that from *primary* to *antithetical* or from *antithetical* to *primary* again. Nor can anything intervene. He must be aware of nothing but the conflict, his despair is necessary, he is of all men the most tempted—"Eloi, Eloi, why hast thou forsaken me?"

PHASE NINE

Will—Belief instead of Individuality.

Mask (from Phase 23). *True*—Facility. *False*—Obscurity.

Creative Mind (from Phase 21). *True*—Self-dramatisation. *False*—Anarchy.

Body of Fate (from Phase 7)—Enforced Sensuality.

Example: An unnamed artist.

Out of phase, blundering and ignorant, the man becomes when in phase powerful and accomplished; all that strength as of metallic rod and wheel discovered within himself. He should seek to liberate the *Mask* by the help of the *Creative Mind* from the *Body of Fate*— that is to say, to carve out and wear the now free *Mask* and so to protect and to deliver the Image. In so far as he does so, there is immense confidence in self-expression, a vehement self, working through mathematical calculation, a delight in straight line and right angle; but if he seek to live according to the *primary tincture*, to use the *Body of Fate* to rid the *Creative Mind* of its *Mask*, to live with objective ambition and curiosity, all is confused, the *Will* asserts itself with a savage, terrified violence. All these phases of incipient personality when out of phase are brutal, but after Phase 12, when true personality begins, brutality gives place to an evasive capricious coldness—"false, fleeting, perjured Clarence"—a lack of good faith in their *primary* relation, often accompanied in their *antithetical* relation by the most self-torturing scruples. When an *antithetical* man is out of phase, he reproduces the *primary* condition, but with an emotional inversion, love for Image or *Mask* becomes dread, or after Phase 15, hatred, and the *Mask* clings to the man or pursues him in the Image. It may even be that he is haunted by a delusive hope, cherished in secret, or bragged of aloud, that he may inherit the *Body of Fate* and *Mask* of a phase opposed to his own. He seeks to avoid *antithetical* conflict by accepting what opposes him, and his *antithetical* life is invaded. At Phase 9, the *Body of Fate* that could purify from an unreal unity the mind of a Carlyle, or of a Whitman, breaks with sensuality (the rising flood of instinct from Phase 7), a new real unity, and the man instead of mastering this sensuality, through his dramatisation of himself as a form of passionate self-mastery, instead of seeking some like form as Image, becomes stupid and blundering. Hence one finds at this phase, more often than at any other, men who dread, despise and persecute the women whom they love. Yet behind all that muddy, flooded, brutal self, there is perhaps a vague timid soul knowing itself caught in an antithesis, an alternation it cannot control. It is said of it, "The soul having found its weakness at Phase 8 begins the inward discipline of the soul in the fury of Phase 9". And again, "Phase 9 has the most sincere belief any man has ever had in his own desire".

There is a certain artist who said to a student of these symbols, speaking of a notable man, and his mistress and their children, "She no longer cares for his work, no longer gives him the sympathy he needs, why does he not leave her, what does he owe to her or to her children?" The student discovered this artist to be a Cubist of powerful imagination and noticed that his head suggested a sullen obstinacy, but that his manner and his speech were generally sympathetic and gentle.

PHASE TEN

Will—The Image-Breaker.

Mask (from Phase 24). *True*—Organisation. *False*—Inertia.

Creative Mind (from Phase 20). *True*—Domination through emotional construction. *False*—Reformation.

Body of Fate (from Phase 6)—Enforced emotion.

Example: Parnell.

If he live like the opposite phase, conceived as *primary* condition—the phase where ambition dies—he lacks all emotional power (False *Mask*: "Inertia"), and gives himself up to rudderless change, reform without a vision of form. He accepts what form (*Mask* and Image) those about him admire and, on discovering that it is alien, casts it away with brutal violence, to choose some other form as alien. He disturbs his own life, and he disturbs all who come near him more than does Phase 9, for Phase 9 has no interest in others except in relation to itself. If, on the other hand, he be true to phase, and use his intellect to liberate from mere race (*Body of Fate* at Phase 6 where race is codified), and so create some code of personal conduct, which implies always "divine right", he becomes proud, masterful and practical. He cannot wholly escape the influence of his *Body of Fate*, but he will be subject to its most personal form; instead of gregarious sympathies, to some woman's tragic love almost certainly. Though the *Body of Fate* must seek to destroy his *Mask*, it may now impose upon him a struggle which leaves victory still possible. As *Body of Fate* phase and *Mask* phase approach one another they share somewhat of each other's nature; the effect of mutual hate grows more diffused, less harsh and obvious. The effect of the *Body of Fate* of Phase 10, for instance, is slightly less harsh and obvious than that of the "enforced sensuality" of Phase 9. It is now "enforced emotion". Phase 9 was without restraint, but now restraint has come and with it pride; there is less need to insist on the brutality of facts of life that he may escape from their charm; the subjective fury is less uncalculating, and the opposition of *Will* and *Mask* no longer produces a delight in an impersonal

precision and power like that of machinery (machinery
that is emotion and thought) but rather a kind of burning restraint, a something that suggests a savage statue
to which one offers sacrifice. This sacrifice is code, personality no longer perceived as power only. He seeks by
its help to free the creative power from mass emotion,
but never wholly succeeds, and so the life remains
troubled, a conflict between pride and race, and passes
from crisis to crisis. At Phase 9 there was little sexual
discrimination, and now there is emotion created by
circumstance rather than by any unique beauty of body
or of character. One remembers Faust, who will find
every wench a Helen, now that he has drunk the
witches' dram, and yet loves his Gretchen with all his
being. Perhaps one thinks of that man who gave a
lifetime of love because a young woman in capricious
idleness had written his name with her umbrella upon
the snow. Here is rage, desire to escape but not now
by mere destruction of the opposing fate; for a vague
abstract sense of some world, some image, some circumstance, harmonious to emotion, has begun, or of something harmonious to emotion that may be set upon the
empty pedestal, once visible world, image, or circumstance has been destroyed. With less desire of expression
than at Phase 9, and with more desire of action and of
command, the man (*Creative Mind* from Phase 20, phase
of greatest dramatic power) sees all his life as a stage
play where there is only one good acting part; yet no
one will accuse him of being a stage player, for he
will wear always that stony *Mask* (Phase 24, "The end
of ambition", *antithetically* perceived). He, too, if he
triumph, may end ambition through the command of
mul·itudes, for he is like that god of Norse mythology

who hung from the cliff's side for three days, a sacrifice to himself. Perhaps Moses when he descended the mountain-side had a like stony *Mask*, and had cut Tables and *Mask* out of the one rock.

John Morley says of Parnell, whose life proves him of the phase, that he had the least discursive mind he had ever known, and that is always characteristic of a phase where all practical curiosity has been lost wherever some personal aim is not involved, while philosophical and artistic curiosity are still undiscovered. He made upon his contemporaries an impression of impassivity, and yet a follower has recorded that, after a speech that seemed brutal and callous, his hands were full of blood because he had torn them with his nails. One of his followers was shocked during the impassioned discussion in Committee Room No. 15 that led to his abandonment, by this most reticent man's lack of reticence in allusion to the operations of sex, an indifference as of a mathematician dealing with some arithmetical quantity, and yet Mrs. Parnell tells how upon a night of storm on Brighton pier, and at the height of his power, he held her out over the waters and she lay still, stretched upon his two hands, knowing that if she moved, he would drown himself and her.

Phase Eleven

Will—The Consumer.

Mask (from Phase 25). *True*—Rejection. *False*—Moral indifference.

Creative Mind (from Phase 19). *True*—Moral iconoclasm. *False*—Self-assertion.

Body of Fate (from Phase 5)—Enforced belief.
Examples: Spinoza, Savonarola.

While Phase 9 was kept from its subjectivity by personal relations, by sensuality, by various kinds of grossness; and Phase 10 by associations of men for practical purposes, and by the emotions that arise out of such associations, or by some tragic love where there is an element of common interest; Phase 11 is impeded by the excitement of conviction, by the contagion of organised belief, or by its interest in organisation for its own sake. The man of the phase is a half-solitary, one who defends a solitude he cannot or will not inhabit, his *Mask* being from a phase of abstract belief, which offers him always some bundle of mathematical formulae, or its like, opposed to his nature. It will presently be seen that the man of Phase 25, where the *Mask* is, creates a system of belief, just as Phase 24 creates a code, to exclude all that is too difficult for dolt or knave; but the man of Phase 11 systematises, runs to some frenzy of conviction, to make intellect, intellect for its own sake, possible, and perhaps, in his rage against rough-and-ready customary thought, to make all but intellect impossible. He will be the antithesis of all this, should he be conquered by his *Body of Fate* (from Phase 5, where the common instinct first unites itself to reflection), being carried off by some contagion of belief, some general interest, and compelled to substitute for intellectual rage some form of personal pride and so to become the proud prelate of tradition.

In Spinoza one finds the phase in its most pure and powerful shape. He saw the divine energy in whatever was the most individual expression of the soul, and spent his life in showing that such expression was for the world's welfare and not, as might seem, a form of anarchy. His *Mask*, under the influence of his *Body of Fate*, would force him to seek happiness in submission to something hard and exterior; but the *Mask*, set free by a *Creative Mind* that would destroy exterior popular sanction, makes possible for the first time the solitary conception of God. One imagines him among the theologians of his time, who sought always some formula perhaps, some sheep-dog for common minds, turning himself into pure wolf, and making for the wilderness. Certainly his pantheism, however pleasing to his own bare bench of scholars, was little likely to help the oratory of any bench of judges or of bishops. Through all his cold definitions, on whose mathematical form he prided himself, one divines a quarrel with the thought of his fathers and his kin, forced upon him perhaps almost to the breaking of his heart: no nature without the stroke of fate divides itself in two.

Phase Twelve

Will—The Forerunner.

Mask (from Phase 26). *True*—Self-exaggeration. *False* —Self-abandonment.

Creative Mind (from Phase 18). *True*—Subjective philosophy. *False*—War between two forms of expression.

Body of Fate (from Phase 4)—Enforced intellectual action.

Example: Nietzsche.

The man of this phase, out of phase, is always in re-
action, is driven from one self-conscious pose to another,
is full of hesitation; true to phase, he is a cup that remembers but its own fullness. His phase is called the
"Forerunner" because fragmentary and violent. The
phases of action where the man mainly defines himself
by his practical relations are finished, or finishing, and
the phases where he defines himself mainly through an
image of the mind begun or beginning; phases of hatred
for some external fate are giving way to phases of self-
hatred. It is a phase of immense energy because the
Four Faculties are equidistant. The *oppositions* (*Will* and
Mask, Creative Mind and *Body of Fate*) are balanced by the
discords, and these, being equidistant between *identity* and
opposition, are at their utmost intensity. The nature is
conscious of the most extreme degree of *deception*, and
is wrought to a frenzy of desire for truth of self. If
Phase 9 had the greatest possible "belief in its own
desire", there is now the greatest possible belief in all
values created by personality. It is therefore before all
else the phase of the hero, of the man who overcomes
himself, and so no longer needs, like Phase 10, the
submission of others, or, like Phase 11, conviction of
others to prove his victory. Solitude has been born at
last, though solitude invaded, and hard to defend. Nor
is there need any longer of the bare anatomy of Phase
11; every thought comes with sound and metaphor, and
the sanity of the being is no longer from its relation to
facts, but from its approximation to its own unity, and
from this on we shall meet with men and women to
whom facts are a dangerous narcotic or intoxicant.
Facts are from the *Body of Fate*, and the *Body of Fate* is
from the phase where instinct, before the complications

of reflection, reached its most persuasive strength. The
man is pursued by a series of accidents, which, unless
he meet them *antithetically*, drive him into all sorts of
temporary ambitions, opposed to his nature, unite him
perhaps to some small protesting sect (the family or
neighbourhood of Phase 4 intellectualised); and these
ambitions he defends by some kind of superficial intellectual action, the pamphlet, the violent speech,
the sword of the swashbuckler. He spends his life
in oscillation between the violent assertion of some
commonplace pose, and a dogmatism which means nothing apart from the circumstance that created it.

   If, however, he meets these accidents by the awakening
of his *antithetical* being, there is a noble extravagance, an
overflowing fountain of personal life. He turns towards
the True *Mask* and having by philosophic intellect
(*Creative Mind*) delivered it from all that is topical and
temporary, announces a philosophy which is the logical
expression of a mind alone with the object of its desire.
The True *Mask*, derived from the terrible Phase 26,
called the phase of the Hunchback, is the reverse of all
that is emotional, being emotionally cold; not mathematical, for intellectual abstraction ceased at Phase 11,
but marble pure. In the presence of the *Mask*, the
Creative Mind has the isolation of a fountain under moon-
light; yet one must always distinguish between the
emotional *Will*—now approaching the greatest subtlety
of sensitiveness, and more and more conscious of its
frailty—and that which it would be, the lonely, imper-
turbable, proud *Mask*, as between the *Will* and its *discord*
in the *Creative Mind* where is no shrinking from life.
The man follows an Image, created or chosen by the
Creative Mind from what Fate offers; would persecute

and dominate it; and this Image wavers between the concrete and sensuous Image. It has become personal; there
is now, though not so decisively as later, but one form
of chosen beauty, and the sexual *Image* is drawn as with
a diamond, and tinted those pale colours sculptors
sometimes put upon a statue. Like all before Phase 15
the man is overwhelmed with the thought of his own
weakness and knows of no strength but that of Image
and *Mask*.

PHASE THIRTEEN

Will—The Sensuous Man.

Mask (from Phase 27). *True*—Self-expression. *False*—
Self-absorption.

Creative Mind (from Phase 17). *True*—Subjective
truth. *False*—Morbidity.

Body of Fate (from Phase 3)—Enforced love of another.

Examples: Baudelaire, Beardsley, Ernest Dowson.

This is said to be the only phase where entire
sensuality is possible, that is to say, sensuality without
the intermixture of any other element. There is now a
possible complete intellectual unity, Unity of Being
apprehended through the images of the mind; and this
is opposed by the Fate (Phase 3 where body becomes
deliberate and whole) which offers an equal roundness
and wholeness of sensation. The *Will* is now a mirror of
emotional experience, or sensation, according to whether
it is swayed by *Mask* or Fate. Though wax to every impression of emotion, or of sense, it would yet through
its passion for truth (*Creative Mind*) become its opposite
and receive from the *Mask* (Phase 27), which is at the
phase of the Saint, a virginal purity of emotion. If it

live objectively, that is to say, surrender itself to sensation, it becomes morbid, it sees every sensation separate
from every other under the light of its perpetual analysis
(*Creative Mind* at a phase of dispersal). Phase 13 is a
phase of great importance, because the most intellectually subjective phase, and because only here can be
achieved in perfection that in the *antithetical* life which
corresponds to sanctity in the *primary*: not self-denial
but expression for expression's sake. Its influence indeed
upon certain writers has caused them in their literary
criticism to exalt intellectual sincerity to the place in
literature which is held by sanctity in theology. At this
phase the self discovers, within itself, while struggling
with the *Body of Fate*, forms of emotional morbidity
which others recognise as their own; as the Saint may
take upon himself the physical diseases of others. There
is almost always a preoccupation with those metaphors
and symbols and mythological images through which
we define whatever seems most strange or most morbid.
Self-hatred now reaches its height, and through this
hatred comes the slow liberation of intellectual love.
There are moments of triumph and moments of defeat,
each in its extreme form, for the subjective intellect
knows nothing of moderation. As the *primary tincture*
has weakened, the sense of quantity has weakened, for
the *antithetical tincture* is preoccupied with quality.

From now, if not from Phase 12, and until Phase 17
or Phase 18 has passed, happy love is rare, for seeing that
the man must find a woman whose *Mask* falls within or
but just outside his *Body of Fate* and *Mask*, if he is to find
strong sexual attraction, the range of choice grows
smaller, and all life grows more tragic. As the woman
grows harder to find, so does every beloved object.

Lacking suitable objects of desire, the relation between man and *Daimon* becomes more clearly a struggle or even a relation of enmity.

PHASE FOURTEEN

Will—The Obsessed Man.

Mask (from Phase 28). *True*—Serenity. *False*—Self-distrust.

Creative Mind (from Phase 16). *True*—Emotional will. *False*—Terror.

Body of Fate (from Phase 2)—Enforced love of the world.

Examples: Keats, Giorgione, many beautiful women.

As we approach Phase 15 personal beauty increases and at Phase 14 and Phase 16 the greatest human beauty becomes possible. The aim of the being should be to disengage those objects which are images of desire from the excitement and disorder of the *Body of Fate*, and under certain circumstances to impress upon these the full character of the *Mask* which, being from Phase 28, is a folding up, or fading into themselves. It is this act of the intellect, begun at conception, which has given the body its beauty. The *Body of Fate*, derived from the phase of the utmost possible physical energy, but of an energy without aim, like that of a child, works against this folding up, yet offers little more of objects than their excitement, their essential honey. The images of desire, disengaged and subject to the *Mask*, are separate and still (*Creative Mind* from a phase of violent scattering). The images of Phase 13 and even of Phase 12 have in a lesser degree this character. When we compare these images with those of any subsequent phase, each seems studied for its own sake; they float as in serene air, or lie hidden in some valley, and if they move it is to music that returns always to the same note, or in a dance that so returns into itself that they seem immortal.

When the being is out of phase, when it is allured by *primary* curiosity, it is aware of its *primary* feebleness and its intellect becomes but a passion of apprehension, or a shrinking from solitude; it may even become mad; or it may use its conscious feebleness and its consequent terror as a magnet for the sympathy of others, as a means of domination. At Phase 16 will be discovered a desire to accept every possible responsibility; but now responsibility is renounced and this renunciation becomes an instrument of power, dropped burdens being taken up by others. Here are born those women who are most touching in their beauty. Helen was of the phase; and she comes before the mind's eye elaborating a delicate personal discipline, as though she would make her whole life an image of a unified *antithetical* energy. While seeming an image of softness and of quiet, she draws perpetually upon glass with a diamond. Yet she will not number among her sins anything that does not break that personal discipline, no matter what it may seem according to others' discipline; but if she fail in her own discipline she will not deceive herself, and for all the languor of her movements, and her indifference to the acts of others, her mind is never at peace. She will wander much alone as though she consciously meditated her masterpiece that shall be at the full moon, yet unseen by human eyes, and when she returns to her house she will look upon her household with timid eyes, as though she knew that all powers of self-protection had been taken away, that of her once violent *primary tincture* nothing remained but a strange irresponsible innocence. Her early life has perhaps been perilous because of that nobility, that excess of *antithetical* energies, which may have so constrained the fading *primary* that, instead of its becoming the expression of those energies, it is but a vague beating of the wings, or their folding up into a melancholy stillness. The greater the peril the nearer has she approached to the final union of *primary* and *antithetical*, where she will desire nothing; already perhaps, through weakness of desire, she understands nothing yet seems to understand everything; already serves nothing, while alone seeming of service. Is it not because she desires so little, gives so little that men will die and murder in her service? One thinks of the "Eternal Idol" of Rodin: that kneeling man with hands clasped behind his back in humble adoration, kissing a young girl a little below the breast, while she gazes down, without comprehending, under her half-closed eyelids. Perhaps, could we see her a little later, with flushed cheeks casting her money upon some gaming-table, we would wonder that action and form could so belie each other, not understanding that the Fool's *Mask* is her chosen motley, nor her terror before death and stillness. One thinks too of the women of Burne-Jones, but not of Botticelli's women, who have too much curiosity, nor Rossetti's women, who have too much passion; and as we see before the mind's eye those pure faces gathered about the "Sleep of Arthur," or crowded upon the "Golden Stair," we wonder if they too would not have filled us with surprise, or dismay, because of some craze, some passion for mere excitement, or slavery to a drug.

In the poets too, who are of the phase, one finds the impression of the *Body of Fate* as intoxication or narcotic. Wordsworth, shuddering at his solitude, has filled his art in all but a few pages with common opinion, common sentiment; while in the poetry of Keats there is, though little sexual passion, an exaggerated sensuousness that compels us to remember the pepper on the tongue as though that were his symbol. Thought is disappearing into image; and in Keats, in some ways a perfect type, intellectual curiosity is at its weakest; there is scarcely an image, where his poetry is at its best, whose subjectivity has not been heightened by its use in many great poets, painters, sculptors, artificers. The being has almost reached the end of that elaboration of itself which has for its climax an absorption in time, where space can be but symbols or images in the mind. There is little observation even in detail of expression, all is reverie, while in Wordsworth the soul's deepening solitude has reduced mankind, when seen objectively, to a few slight figures outlined for a moment amid mountain and lake. The corresponding genius in painting is that of Monticelli, after 1870, and perhaps that of Conder, though in Conder there are elements suggesting the preceding phase.

All born at *antithetical* phases before Phase 15 are subject to violence, because of the indeterminate energy of the *Body of Fate*; this violence seems accidental, unforeseen and cruel—and here are women carried off by robbers and ravished by clowns.

Phase Fifteen

Will.	No description ex-
Mask (from Phase 1).	cept that this is a
Creative Mind (from Phase 15).	phase of complete
Body of Fate (from Phase 1).	beauty.

Body of Fate and *Mask* are now identical; and *Will* and *Creative Mind* identical; or rather the *Creative Mind* is dissolved in the *Will* and the *Body of Fate* in the *Mask*. Thought and will are indistinguishable, effort and attainment are indistinguishable; and this is the consummation of a slow process; nothing is apparent but dreaming *Will* and the Image that it dreams. Since Phase 12 all images, and cadences of the mind, have been satisfying to that mind just in so far as they have expressed this converging of will and thought, effort and attainment. The words "musical", "sensuous", are but descriptions of that converging process. Thought has been pursued, not as a means but as an end—the poem, the painting, the reverie has been sufficient of itself. It is not possible, however, to separate in the understanding this running into one of *Will* and *Creative Mind* from the running into one of *Mask* and *Body of Fate*. Without *Mask* and *Body of Fate* the *Will* would have nothing to desire, the *Creative Mind* nothing to apprehend. Since Phase 12 the *Creative Mind* has been so interfused by the *antithetical tincture* that it has more and more confined its contemplation of actual things to those that resemble images of the mind desired by the *Will*. The being has selected, moulded and remoulded, narrowed its circle of living, been more and more the artist, grown more and more "distinguished" in all preference. Now contemplation and desire, united into one, inhabit a world where every beloved image has bodily form, and every bodily form is loved. This love knows nothing of desire, for desire implies effort, and though there is still separation from the loved object, love accepts the separation as necessary to its own existence. *Fate* is known for the boundary that gives our *Destiny* its form, and—as we can desire nothing outside that form—as an expression of our freedom. Chance and Choice have become interchangeable without losing their identity. As all effort has ceased, all thought has become image, because no thought could exist if it were not carried towards its own extinction, amid fear or in contemplation; and every image is separate from every other, for if image were linked to image, the soul would awake from its immovable trance. All that the being has experienced as thought is visible to its eyes as a whole, and in this way it perceives, not as they are to others, but according to its own perception, all orders of existence. Its own body possesses the greatest possible beauty, being indeed that body which the soul will permanently inhabit, when all its phases have been repeated according to the number allotted: that which we call the clarified or Celestial Body. Where the being has lived out of phase, seeking to live through *antithetical* phases as though they had been *primary*, there is now terror of solitude, its forced, painful and slow acceptance, and a life haunted by terrible dreams. Even for the most perfect, there is a time of pain, a passage through a vision, where evil reveals itself in its final meaning. In this passage Christ, it is said, mourned over the length of time and the unworthiness of man's lot to man, whereas his forerunner mourned and his successor will mourn over the shortness of time and the unworthiness of man to his lot; but this cannot yet be understood.

Will—The Positive Man.

Mask (from Phase 2). *True*—Illusion. *False*—Delusion.

Creative Mind (from Phase 14). *True*—Vehemence. *False*—Opinionated will.

Body of Fate (from Phase 28)—Enforced Illusion.

Examples: William Blake, Rabelais, Aretino, Paracelsus, some beautiful women.

Phase 16 is in contrast to Phase 14, in spite of their resemblance of extreme subjectivity, in that it has a *Body of Fate* from the phase of the Fool, a phase of absorption, and its *Mask* from what might have been called the phase of the Child, a phase of aimless energy, of physical life for its own sake; whereas Phase 14 had its *Body of Fate* from the phase of the Child and its *Mask* from that of the Fool. Fate thrusts an aimless excitement upon Phase 14. Phase 14 finds within itself an *antithetical* self-absorbing dream. Phase 16 has a like dream thrust upon it and finds within itself an aimless excitement. This excitement, and this dream, are both illusions, so that the *Will*, which is itself a violent scattering energy, has to use its intellect (*Creative Mind*) to discriminate between illusions. They are both illusions, because, so small is the *primary* nature, sense of fact is an impossibility. If it use its intellect, which is the most narrow, the most unflinching, even the most cruel possible to man, to disengage the aimless child (*i.e.* to find *Mask* and Image in the child's toy), it finds the

soul's most radiant expression and surrounds itself
with some fairyland, some mythology of wisdom or
laughter. Its own mere scattering, its mere rushing out
into the disordered and unbounded, after the still trance
of Phase 15, has found its antithesis, and therefore self-
knowledge and self-mastery.

If, however, it subordinate its intellect to the *Body of
Fate*, all the cruelty and narrowness of that intellect are
displayed in service of preposterous purpose after purpose till there is nothing left but the fixed idea and some
hysterical hatred. By these purposes, derived from a phase
of absorption, the *Body of Fate* drives the *Will* back upon
its subjectivity, deforming the *Mask* until the *Will* can
only see the object of its desire in these purposes. It does
not hate opposing desire, as do the phases of increasing
antithetical emotion, but hates that which opposes desire.
Capable of nothing but an incapable idealism (for it has
no thought but in myth, or in defence of myth), it must,
because it sees one side as all white, see the other side all
black; what but a dragon could dream of thwarting a
St. George? In men of the phase there will commonly
be both natures, for to be true to phase is a ceaseless
struggle. At one moment they are full of hate—Blake
writes of "Flemish and Venetian demons" and of some
picture of his own destroyed "by some vile spell of
Stoddart's"—and their hate is always close to madness;
and at the next they produce the comedy of Aretino and
of Rabelais or the mythology of Blake, and discover
symbolism to express the overflowing and bursting of
the mind. There is always an element of frenzy, and
almost always a delight in certain glowing or shining
images of concentrated force: in the smith's forge; in
the heart; in the human form in its most vigorous

development; in the solar disc; in some symbolical representation of the sexual organs; for the being must brag of its triumph over its own incoherence.

Since Phase 8 the man has more and more judged what is right in relation to time: a right action, or a right motive, has been one that he thought possible or desirable to think or do eternally; his soul would "come into possession of itself for ever in one single moment"; but now he begins once more to judge an action or motive in relation to space. A right action or motive must soon be right for any other man in similar circumstance. Hitherto an action, or motive, has been right precisely because it is exactly right for one person only, though for that person always. After the change, the belief in the soul's immortality declines, though the decline is slow, and it may only be recovered when Phase 1 is passed.

Among those who are of this phase may be great satirists, great caricaturists, but they pity the beautiful, for that is their *Mask*, and hate the ugly, for that is their *Body of Fate*, and so are unlike those of the *primary* phases, Rembrandt for instance, who pity the ugly, and sentimentalise the beautiful, or call it insipid, and turn away or secretly despise and hate it. Here too are beautiful women, whose bodies have taken upon themselves the image of the True *Mask*, and in these there is a radiant intensity, something of "The Burning Babe" of the Elizabethan lyric. They walk like queens, and seem to carry upon their backs a quiver of arrows, but they are gentle only to those whom they have chosen or subdued, or to the dogs that follow at their heels. Boundless in generosity, and in illusion, they will give themselves to a beggar because he resembles a religious picture and be faithful all their lives, or if they take another turn and choose a dozen lovers, die convinced that none but the first or last has ever touched their lips, for they are of those whose "virginity renews itself like the moon". Out of phase they turn termagant, if their lover take a wrong step in a quadrille where all the figures are of their own composition and changed without notice when the fancy takes them. Indeed, perhaps if the body have great perfection, there is always something imperfect in the mind, some rejection of or inadequacy of *Mask*: Venus out of phase chose lame Vulcan. Here also are several very ugly persons, their bodies torn and twisted by the violence of the new *primary*, but where the body has this ugliness great beauty of mind is possible. This is indeed the only *antithetical* phase where ugliness is possible, it being complementary to Phase 2, the only *primary* phase where beauty is possible.

From this phase on we meet with those who do violence, instead of those who suffer it; and prepare for those who love some living person, and not an image of the mind, but as yet this love is hardly more than the "fixed idea" of faithfulness. As the new love grows the sense of beauty will fade.

PHASE SEVENTEEN

Will—The *Daimonic* Man.

Mask (from Phase 3). *True*—Simplification through intensity. *False*—Dispersal.

Creative Mind (from Phase 13). *True*—Creative imagination through *antithetical* emotion. *False*—Enforced self-realization.

Body of Fate (from Phase 27)—Loss.
Examples: Dante, Shelley, Landor.

He is called the *Daimonic* man because Unity of
Being, and consequent expression of *Daimonic* thought,
is now more easy than at any other phase. As contrasted
with Phase 13 and Phase 14, where mental images were
separated from one another that they might be subject
to knowledge, all now flow, change, flutter, cry out, or
mix into something else; but without, as at Phase 16,
breaking and bruising one another, for Phase 17, the
central phase of its triad, is without frenzy. The *Will* is
falling asunder, but without explosion and noise. The
separated fragments seek images rather than ideas, and
these the intellect, seated in Phase 13, must synthesise
in vain, drawing with its compass-point a line that
shall but represent the outline of a bursting pod. The
being has for its supreme aim, as it had at Phase 16
(and as all subsequent *antithetical* phases shall have), to
hide from itself and others this separation and disorder,
and it conceals them under the emotional *Image* of
Phase 3; as Phase 16 concealed its greater violence under
that of Phase 2. When true to phase the intellect must
turn all its synthetic power to this task. It finds, not
the impassioned myth that Phase 16 found, but a
Mask of simplicity that is also intensity. This *Mask*
may represent intellectual or sexual passion; seem
some Ahasuerus or Athanase; be the gaunt Dante of
the *Divine Comedy*; its corresponding Image may be
Shelley's Venus Urania, Dante's Beatrice, or even the
Great Yellow Rose of the *Paradiso*. The *Will*, when
true to phase, assumes, in assuming the *Mask*, an intensity which is never dramatic but always lyrical and

personal, and this intensity, though always a deliberate assumption, is to others but the charm of the being; and yet the *Will* is always aware of the *Body of Fate*, which perpetually destroys this intensity, thereby leaving the *Will* to its own "dispersal".

At Phase 3, not as *Mask* but as phase, there should be perfect physical well-being or balance, though not beauty or emotional intensity, but at Phase 27 are those who turn away from all that Phase 3 represents and seek all those things it is blind to. The *Body of Fate*, therefore, derived from a phase of renunciation, is "loss", and works to make impossible "simplification by intensity". The being, through the intellect, selects some object of desire for a representation of the *Mask* as Image, some woman perhaps, and the *Body of Fate* snatches away the object. Then the intellect (*Creative Mind*), which in the most *antithetical* phases were better described as imagination, must substitute some new image of desire; and in the degree of its power and of its attainment of unity, relate that which is lost, that which has snatched it away, to the new image of desire, that which threatens the new image to the being's unity. If its unity be already past, or if unity be still to come, it may for all that be true to phase. It will then use its intellect merely to isolate *Mask* and Image, as chosen forms or as conceptions of the mind.

If it be out of phase it will avoid the subjective conflict, acquiesce, hope that the *Body of Fate* may die away; and then the *Mask* will cling to it and the Image lure it. It will feel itself betrayed, and persecuted till, entangled in *primary* conflict, it rages against all that destroys *Mask* and Image. It will be subject to nightmare, for its *Creative Mind* (deflected from the *Image* and

Mask to the *Body of Fate*) gives an isolated mythological
or abstract form to all that excites its hatred. It may
even dream of escaping from ill-luck by possessing the
impersonal *Body of Fate* of its opposite phase and of
exchanging passion for desk and ledger. Because of the
habit of synthesis, and of the growing complexity of the
energy, which gives many interests, and the still faint
perception of things in their weight and mass, men of
this phase are almost always partisans, propagandists
and gregarious; yet because of the *Mask* of simplification,
which holds up before them the solitary life of hunters
and of fishers and "the groves pale passion loves", they
hate parties, crowds, propaganda. Shelley out of phase
writes pamphlets, and dreams of converting the world,
or of turning man of affairs and upsetting governments,
and yet returns again and again to these two images of
solitude, a young man whose hair has grown white from
the burden of his thoughts, an old man in some shell-
strewn cave whom it is possible to call, when speaking
to the Sultan, "as inaccessible as God or thou". On the
other hand, how subject he is to nightmare! He sees the
devil leaning against a tree, is attacked by imaginary
assassins, and, in obedience to what he considers a supernatural voice, creates *The Cenci* that he may give to
Beatrice Cenci her incredible father. His political
enemies are monstrous, meaningless images. And unlike
Byron, who is two phases later, he can never see anything
that opposes him as it really is. Dante, who lamented
his exile as of all possible things the worst for such as
he, and sighed for his lost solitude, and yet could never
keep from politics, was, according to a contemporary,
such a partisan, that if a child, or a woman, spoke against
his party he would pelt this child or woman with stones.

Yet Dante, having attained, as poet, to Unity of Being, as poet saw all things set in order, had an intellect that served the *Mask* alone, that compelled even those things that opposed it to serve, and was content to see both good and evil. Shelley, upon the other hand, in whom even as poet unity was but in part attained, found compensation for his "loss", for the taking away of his children, for his quarrel with his first wife, for later sexual disappointment, for his exile, for his obloquy—there were but some three or four persons, he said, who did not consider him a monster of iniquity—in his hopes for the future of mankind. He lacked the Vision of Evil, could not conceive of the world as a continual conflict, so, though great poet he certainly was, he was not of the greatest kind. Dante suffering injustice and the loss of Beatrice, found divine justice and the heavenly Beatrice, but the justice of *Prometheus Unbound* is a vague propagandist emotion and the women that await its coming are but clouds. This is in part because the age in which Shelley lived was in itself so broken that true Unity of Being was almost impossible, but partly because, being out of phase so far as his practical reason was concerned, he was subject to an *automatonism* which he mistook for poetical invention, especially in his longer poems. *Antithetical* men (Phase 15 once passed) use this *automatonism* to evade hatred, or rather to hide it from their own eyes; perhaps all at some time or other, in moments of fatigue, give themselves up to fantastic, constructed images, or to an almost mechanical laughter.

Landor has been examined in *Per Amica Silentia Lunae.* The most violent of men, he uses his intellect to disengage a visionary image of perfect sanity (*Mask* at

Phase 3) seen always in the most serene and classic art imaginable. He had perhaps as much Unity of Being as his age permitted, and possessed, though not in any full measure, the Vision of Evil.

Will—The Emotional Man.

Mask (from Phase 4). *True*—Intensity through emotion. *False*—Curiosity.

Creative Mind (from Phase 12). *True*—Emotional philosophy. *False*—Enforced lure.

Body of Fate (from Phase 26)—Enforced disillusionment.

Examples: Goethe, Matthew Arnold.

The *antithetical tincture* closes during this phase, the being is losing direct knowledge of its old antithetical life. The conflict between that portion of the life of feeling which appertains to his unity, and that portion he has in common with others, coming to an end, has begun to destroy that knowledge. "A Lover's Nocturne" or "An Ode to the West Wind" are probably no more possible, certainly no more characteristic. He can hardly, if action and the intellect that concerns action are taken from him, recreate his dream life; and when he says "Who am I?", he finds it difficult to examine his thoughts in relation to one another, his emotions in relation to one another, but begins to find it easy to examine them in relation to action. He can examine those actions themselves with a new clearness. Now for the first time since Phase 12, Goethe's saying is almost true: "Man knows himself by action only, by thought never".

Meanwhile the *antithetical tincture* begins to attain, without previous struggle or self-analysis, its active form which is love—love being the union of emotion and instinct—or when out of phase, sentimentality. The *Will* seeks by some form of emotional philosophy to free a form of emotional beauty (*Mask*) from a "disillusionment" differing from the "illusions" of Phase 16, which are continuous, in that it permits intermittent awakening. The *Will*, with its closing *antithetical*, is turning away from the life of images to that of ideas, it is vacillating and curious, and it seeks in this *Mask* (from a phase where all the functions can be perfect), what becomes, when considered *antithetically*, a wisdom of the emotions.

At its next phase it will have fallen asunder; already it can only preserve its unity by a deliberate balancing of experiences (*Creative Mind* at Phase 12, *Body of Fate* at Phase 26), and so it must desire that phase (though that transformed into the emotional life), where wisdom seems a physical accident. Its object of desire is no longer a single image of passion, for it must relate all to social life; the man seeks to become not a sage, not Ahasuerus, but a wise king, and seeks a woman who looks the wise mother of children. Perhaps now, and for the first time, the love of a living woman ("disillusionment" once accepted) as apart from beauty or function, is an admitted aim, though not yet wholly achieved. The *Body of Fate* is from the phase where the "wisdom of knowledge" has compelled *Mask* and Image to become not objects of desire but objects of knowledge. Goethe did not, as Beddoes said, marry his cook, but he certainly did not marry the woman he had desired, and his grief at her death showed that, unlike Phase 16 or Phase 17, which forget their broken toys, he could love what disillusionment gave. When he seeks to live objectively, he will substitute curiosity for emotional wisdom, he will invent objects of desire artificially, he will say perhaps, though this was said by a man who was probably still later in phase, "I was never in love with a serpent-charmer before"; the False *Mask* will press upon him, pursue him, and, refusing conflict, he will fly from the True *Mask* at each artificial choice. The nightingale will refuse the thorn and so remain among images instead of passing to ideas. He is still disillusioned, but he can no longer through philosophy substitute for the desire that life has taken away, love for what life has brought. The *Will* is near the place marked Head upon the great chart, which enables it to choose its *Mask* even when true to phase almost coldly and always deliberately, whereas the *Creative Mind* is derived from the place marked Heart, and is therefore more impassioned and less subtle and delicate than if Phase 16 or Phase 17 were the place of the *Will*, though not yet argumentative or heated. The *Will* at Head uses the heart with perfect mastery and, because of the growing *primary*, begins to be aware of an audience, though as yet it will not dramatise the *Mask* deliberately for the sake of effect as will Phase 19.

PHASE NINETEEN

Will—The Assertive Man.

Mask (from Phase 5). *True*—Conviction. *False*—Domination.

Creative Mind (from Phase 11). *True*—Emotional intellect. *False*—The Unfaithful.

Body of Fate (from Phase 25)—Enforced failure of action.

Examples: Gabriele d'Annunzio (perhaps), Oscar Wilde, Byron, a certain actress.

This phase is the beginning of the artificial, the abstract, the fragmentary, and the dramatic. Unity of Being is no longer possible, for the being is compelled to live in a fragment of itself and to dramatise that fragment. The *primary tincture* is closing, direct knowledge of self in relation to action is ceasing to be possible. The being only completely knows that portion of itself which judges fact for the sake of action. When the man lives according to phase, he is now governed by conviction, instead of by a ruling mood, and is effective only in so far as he can find this conviction. His aim is so to use an intellect which turns easily to declamation, emotional emphasis, that it serves conviction in a life where effort, just in so far as its object is passionately desired, comes to nothing. He desires to be strong and stable, but as Unity of Being and self-knowledge are both gone, and it is too soon to grasp at another unity through *primary* mind, he passes from emphasis to emphasis. The strength from conviction, derived from a *Mask* of the first quarter *antithetically* transformed, is not founded upon social duty, though that may seem so to others, but is temperamentally formed to fit some crisis of personal life. His thought is immensely effective and dramatic, arising always from some immediate situation, a situation found or created by himself, and may have great permanent value as the expression of an exciting personality. This thought is always an open attack; or a sudden emphasis, an extravagance, or an impassioned declamation of some general idea, which is a more veiled attack. The *Creative Mind* being derived from Phase 11, he is doomed to attempt the destruction of all that breaks or encumbers personality, but this personality is conceived of as a fragmentary, momentary intensity. The mastery of images, threatened or lost at Phase 18, may, however, be completely recovered, but there is less symbol, more fact. Vitality from dreams has died out, and a vitality from fact has begun which has for its ultimate aim the mastery of the real world. The watercourse after an abrupt fall continues upon a lower level; ice turns to water, or water to vapour: there is a new chemical phase.

When lived out of phase there is a hatred or contempt of others, and instead of seeking conviction for its own sake, the man takes up opinions that he may impose himself upon others. He is tyrannical and capricious, and his intellect is called "The Unfaithful", because, being used for victory alone, it will change its ground in a moment and delight in some new emphasis, not caring whether old or new have consistency. The *Mask* is derived from that phase where perversity begins, where artifice begins, and has its *discord* from Phase 25, the last phase where the artificial is possible; the *Body of Fate* is therefore enforced failure of action, and many at this phase desire action above all things as a means of expression. Whether the man be in or out of phase, there is the desire to escape from Unity of Being or any approximation towards it, for Unity can be but a simulacrum now. And in so far as the soul keeps its memory of that potential Unity there is conscious *antithetical* weakness. He must now dramatise the *Mask* through the *Will* and dreads the Image, deep within, of the old *anti-*

thetical tincture at its strongest, and yet this *Image* may seem infinitely desirable if he could but find the desire. When so torn into two, escape when it comes may be so violent that it brings him under the False *Mask* and the False *Creative Mind*. A certain actress is typical, for she surrounds herself with drawings by Burne-Jones in his latest period, and reveres them as they were holy pictures, while her manners are boisterous, dominating and egotistical. They are faces of silent women, and she is not silent for a moment; yet these faces are not, as I once thought, the True *Mask* but a part of that incoherence the True *Mask* must conceal. Were she to surrender to their influence she would become insincere in her art and exploit an emotion that is no longer hers. I find in Wilde, too, something pretty, feminine, and insincere, derived from his admiration for writers of the 17th and earlier phases, and much that is violent, arbitrary and insolent, derived from his desire to escape.

The *antithetical Mask* comes to men of Phase 17 and Phase 18 as a form of strength, and when they are tempted to dramatise it, the dramatisation is fitful, and brings no conviction of strength, for they dislike emphasis; but now the weakness of the *antithetical* has begun, for though still the stronger it cannot ignore the growing *primary*. It is no longer an absolute monarch, and it permits power to pass to statesman or demagogue, whom, however, it will constantly change.

Here one finds men and women who love those who rob them or beat them, as though the soul were intoxicated by its discovery of human nature, or found even a secret delight in the shattering of the image of its desire. It is as though it cried, "I would be possessed by" or "I would possess that which is Human. What

do I care if it is good or bad?" There is no "disillusionment", for they have found that which they have
sought, but that which they have sought and found is
a fragment.

Will—The Concrete Man.

Mask (from Phase 6). *True*—Fatalism. *False*—Superstition.

Creative Mind (from Phase 10). *True*—Dramatisation
of *Mask*. *False*—Self-desecration.

Body of Fate (from Phase 24)—Enforced success of
action.

Examples: Shakespeare, Balzac, Napoleon.

Like the phase before it, and those that follow it
immediately, a phase of the breaking up and subdivision of the being. The energy is always seeking those
facts which being separable can be seen more clearly,
or expressed more clearly, but when there is truth to
phase there is a similitude of the old unity, or rather a
new unity, which is not a Unity of Being but a unity of
the creative act. He no longer seeks to unify what is
broken through conviction, by imposing those very convictions upon himself and others, but by projecting a
dramatisation or many dramatisations. He can create,
just in that degree in which he can see these dramatisations as separate from himself, and yet as an epitome
of his whole nature. His *Mask* is derived from Phase 6,
where man first becomes a generalised form, according
to the *primary tincture*, as in the poetry of Walt Whitman, but this *Mask* he must by dramatisation rescue
from a *Body of Fate* derived from Phase 24, where moral

domination dies out before that of the exterior world
conceived as a whole. The *Body of Fate* is called
"enforced success", a success that rolls out and smooths
away, that dissolves through creation, that seems to
delight in all outward flowing, that drenches all with
grease and oil; that turns dramatisation into desecra-
tion: "I have made myself a motley to the view".
Owing to the need of seeing the dramatic image, or
images, as individuals, that is to say as set amongst
concrete or fixed surroundings, he seeks some field of
action, some mirror not of his own creation. Unlike
Phase 19 he fails in situations wholly created by himself, or in works of art where character or story has
gained nothing from history. His phase is called "The
Concrete Man", because the isolation of parts that
began at Phase 19 is overcome at the second phase
of the triad; subordination of parts is achieved by the
discovery of concrete relations. His abstraction too,
affected by these relations, may be no more than an
emotional interest in such generalisations as "God",
"Man", a Napoleon may but point to the starry
heavens and say that they prove the existence of God.
There is a delight in concrete images that, unlike the
impassioned images of Phase 17 and Phase 18, or the
declamatory images of Phase 19, reveal through com-
plex suffering the general destiny of man. He must,
however, to express this suffering, personify rather than
characterise, create not observe that multitude, which
is but his *Mask* as in a multiplying mirror, for the
primary is not yet strong enough to substitute for the
lost Unity of Being that of the external world perceived
as fact. In a man of action this multiplicity gives the
greatest possible richness of resource where he is not

thwarted by his horoscope, great ductability, a gift for adopting any rôle that stirs imagination, a philosophy of impulse and audacity; but in the man of action a part of the nature must be crushed, one main dramatisation or group of images preferred to all others.

Napoleon sees himself as Alexander moving to the conquest of the East, *Mask* and Image must take an historical and not a mythological or dream form, a form found but not created; he is crowned in the dress of a Roman Emperor. Shakespeare, the other supreme figure of the phase, was—if we may judge by the few biographical facts, and by such adjectives as "sweet" and "gentle" applied to him by his contemporaries—a man whose actual personality seemed faint and passionless. Unlike Ben Jonson he fought no duels; he kept out of quarrels in a quarrelsome age; not even complaining when somebody pirated his sonnets; he dominated no Mermaid Tavern, but—through *Mask* and Image, reflected in a multiplying mirror—he created the most passionate art that exists. He was the greatest of modern poets, partly because entirely true to phase, creating always from *Mask* and *Creative Mind*, never from situation alone, never from *Body of Fate* alone; and if we knew all we would find that success came to him, as to others of this phase, as something hostile and unforeseen; something that sought to impose an intuition of Fate (the condition of Phase 6) as from without and therefore as a form of superstition. Both Shakespeare and Balzac used the False *Mask* imaginatively, explored it to impose the True, and what Thomas Lake Harris,[1] the half-charlatan

---

[1] I quote from a book circulated privately among his followers. I saw it years ago but seem to remember it as now vague, now vulgar, and now magnificent in style.

American visionary, said of Shakespeare might be said of both: "Often the hair of his head stood up and all life became the echoing chambers of the tomb".

At Phase 19 we create through the externalised *Mask* an imaginary world, in whose real existence we believe, while remaining separate from it; at Phase 20 we enter that world and become a portion of it; we study it, we amass historical evidence, and, that we may dominate it the more, drive out myth and symbol, and compel it to seem the real world where our lives are lived.

A phase of ambition; in Napoleon the dramatist's own ambition; in Shakespeare that of the persons of his art; and this ambition is not that of the solitary law-giver, that of Phase 10 (where the *Creative Mind* is placed) which rejects, resists and narrows, but a creative energy.

PHASE TWENTY-ONE

Will—The Acquisitive Man.

Mask (from Phase 7). *True*—Self-analysis. *False*—Self-adaptation.

Creative Mind (from Phase 9). *True*—Domination of the intellect. *False*—Distortion.

Body of Fate (from Phase 23)—Enforced triumph of achievement.

Examples: Lamarck, Mr. Bernard Shaw, Mr. Wells. George Moore.

The *antithetical tincture* has a predominance so slight that the *Creative Mind* and *Body of Fate* almost equal it in control of desire. The *Will* can scarcely conceive of a *Mask* separate from or predominant over *Creative Mind* and *Body of Fate*, yet because it can do so there is personality not character. It is better, however, to use a different word, and therefore Phases 21, 22 and 23 are described as, like the phases opposite, phases of individuality where the *Will* is studied less in relation to the *Mask* than in relation to itself. At Phase 23 the new relation to the *Mask*, as something to escape from, will have grown clear.

The *antithetical tincture* is noble, and, judged by the standards of the *primary*, evil, whereas the *primary* is good and banal; and this phase, the last before the *antithetical* surrenders its control, would be almost wholly good did it not hate its own banality. Personality has almost the rigidity, almost the permanence of character, but it is not character, for it is still always assumed. When we contemplate Napoleon we can see ourselves, perhaps even think of ourselves as Napoleons, but a man of Phase 21 has a personality that seems a creation of his circumstance and his faults, a manner peculiar to himself and impossible to others. We say at once, "How individual he is". In theory whatever one has chosen must be within the choice of others, at some moment or for some purpose, but we find in practice that nobody of this phase has personal imitators, or has given his name to a form of manners. The *Will* has driven intellectual complexity into its final entanglement, an entanglement created by the continual adaptation to new circumstances of a logical sequence; and the aim of the individual, when true to phase, is to realise, by his own complete domination over all circumstance, a self-analysing, self-conscious simplicity. Phase 7 shuddered at its intellectual simplicity, whereas he must shudder at his complexity.

Out of phase, instead of seeking this simplicity

through his own dominating constructive will, he will parade an imaginary naïveté, even blunder in his work, encourage in himself stupidities of spite or sentiment, or commit calculated indiscretions simulating impulse. He is under the False *Mask* (emotional self-adaptation) and the False *Creative Mind* (distortion: the furious Phase 9 acted upon by "enforced sensuality"). He sees the *antithetical* as evil, and desires the evil, for he is subject to a sort of possession by the devil, which is in reality but a theatrical scene. Precisely because his adaptability can be turned in any direction, when lived according to the *primary*, he is driven into all that is freakish or grotesque, mind-created passions, simulated emotions; he adopts all that can suggest the burning heart he longs for in vain; he turns braggart or buffoon. Like somebody in Dostoieffsky's *Idiot*, he will invite others to tell their worst deeds that he may himself confess that he stole a half-crown and left a servant-girl to bear the blame. When all turn upon him he will be full of wonder, for he knows that the confession is not true, or if true, that the deed itself was but a trick, or a pose, and that all the time he is full of a goodness that fills him with shame. Whether he live according to phase and regard life without emotion, or live out of phase and simulate emotion, his *Body of Fate* drags him away from intellectual unity; but in so far as he lives out of phase he weakens conflict, refuses to resist, floats upon the stream. In phase he strengthens conflict to the utmost by refusing all activity that is not *antithetical*: he becomes intellectually dominating, intellectually unique. He apprehends the simplicity of his opposite phase as some vast systematisation, in which the will imposes itself upon the multiplicity of living images, or events, upon all in Shakespeare, in Napoleon even, that delighted in its independent life; for he is a tyrant and must kill his adversary. If he is a novelist, his characters must go his road, and not theirs, and perpetually demonstrate his thesis; he will love construction better than the flow of life, and as a dramatist he will create character and situation without passion, and without liking, and yet he is a master of surprise, for one can never be sure where even a charge of shot will fall. Style exists now but as a sign of work well done, a certain energy and precision of movement; in the artistic sense it is no longer possible, for the tension of the will is too great to allow of suggestion. Writers of the phase are great public men and they exist after death as historical monuments, for they are without meaning apart from time and circumstance.

Phase Twenty-two

Will—Balance between ambition and contemplation.

Mask (from Phase 8). *True*—Self-immolation. *False*—Self-assurance.

Creative Mind (from Phase 8). *True*—Amalgamation. *False*—Despair.

Body of Fate (from Phase 22)—The Temptation through Strength.

Examples: Flaubert, Herbert Spencer, Swedenborg, Dostoieffsky, Darwin.

The aim of the being, until the point of balance has been reached, will be that of Phase 21 except that synthesis will be more complete, and the sense of identity between the individual and his thought, between his

desire and his synthesis will be closer; but the character
of the phase is precisely that here balance is reached
and passed, though it is stated that the individual may
have to return to this phase more than once, though not
more than four times, before it is passed. Once balance
has been reached, the aim must be to use the *Body of
Fate* to deliver the *Creative Mind* from the *Mask*, and not
to use the *Creative Mind* to deliver the *Mask* from the
Body of Fate. The being does this by so using the intellect
upon the facts of the world that the last vestige of
personality disappears. The *Will*, engaged in its last
struggle with external fact (*Body of Fate*), must submit,
until it sees itself as inseparable from nature perceived
as fact, and it must see itself as merged into that nature
through the *Mask*, either as a conqueror lost in what he
conquers, or dying at the moment of conquest, or as
renouncing conquest, whether it come by might of
logic, or might of drama, or might of hand. The *Will*
since Phase 8 has more and more seen itself as a *Mask*,
as a form of personal power, but now it must see that
power broken. From Phase 12 to Phase 18 it was or
should have been a power wielded by the whole nature;
but since Phase 19 it has been wielded by a fragment
only, as something more and more professional, tem-
peramental or technical.

It has become abstract, and the more it has sought the
whole of natural fact, the more abstract it has become.
One thinks of some spilt liquid which grows thinner the
wider it spreads till at last it is but a film. That which at
Phase 21 was a longing for self-conscious simplicity, as
an escape from logical complication and subdivision, is
now (through the *Mask* from Phase 8) a desire for the death
of the intellect. At Phase 21 it still sought to change the

world, could still be a Shaw, a Wells, but now it will
seek to change nothing, it needs nothing but what it
may call "reality", "truth", "God's Will": confused
and weary, through trying to grasp too much, the hand
must loosen.

Here takes place an interchange between portions of
the mind which resembles the interchange between the
old and new *primary*, the old and new *antithetical* at
Phase 1 and Phase 15. It is reflected, however, from the
Wheel of the *Principles* I shall describe in Book II. The
mind that has shown a predominantly emotional character, called that of the *Victim*, through the *antithetical*
phases, now shows a predominantly intellectual character, called that of the *Sage* (though until Phase 1 has
been passed it can but use intellect when true to phase
to eliminate intellect); whereas the mind that has been
predominantly that of the *Sage* puts on *Victimage*. An
element in the nature is exhausted at the point of
balance, and the opposite element controls the mind.
One thinks of the gusts of sentimentality that overtake
violent men, the gusts of cruelty that overtake the sentimental. At Phase 8, a blinded and throttled phase, there
is not a similar interchange. I will return to this omis-
sion in Book II. A man of Phase 22 will commonly not
only systematise, to the exhaustion of his will, but discover this exhaustion of will in all that he studies. If
Lamarck, as is probable, was of Phase 21, Darwin was
probably a man of Phase 22, for his theory of development by the survival of fortunate accidental varieties
seems to express this exhaustion. The man himself is
never weak, never vague or fluctuating in his thought,
for if he brings all to silence, it is a silence that results
from tension, and till the moment of balance, nothing

interests him that is not wrought up to the greatest effort of which it is capable. Flaubert is the supreme literary genius of the phase, and his *Temptation of St. Anthony* and his *Bouvard and Pécuchet* are the sacred books of the phase, one describing its effect upon a mind where all is concrete and sensuous, the other upon the more logical, matter-of-fact, curious, modern mind. In both the mind exhausts all knowledge within its reach and sinks exhausted to a conscious futility. But the matter is not more of the phase than is the method. One never doubts for a moment that Flaubert was of the phase; all must be impersonal; he must neither like nor dislike character or event; he is "the mirror dawdling down a road" of Stendhal, with a clear brightness that is not Stendhal's; and when we make his mind our own, we seem to have renounced our own ambition under the influence of some strange, far-reaching, impartial gaze.

We feel too that this man who systematised by but linking one emotional association to another has become strangely hard, cold and invulnerable, that this mirror is not brittle but of unbreakable steel. "Systematised" is the only word that comes to mind, but it implies too much deliberation, for association has ranged itself by association as little bits of paper and little chips of wood cling to one another upon the water in a bowl. In Dostoieffsky the "amalgamation" is less intellectual, less orderly, he, one feels, has reached the point of balance through life, not through the deliberate process of his art; his Whole will, not merely his intellectual will, has been shaken. His characters, in whom is reflected this broken will, are aware, unlike those of *Bouvard and Pécuchet*, those of the *Temptation* even, of

some ungraspable Whole to which they have given the
name of God. For a moment that fragment, that relation, which is our very being, is broken; they are at
Udan Adan "wailing upon the edge of nonentity, wailing for Jerusalem, with weak voices almost inarticu-
late"; yet full submission has not come.

Swedenborg passes through his balance after fifty,
a mind incredibly dry and arid, hard, tangible and cold,
like the minerals he assayed for the Swedish government, studies a new branch of science: the economics,
the natural history of Heaven; notes that there nothing
but emotion, nothing but the ruling love exists. The
desire to dominate has so completely vanished, "amalgamation" has pushed its way so far into the subconscious, into that which is dark, that we call it a
vision. Had he been out of phase, had he attempted to
arrange his life according to the personal *Mask*, he would
have been pedantic and arrogant, a Bouvard, or a
Pécuchet, passing from absurdity to absurdity, hopeless
and insatiable.

In the world of action such absurdity may become
terrible, for men will die and murder for an abstract
synthesis, and the more abstract it is the further it
carries them from compunction and compromise; and
as obstacles to that synthesis increase, the violence of
their will increases. It is a phase as tragic as its opposite,
and more terrible, for the man of this phase may, before
the point of balance has been reached, become a destroyer
and persecutor, a figure of tumult and of violence; or as
is more probable—for the violence of such a man must be
checked by moments of resignation or despair, premoni-
tions of balance—his system will become an instrument
of destruction and of persecution in the hands of others.

The seeking of Unity of Fact by a single faculty, instead of Unity of Being by the use of all, has separated a man from his genius. This is symbolised in the Wheel by the gradual separation (as we recede from Phase 15) of *Will* and *Creative Mind*, *Mask* and *Body of Fate*. During the supernatural incarnation of Phase 15, we were compelled to assume an absolute identity of the *Will*, or self, with its creative power, of beauty with body; but for some time self and creative power, though separating, have been neighbours and kin. A Landor, or a Morris, however violent, however much of a child he seem, is always a remarkable man; in Phases 19, 20 and 21 genius grows professional, something taken up when work is taken up, it begins to be possible to record the stupidities of men of genius in a scrapbook; Bouvard and Pécuchet have that refuge for their old age. Someone has said that Balzac at noonday was a very ignorant man, but at midnight over a cup of coffee knew everything in the world. In the man of action, in a Napoleon, let us say, the stupidities lie hidden, for action is a form of abstraction that crushes everything it cannot express. At Phase 22 stupidity is obvious, one finds it in the correspondence of Karl Marx, in his banal abusiveness, while to Goncourt, Flaubert, as man, seemed full of unconsidered thought. Flaubert, says Anatole France, was not intelligent. Dostoieffsky, to those who first acclaimed his genius, seemed when he laid down his pen an hysterical fool. One remembers Herbert Spencer dabbing the grapes upon a lodging-house carpet with an inky cork that he might tint them to his favourite colour, "impure purple". On the other hand, as the *Will* moves further from the *Creative Mind*, it approaches the *Body of Fate*, and with this comes an increasing delight in impersonal energy and in inanimate objects, and as the *Mask* separates from the *Body of Fate* and approaches the *Creative Mind* we delight more and more in all that is artificial, all that is deliberately invented. Symbols may become hateful to us, the ugly and the arbitrary delightful, that we may the more quickly kill all memory of Unity of Being. We identify ourselves in our surroundings—in our surroundings perceived as fact —while at the same time the intellect so slips from our grasp, as it were, that we contemplate its energies as something we can no longer control, and give to each of those energies an appropriate name as though it were an animate being. Now that *Will* and *Body of Fate* are one, *Creative Mind* and *Mask* one also, we are no longer four but two; and life, the balance reached, becomes an act of contemplation. There is no longer a desired object, as distinct from thought itself, no longer a *Will*, as distinct from the process of nature seen as fact; and so thought itself, seeing that it can neither begin nor end, is stationary. Intellect knows itself as its own object of desire; and the *Will* knows itself to be the world; there is neither change nor desire of change. For the moment the desire for a form has ceased and an absolute realism becomes possible.

PHASE TWENTY-THREE

Will—The Receptive Man.

Mask (from Phase 9). *True*—Wisdom. *False*—Self-pity.

Creative Mind (from Phase 7). *True*—Creation through pity. *False*—Self-driven desire.

Body of Fate (from Phase 21)—Success.

Examples: Rembrandt, Synge.

When out of phase, for reasons that will appear later, he is tyrannical, gloomy and self-absorbed. In phase his energy has a character analogous to the longing of Phase 16 to escape from complete subjectivity: it escapes in a condition of explosive joy from systematisation and abstraction. The clock has run down and must be wound up again. The *primary tincture* is now greater than the *antithetical*, and the man must free the intellect from all motives founded upon personal desire, by the help of the external world, now for the first time studied and mastered for its own sake. He must kill all thought that would systematise the world, by doing a thing, not because he wants to, or because he should, but because he can; that is to say, he sees all things from the point of view of his own technique, touches and tastes and investigates technically. He is, however, because of the nature of his energy, violent, anarchic, like all who are of the first phase of a quarter. Because he is without systematisation he is without a master, and only by his technical mastery can he escape from the sense of being thwarted and opposed by other men; and his technical mastery must exist, not for its own sake, though for its own sake it has been done, but for that which it reveals, for its laying bare—to hand and eye, as distinguished from thought and emotion—general humanity. Yet this laying bare is a perpetual surprise, is an unforeseen reward of skill. And unlike *antithetical* man he must use his *Body of Fate* (now always his "success") to liberate his intellect from personality, and only when he has done this, only when he escapes the voluntary *Mask*, does he find his true intellect, is he found by his True *Mask*.

The True *Mask* is from the frenzied Phase 9 where

personal life is made visible for the first time, but from
that phase mastered by its *Body of Fate*, "enforced
sensuality", derived from Phase 7 where the instinctive
flood is almost above the lips. It is called "wisdom" and
this wisdom (personality reflected in a *primary* mirror)
is general humanity experienced as a form of involuntary emotion and involuntary delight in the "minute
particulars" of life. The man wipes his breath from the
window-pane, and laughs in his delight at all the varied
scene. Because his *Creative Mind* is at Phase 7, where instinctive life, all but reaching utmost complexity, suffers
an external abstract synthesis, his *Body of Fate* which
drives him to intellectual life, at Phase 21; his *Will*
at a phase of revolt from every intellectual summary,
from all intellectual abstraction, this delight is not
mere delight, he would construct a whole, but that
whole must seem all event, all picture. That whole must
not be instinctive, bodily, natural, however, though it
may seem so, for in reality he cares only for what is
human, individual and moral. To others he may seem
to care for the immoral and inhuman only, for he will
be hostile, or indifferent to moral as to intellectual
summaries; if he is Rembrandt he discovers his Christ
through anatomical curiosity, or through curiosity as to
light and shade, and if he is Synge he takes a malicious
pleasure in the contrast between his hero, whom he discovers through his instinct for comedy, and any hero
in men's minds. Indeed, whether he be Synge or Rembrandt, he is ready to sacrifice every convention, perhaps
all that men have agreed to reverence, for a startling
theme, or a model one delights in painting; and yet all
the while, because of the nature of his *Mask*, there is
another summary working through bone and nerve. He

is never the mere technician that he seems, though when you ask his meaning he will have nothing to say, or will say something irrelevant or childish.

Artists and writers of Phase 21 and Phase 22 have eliminated all that is personal from their style, seeking cold metal and pure water, but he will delight in colour and idiosyncrasy, though these he must find rather than create. Synge must find rhythm and syntax in the Aran Islands, Rembrandt delight in all accidents of the visible world; yet neither, no matter what his delight in reality, shows it without exaggeration, for both delight in all that is wilful, in all that flouts intellectual coherence, and conceive of the world as if it were an overflowing cauldron. Both will work in toil and in pain, finding what they do not seek, for, after Phase 22, desire creates no longer, will has taken its place; but that which they reveal is joyous. Whereas Shakespeare showed, through a style full of joy, a melancholy vision sought from afar; a style at play, a mind that served; Synge must fill many notebooks, clap his ear to that hole in the ceiling; and what patience Rembrandt must have spent in the painting of a lace collar though to find his subject he had but to open his eyes. When out of phase, when the man seeks to choose his *Mask*, he is gloomy with the gloom of others, and tyrannical with the tyranny of others, because he cannot create. Phase 9 was dominated by desire, was described as having the greatest belief in its own desire possible to man, yet from it Phase 23 receives not desire but pity, and not belief but wisdom. Pity needs wisdom as desire needs belief, for pity is *primary*, whereas desire is *antithetical*. When pity is separated from wisdom we have the False *Mask*, a pity like that of a drunken man, self-pity, whether offered in seeming to another or only to oneself: pity corrupted by desire. Who does not feel the pity in Rembrandt, in Synge, and know that it is inseparable from wisdom? In the works of Synge there is much self-pity, ennobled to a pity for all that lived; and once an actress, playing his Deirdre, put all into a gesture. Concubar, who had murdered Deirdre's husband and her friends, was in altercation with Fergus, who had demanded vengeance; "Move a little further off", she cried, "with the babbling of fools"; and a moment later, moving like a somnambulist, she touched Concubar upon the arm, a gesture full of gentleness and compassion, as though she had said, "You also live". In Synge's early unpublished work, written before he found the dialects of Aran and of Wicklow, there is brooding melancholy and morbid self-pity. He had to undergo an aesthetic transformation, analogous to religious conversion, before he became the audacious, joyous, ironical man we know. The emotional life in so far as it was deliberate had to be transferred from Phase 9 to Phase 23, from a condition of self-regarding melancholy to its direct opposite. This transformation must have seemed to him a discovery of his true self, of his true moral being; whereas Shelley's came at the moment when he first created a passionate image which made him forgetful of himself. It came perhaps when he had passed from the litigious rhetoric of *Queen Mab* to the lonely reveries of *Alastor*. *Primary* art values above all things sincerity to the self or *Will* but to the self active, transforming, perceiving.

The quarter of Intellect was a quarter of dispersal and generalisation, a play of shuttlecock with the first quarter of animal burgeoning, but the fourth quarter is

a quarter of withdrawal and concentration, in which
active moral man should receive into himself, and transform into *primary* sympathy the emotional self-realisation
of the second quarter. If he does not so receive and
transform he sinks into stupidity and stagnation, perceives nothing but his own interests, or becomes a tool
in the hands of others; and at Phase 23, because there
must be delight in the unforeseen, he may be brutal and
outrageous. He does not, however, hate, like a man of
the third quarter, being but ignorant of or indifferent
to the feelings of others. Rembrandt pitied ugliness, for
what we call ugliness was to him an escape from all that
is summarised and known, but had he painted a beautiful face, as *antithetical* man understands beauty, it would
have remained a convention, he would have seen it
through a mirage of boredom.

When one compares the work of Rembrandt with
that of David, whose phase was Phase 21; the work
of Synge with that of Mr. Wells; one compares men
whose *antithetical tincture* is breaking up and dissolving,
with men in whom it is, as for a last resistance, tightening,
concentrating, levelling, transforming, tabulating. Rembrandt and Synge but look on and clap their hands.
There is indeed as much selection among the events in
one case as in the other, but at Phase 23 events seem
startling because they elude intellect.

All phases after Phase 15 and before Phase 22 un-
weave that which is woven by the equivalent phases
before Phase 15 and after Phase 8.

The man of Phase 23 has in the *Mask*, at Phase 9, a
contrary that seems his very self until he use the discord
of that contrary, his *Body of Fate* at Phase 21, to drive
away the *Mask* and free the intellect and rid pity of

desire and turn belief into wisdom. The *Creative Mind*, a discord to the *Will*, is from a phase of instinctive dispersal, and must turn the violent objectivity of the self or *Will* into a delight in all that breathes and moves: "The gay fishes on the wave when the moon sucks up the dew".

PHASE TWENTY-FOUR

Will—The end of ambition.

Mask (from Phase 10). *True*—Self-reliance. *False*—Isolation.

Creative Mind (from Phase 6). *True*—Humanitarianism. through constructive emotion. *False*—Authority.

Body of Fate (from Phase 20)—Objective action.

Examples: Queen Victoria, Galsworthy, Lady Gregory.

As the *Mask* now seems the natural self, which he must escape, the man labours to turn all within him that is from Phase 10 into some quality of Phase 24. At Phase 23, when in what seemed the natural self, the man was full of gloomy self-absorption and its appropriate abstractions, but now the abstractions are those that feed self-righteousness and scorn of others, the nearest the natural self can come to the self-expressing mastery of Phase 10. Morality, grown passive and pompous, dwindles to unmeaning forms and formulae. Under the influence of the *Body of Fate*, the unweaver and *discord* of Phase 10, the man frees the intellect from the *Mask* by unflagging impersonal activity. Instead of burning, as did Phase 23, intellectual abstraction in a technical fire, it grinds moral abstraction in a mill. This mill, created by the freed intellect, is a code of personal conduct, which, being formed from social and historical tradition, remains always concrete in the mind. All is sacrificed to this code; moral strength reaches its climax; the rage of Phase 10 to destroy all that trammels the being from without is now all self-surrender. There is great humility—"she died every day she lived"—and pride as great, pride in the code's acceptance, an impersonal pride, as though one were to sign "servant of servants". There is no philosophic capacity, no intellectual curiosity, but there is no dislike for either philosophy or science; they are a part of the world and that world is accepted. There may be great intolerance for all who break or resist the code, and great tolerance for all the evil of the world that is clearly beyond it whether above it or below. The code must rule, and because that code cannot be an intellectual choice, it is always a tradition bound up with family, or office, or trade, always a part of history. It is always seemingly fated, for its subconscious purpose is to compel surrender of every personal ambition; and though it is obeyed in pain—can there be mercy in a rigid code?—the man is flooded with the joy of self-surrender; and flooded with mercy —what else can there be in self-surrender?—for those over whom the code can have no rights, children and the nameless multitude. Unmerciful to those who serve and to himself, merciful in contemplating those who are served, he never wearies of forgiveness.

Men and women of the phase create an art where individuals only exist to express some historical code, or some historical tradition of action and of feeling, things written in what Raftery called the Book of the People, or settled by social or official station, even as set forth in Directory or Peerage. The judge upon the bench is but

a judge, the prisoner in the dock is but the eternal
offender, whom we may study in legend or in Blue
Book. They despise the Bohemian above all men till he
turns gypsy, tinker, convict, or the like, and so finds
historical sanction, attains as it were to some inherited
code or recognised relation to such code. They submit
all their actions to the most unflinching examination,
and yet are without psychology, or self-knowledge, or
self-created standard of any kind, for they but ask without ceasing, "Have I done my duty as well as So-and-so?"
"Am I as unflinching as my fathers before me?" and
though they can stand utterly alone, indifferent though
all the world condemn, it is not that they have found
themselves, but that they have been found faithful. The
very Bohemians are not wholly individual men in their
eyes, and but fulfil the curse, laid upon them before
they were born, by God or social necessity.

Out of phase, seeking emotion instead of impersonal
action, there is—desire being impossible—self-pity, and
therefore discontent with people and with circumstance,
and an overwhelming sense of loneliness, of being
abandoned. All criticism is resented, and small personal
rights and predilections, especially if supported by habit
or position, are asserted with violence; there is great
indifference to others' rights and predilections; we have
the bureaucrat or the ecclesiastic of satire, a tyrant who
is incapable of insight or of hesitation.

Their intellect being from Phase 6, but their energy,
or will, or bias, from Phase 24, they must, if in phase,
see their code expressed in multiform human life, the
mind of Victoria at its best, as distinguished from that
of Walt Whitman. Their emotional life is a reversal of
Phase 10, as what was autocratic in Victoria reversed the

personal autocracy of Parnell. They fly the *Mask*, that it may become, when enforced, that form of pride and of humility that holds together a professional or social order.

When out of phase they take from Phase 10 isolation, which is good for that phase but destructive to a phase that should live for others and from others; and they take from Phase 6 a bundle of race instincts, and turn them to abstract moral or social convention, and so contrast with Phase 6, as the mind of Victoria at its worst contrasts with that of Walt Whitman. When in phase they turn these instincts to a concrete code, founded upon dead or living example.

That which characterises all phases of the last quarter, with an increasing intensity, begins now to be plain: persecution of instinct—race is transformed into a moral conception—whereas the intellectual phases, with increasing intensity as they approached Phase 22, persecuted emotion. Morality and intellect persecute instinct and emotion respectively, which seek their protection.

PHASE TWENTY-FIVE

Will—The Conditional Man.

Mask (from Phase 11). *True*—Consciousness of self. *False*—Self-consciousness.

Creative Mind (from Phase 5). *True*—Rhetoric. *False*—Spiritual arrogance.

Body of Fate (from Phase 19)—Persecution.

Examples: Cardinal Newman, Luther, Calvin, George Herbert, George Russell (A. E.).

Born as it seems to the arrogance of belief, as Phase 24 was born to moral arrogance, the man of the phase must reverse himself, must change from Phase 11 to Phase 25; use the *Body of Fate* to purify the intellect from the *Mask*, till this intellect accepts some social order, some condition of life, some organised belief: the convictions of Christendom perhaps. He must eliminate all that is personal from belief; eliminate the necessity for intellect by the contagion of some common agreement, as did Phase 23 by its technique, Phase 24 by its code. With a *Will* of subsidence, an intellect of loosening and separating, he must, like Phase 23 or Phase 24, find himself in such a situation that he is compelled to concrete synthesis (*Body of Fate* at Phase 19 the *discord* of Phase 11), but this situation compels the *Will*, if it pursue the False *Mask*, to the persecution of others if found by the True *Mask*, to suffer persecution. Phase 19, phase of the *Body of Fate*, is a phase of breaking, and when the *Will* is at Phase 25, of breaking by belief or by condition. In this it finds impulse and joy. It is called the *Conditional Man*, perhaps because all the man's thought arises out of some particular condition of actual life, or is an attempt to change that condition through social conscience. He is strong, full of initiative, full of social intellect; absorption has scarce begun; but his object is to limit and bind, to make men better, by making it impossible that they should be otherwise, to so arrange prohibitions and habits that men may be naturally good, as they are naturally black, or white, or yellow. There may be great eloquence, a mastery of all concrete imagery that is not personal expression, because though as yet there is no sinking into the world but much distinctness, clear identity, there is an overflowing social conscience. No man of any other phase can produce the same instant effect upon great crowds; for codes have passed, the universal conscience takes their place. He should not appeal to a personal interest, should make little use of argument which requires a long train of reasons, or many technical terms, for his power rests in certain simplifying convictions which have grown with his character; he needs intellect for their expression, not for proof, and taken away from these convictions is without emotion and momentum. He has but one overwhelming passion, to make all men good, and this good is something at once concrete and impersonal; and though he has hitherto given it the name of some church, or state, he is ready at any moment to give it a new name, for, unlike Phase 24, he has no pride to nourish upon the past. Moved by all that is impersonal, he becomes powerful as, in a community tired of elaborate meals, that man might become powerful who had the strongest appetite for bread and water.

When out of phase he may, because Phase 11 is a phase of diffused personality and pantheistic dreaming, grow sentimental and vague, drift into some emotional abstract, his head full of images long separated from life, and ideas long separated from experience, turn tactless and tasteless, affirm his position with the greatest arrogance possible to man. Even when nearly wholly good he can scarce escape from arrogance; what old friend did Cardinal Newman cut because of some shade of theological difference?

Living in the False *Creative Mind* produces, in all *primary* phases, insensitiveness, as living in the False *Mask* produces emotional conventionality and banality, because that False *Creative Mind*, having received no influence from the *Body of Fate*, no mould from individuals and interests, is as it were self-suspended. At

Phase 25 this insensitiveness may be that of a judge who orders a man to the torture, that of a statesman who accepts massacre as an historical necessity. One thinks of Luther's apparent indifference to atrocities committed, now by the peasants, now against them, according to the way his incitements veered.

The genius of Synge and Rembrandt has been described as typical of Phase 23. The first phase of a triad is an expression of unrelated power. They surprised the multitude, they did not seek to master it; while those chosen for examples of Phase 24 turn the multitude into a moral norm. At Phase 25 men seek to master the multitude, not through expressing it, nor through surprising it, but by imposing upon it a spiritual norm. Synge, reborn at Phase 25, might interest himself, not in the *primary* vigour and tragedy of his Aran Island countrymen, but in their conditions, their beliefs, and through some eccentricity (not of phase but horoscope), not in those shared with fellow Catholics, as Newman would, but in those shared with Japanese peasants, or in their belief as a part of all folk belief considered as religion and philosophy He would use this religion and philosophy to kill within himself the last trace of individual abstract speculation, yet this religion and this philosophy, as present before his mind, would be artificial and selected, though always concrete. Subsidence upon, or absorption in, the spiritual *primary* is not yet possible or even conceivable.

Poets of this phase are always stirred to an imaginative intensity by some form of propaganda. George Herbert was doubtless of this phase; and George Russell (A. E.), though the signs are obscured by the influence upon his early years of poets and painters of middle *anti-*

thetical phases. Neither Russell's visionary painting nor his visions of "nature spirits" are, upon this supposition, true to phase. Every poem, where he is moved to write by some form of philosophical propaganda, is precise, delicate and original, while in his visionary painting one discovers the influence of other men, Gustave Moreau, for instance. This painting is like many of his "visions", an attempt to live in the *Mask*, caused by critical ideas founded upon *antithetical* art. What dialect was to Synge, his practical work as a co-operative organiser was to him, and he found precise ideas and sincere emotion in the expression of conviction. He learned practically, but not theoretically, that he must fly the *Mask*. His work should neither be consciously aesthetic nor consciously speculative but imitative of a central Being—the *Mask* as his pursuer—consciously apprehended as something distinct, as something never imminent though eternally united to the soul.

His False *Mask* showed him what purport to be "nature spirits" because all phases before Phase 15 are in nature, as distinguished from God, and at Phase 11 that nature becomes intellectually conscious of its relations to all created things. When he desires the *Mask*, instead of flying that it may follow, it gives, instead of the intuition of God, a simulated intuition of nature. That simulated intuition is arrayed in ideal conventional images of sense, instead of in some form of abstract opinion, because of the character of his horoscope.

PHASE TWENTY-SIX

Will—The Multiple Man, also called "The Hunchback".

Mask (from Phase 12). *True*—Self-realisation. *False*—Self-abandonment.

Creative Mind (from Phase 4). *True*—Beginning of abstract supersensual thought. *False*—Fascination of sin.

Body of Fate (from Phase 18)—The Hunchback is his own *Body of Fate*.

The most difficult of the phases, and the first of those phases for which one can find few or no examples from personal experience. I think that in Asia it might not be difficult to discover examples at least of Phases 26, 27 and 28, final phases of a cycle. If such embodiments occur in our present European civilisation they remain obscure, through lacking the instruments for self-expression. One must create the type from its symbols without the help of experience.

All the old abstraction, whether of morality or of belief, has now been exhausted; but in the seemingly natural man, in Phase 26 out of phase, there is an attempt to substitute a new abstraction, a simulacrum of self-expression. Desiring emotion the man becomes the most completely solitary of all possible men, for all normal communion with his kind, that of a common study, that of an interest in work done, that of a condition of life, a code, a belief shared, has passed; and without personality he is forced to create its artificial semblance. It is perhaps a slander of history that makes us see Nero so, for he lacked the physical deformity which is, we are told, first among this phase's inhibitions of personality. The deformity may be of any kind, great or little, for it is but symbolised in the hump that thwarts what seems the ambition of a Caesar or of an Achilles. He commits crimes, not because he

wants to, or like Phase 23 out of phase because he can,
but because he wants to feel certain that he can; and he
is full of malice because, finding no impulse but in his
own ambition, he is made jealous by the impulse of
others. He is all emphasis, and the greater that emphasis the more does he show himself incapable of
emotion, the more does he display his sterility. If he
live amid a theologically minded people, his greatest
temptation may be to defy God, to become a Judas,
who betrays, not for thirty pieces of silver, but that he
may call himself creator.

In examining how he becomes true to phase, one is
perplexed by the obscure description of the *Body of Fate*,
"The Hunchback is his own *Body of Fate*". This *Body of
Fate* is derived from Phase 18, and (being reflected in
the physical being of Phase 26) can only be such a
separation of function—deformity—as breaks the self-
regarding False *Mask* (Phase 18 being the breaking of
Phase 12). All phases from Phase 26 to Phase 11 inclusive
should be gregarious; and from Phase 26 to Phase 28
there is, when the phase is truly lived, contact with
supersensual life, or a sinking-in of the body upon its
supersensual source, or desire for that contact and sinking. At Phase 26 has come a subconscious exhaustion
of the moral life, whether in belief or in conduct, and
of the life of imitation, the life of judgment and ap-
proval. The *Will* must find a substitute, and as always
in the first phase of a triad energy is violent and fragmentary. The moral abstract being no longer possible,
the *Will* may seek this substitute through the knowledge of the lives of men and beasts, plucked up, as it
were, by the roots, lacking in all mutual relations; there
may be hatred of solitude, perpetual forced bonhomie; yet

that which it seeks is without social morality, something radical and incredible. When Ezekiel lay upon his "right and left side" and ate dung, to raise "other men to a perception of the infinite", he may so have sought, and so did perhaps the Indian sage or saint who coupled with the roe.

If the man of this phase seeks, not life, but knowledge of each separated life in relation to supersensual unity; and above all of each separated physical life, or action, —that alone is entirely concrete—he will, because he can see lives and actions in relation to their source and not in their relations to one another, see their deformities and incapacities with extraordinary acuteness. His own past actions also he must judge as isolated and each in relation to its source; and this source, experienced not as love but as knowledge, will be present in his mind as a terrible unflinching judgment. Hitherto he could say to *primary* man, "Am I as good as So-and-so?" and when still *antithetical* he could say, "After all I have not failed in my good intentions taken as a whole"; he could pardon himself; but how pardon where every action is judged alone and no good action can turn judgment from the evil action by its side? He stands in the presence of a terrible blinding light, and would, were that possible, be born as worm or mole.

From Phase 22 to Phase 25, man is in contact with what is called the physical *primary*, or physical objective; from Phase 26 and Phase 4, the *primary* is spiritual; then for three phases, the physical *primary* returns. Spiritual, in this connection, may be understood as a reality known by analogy alone. How can we know what depends only on the self? In the first and in the last crescents lunar nature is but a thin veil; the eye is fixed upon the sun and dazzles.

PHASE TWENTY-SEVEN

Will—The Saint.

Mask (from Phase 13). *True*—Renunciation. *False*—Emulation.

Creative Mind (from Phase 3). *True*—Supersensual receptivity. *False*—Pride.

Body of Fate (from Phase 17)—None except impersonal action.

Examples: Socrates, Pascal.

In his seemingly natural man, derived from *Mask*, there is an extreme desire for spiritual authority; and thought and action have for their object display of zeal or some claim of authority. Emulation is all the greater because not based on argument but on psychological or physiological difference. At Phase 27, the central phase of the soul, of a triad that is occupied with the relations of the soul, the man asserts when out of phase his claim to faculty or to supersensitive privilege beyond that of other men; he has a secret that makes him better than other men.

True to phase, he substitutes for emulation an emotion of renunciation, and for the old toil of judgment and discovery of sin, a beating upon his breast and an ecstatical crying out that he must do penance, that he is even the worst of men. He does not, like Phase 26, perceive separated lives and actions more clearly than the total life, for the total life has suddenly displayed its source. If he possess intellect he will use it but to serve perception and renunciation. His joy is to be nothing, to do nothing, to think nothing; but to permit the total life, expressed in its humanity, to flow in upon him and to express itself through his acts and thoughts. He is not identical with it, he is not absorbed in it, for if he were he would not know that he is nothing, that he no longer even possesses his own body, that he must renounce even his desire for his own salvation, and that this total life is in love with his nothingness.

Before the self passes from Phase 22 it is said to attain what is called the "Emotion of Sanctity", and this emotion is described as a contact with life beyond death. It comes at the instant when synthesis is abandoned, when fate is accepted. At Phases 23, 24 and 25 we are said to use this emotion, but not to pass from Phase 25 till we have intellectually realised the nature of sanctity itself, and sanctity is described as the renunciation of personal salvation. The "Emotion of Sanctity" is the reverse of that realisation of incipient personality at Phase 8, which the *Will* related to collective action till Phase 11 had passed. After Phase 22 the man becomes aware of something which the intellect cannot grasp, and this something is a supersensual environment of the soul. At Phases 23, 24 and 25 he subdues all attempts at its intellectual comprehension, while relating it to his bodily senses and faculties, through technical achievement, through morality, through belief. At Phases 26, 27 and 28 he permits those senses and those faculties to sink in upon their environment. He will, if it be possible, not even touch or taste or see: "Man does not perceive the truth; God perceives the truth in man".

PHASE TWENTY-EIGHT

Will—The Fool.

Mask (from Phase 14). *True*—Oblivion. *False*—Malignity.

Creative Mind (from Phase 2). *True*—Physical activity.
False—Cunning.

Body of Fate (from Phase 16)—The Fool is his own
Body of Fate.

The natural man, the Fool desiring his *Mask*, grows
malignant, not as the Hunchback, who is jealous of
those that can still feel, but through terror and out of
jealousy of all that can act with intelligence and effect.
It is his true business to become his own opposite, to
pass from a semblance of Phase 14 to the reality of
Phase 28, and this he does under the influence of his
own mind and body—he is his own *Body of Fate*—for
having no active intelligence he owns nothing of the
exterior world but his mind and body. He is but a
straw blown by the wind, with no mind but the wind
and no act but a nameless drifting and turning, and is
sometimes called "The Child of God". At his worst his
hands and feet and eyes, his will and his feelings, obey
obscure subconscious fantasies, while at his best he
would know all wisdom if he could know anything. The
physical world suggests to his mind pictures and events
that have no relation to his needs or even to his desires;
his thoughts are an aimless reverie; his acts are aimless
like his thoughts; and it is in this aimlessness that he
finds his joy. His importance will become clear as the
system elaborates itself, yet for the moment no more
need be said but that one finds his many shapes on
passing from the village fool to the Fool of Shakespeare.

> Out of the pool,
> Where love the slain with love the slayer lies,
> Bubbles the wan mirth of the mirthless fool.

PHASE ONE

Will.

Mask (from Phase 15).
Creative Mind (from Phase 1). } No description except complete plasticity.
Body of Fate (from Phase 15).

This is a supernatural incarnation, like Phase 15, because there is complete objectivity, and human life cannot be completely objective. At Phase 15 mind was completely absorbed by being, but now body is completely absorbed in its supernatural environment. The images of mind are no longer irrelevant even, for there is no longer anything to which they can be relevant, and acts can no longer be immoral or stupid, for there is no one there that can be judged. Thought and inclination, fact and object of desire, are indistinguishable (*Mask* is submerged in *Body of Fate*, *Will* in *Creative Mind*), that is to say, there is complete passivity, complete plasticity. Mind has become indifferent to good and evil, to truth and falsehood; body has become undifferentiated, dough-like; the more perfect be the soul, the more indifferent the mind, the more dough-like the body; and mind and body take whatever shape, accept whatever image is imprinted upon them, transact whatever purpose is imposed upon them, are indeed the instruments of supernatural manifestation, the final link between the living and more powerful beings. There may be great joy; but it is the joy of a conscious plasticity; and it is this plasticity, this liquefaction, or pounding up, whereby all that has been knowledge becomes instinct and faculty. All plasticities do not obey all masters, and when we have considered cycle and horoscope it will be seen how those that are the instruments of subtle supernatural will differ from the instruments of cruder energy; but all, highest and lowest, are alike in being automatic.

Finished at Thoor Ballylee, 1922,

in a time of Civil War.

THE COMPLETED SYMBOL

BOOK II: THE COMPLETED SYMBOL

I

I KNEW nothing of the *Four Principles* when I wrote the last Book: a script had been lost through frustration, or through my own carelessness. The *Faculties* are man's voluntary and acquired powers and their objects; the *Principles* are the innate ground of the *Faculties*, and must act upon one another in the same way, though my instructors, to avoid confusion, have given them a different geometry. The whole system is founded upon the belief that the ultimate reality, symbolised as the Sphere, falls in human consciousness, as Nicholas of Cusa was the first to demonstrate, into a series of antinomies. The *Principles* are the *Faculties* transferred, as it were, from a concave to a convex mirror, or vice versa. They are *Husk, Passionate Body, Spirit* and *Celestial Body. Spirit* and *Celestial Body* are mind and its object (the Divine Ideas in their unity),[1] while *Husk* and *Passionate*

[1] In the following passage from *The Friend* Coleridge writes "reason" where I write "mind". "I shall have no objection to define reason with Jacobi, with my friend Helvetius, as an organ bearing the same relation to its spiritual object, the universal, the eternal, the necessary, as the eye bears to material and contingent phenomena. But then it must be added that it is an organ identical with its appropriate objects. Thus God, the soul, eternal truth etc. are the objects of reason; but they are themselves reason . . . whatever is conscious self-knowledge is reason." Later on he distinguishes between "the outward sense and the mind's eye which is reason"; on the next page between mind and its object, or as we put it *Spirit* and *Celestial Body*, "reasoning (or reason in this its secondary sense) does not consist in the ideas or in their clearness but simply, when they are in the mind, in seeing whether they coincide with each other or no".

Body, which correspond to *Will* and *Mask*, are sense[1] (impulse, images; hearing, seeing, etc., images that we associate with ourselves—the ear, the eye, etc.) and the objects of sense. *Husk* is symbolically the human body. The *Principles* through their conflict reveal reality but create nothing. They find their unity in the *Celestial Body*. The *Faculties* find theirs in the *Mask*.

The wheel or cone of the *Faculties* may be considered to complete its movement between birth and death, that of the *Principles* to include the period between lives as well. In the period between lives, the *Spirit* and the *Celestial Body* prevail, whereas *Husk* and *Passionate Body* prevail during life. Once again, solar day, lunar night. If, however, we were to consider both wheels or cones as moving at the same speed and to place, for purposes of comparison, the *Principles* in a double cone, drawn and numbered like that of the *Faculties*, and superimpose it upon that of the *Faculties*, a line drawn between Phase 1 and Phase 15 on the first would be at right angles to a line drawn between the same phases upon the other. Phase 22 in the cone of the *Principles* would coincide with Phase 1 in the cone of the *Faculties*. "Lunar South in Solar East." In practice, however, we do not divide the wheel of the *Principles* into the days of the month, but into the months of the year.

At death consciousness passes from *Husk* to *Spirit*; *Husk* and *Passionate Body* are said to *disappear*, which corresponds to the *enforcing* of *Will* and *Mask* after Phase 22, and *Spirit* turns from *Passionate Body* and clings to *Celestial Body* until they are one and there is only

[1] Indian Philosophy has active and passive senses. Seeing is passive, walking active.

Spirit; pure mind, containing within itself pure truth, that which depends only upon itself: as in the *Primary* phases, *Creative Mind* clings to *Body of Fate* until mind deprived of its obstacle can create no more and nothing is left but "the spirits at one", unrelated facts and aimless mind, the burning out that awaits all voluntary effort.

Behind the *Husk* (or sense) is the *Daimon's* hunger to make apparent to itself certain *Daimons*, and the organs of sense are that hunger made visible. The *Passionate Body* is the sum of those *Daimons*. The *Spirit*, upon the other hand, is the *Daimon's* knowledge, for in the *Spirit* it knows all other *Daimons* as the Divine Ideas in their unity. They are one in the *Celestial Body*. The *Celestial Body* is identified with necessity; when we perceive the *Daimons* as *Passionate Body*, they are subject to time and space, cause and effect; when they are known to the *Spirit*, they are known as intellectual necessity, because what the *Spirit* knows becomes a part of itself. The *Spirit* cannot know the *Daimons* in their unity until it has first perceived them as the objects of sense, the *Passionate Body* exists that it may "save the *Celestial Body* from solitude". In the symbolism the *Celestial Body* is said to age as the *Passionate Body* grows young, sometimes the *Celestial Body* is a prisoner in a tower rescued by the *Spirit*. Sometimes, grown old, it becomes the personification of evil. It pursues, persecutes and imprisons the *Daimons*.[1]

---

[1] See Blake's *Mental Traveller*. Neither Edwin Ellis nor I, nor any commentator has explained the poem, though one or another has explained certain passages. The student of *A Vision* will understand it at once. Did Blake and my instructors draw upon some unknown historical source, some explanation perhaps of the lunar circuit?

II

And because the *Daimon* seeks through the *Husk* that in *Passionate Body* which it needs, when *Passionate Body* predominates all is *Destiny*; the man dominated by his *Daimon* acts in spite of reason; whereas the man finds through reason or through the direct vision of the *Spirit* Fate or Necessity, which lies outside himself in *Body of Fate* or *Celestial Body*.[1]

The *Passionate Body* is in another of its aspects identical with physical light; not the series of separated images we call by that name, but physical light, as it was understood by mediaeval philosophers, by Berkeley in *Siris*, by Balzac in *Louis Lambert*, the creator of all that is sensible.

It is because of the identification of light with nature that my instructors make the *antithetical* or lunar cone of the *Faculties* light and leave the solar dark. In the cone of the *Principles*, the solar cone is light and the other dark, but their light is thought not nature.[2]

[1] The Hermetic Fragments draw somewhat the same distinction. Necessity comes, they say, upon us through the events of life and must be obeyed. Destiny sows the seeds of those events and impels evil men. One fragment adds "Order" connecting "Necessity" and "Destiny" and identifies it with the Cosmos. The three seem to constitute a Hegelian triad. I am summarising from Scott's *Hermetics* Exc. vii. Exc. viii. and Aeslepius iii. Section 39. The difference between their point of view and mine is that I cannot consider that Destiny inspires only evil men. The Hermetic Fragments are full of Platonic Intellectualism. Destiny becomes evil when the *Passionate Body* is subject to Necessity.

[2] Collyns Simon in his index to *The Principles of Human Knowledge* calls Light a "Sensation, not the condition or cause of one, as some physicists endeavour to teach". Berkeley, according to Hone and Rossi, meant by Light not "Sensation" but that which "brings

III

Spirit is the future, *Passionate Body* the present, *Husk* the past, deriving its name from the husk that is abandoned by the sprouting seed. The *Passionate Body* is the present, creation, light, the objects of sense. *Husk* is the past not merely because the objects are passed before we can know their images, but because those images fall in patterns and recurrences shaped by a past life or lives. At moments it is identified with race or instinct. It is the involuntary self as *Will* the voluntary. I am not, however, certain that I understand the statement that *Spirit* is the future. I would have understood had my instructors said that *Celestial Body* was the future, for the ideal forms are only apparent through hope; perhaps they mean that we do not in reality seek these forms, that while separate from us they are illusionary, but that we do seek *Spirit* as complete self-realisation, and do not

out Sensation . . . a semi-material agent" discoverable by mind alone; but Simon is right, for Berkeley speaks of Light as discoverable by animals, where all to us seems dark, and uses this argument to prove that Light is all-pervading. In the *Commonplace Book* he warned himself to avoid the theologically dangerous theme of personality. Did he in his private thoughts come to regard Light as the creative act of a universal self dwelling in all selves? Grosseteste, Bishop of Lincoln, described Light as corporeality itself, and thought that in conjunction with the first matter, it engendered all bodies. Pierre Duhem analyses his philosophy in *Le Système du Monde*, vol. v, pp. 356, 357, 358. Plotinus describes the Light seen with our eyes open and that seen when we rub our closed eyes, as a light coming from the soul itself. The modern term "Astral Light" implies this source and is probably derived from some seventeenth-century Platonist, who symbolised the soul as a star, but the popular writers who employ it seem to think that the Light seen in Spiritual Vision alone is from that star.

spirits sometimes say, "We have no present,[1] we are the future", meaning that they are reality as we perceive it under the category of the future? From another point of view, the spirits can have neither past nor present, because *Husk* and *Passionate Body* have *disappeared*. My teachers do not characterise the *Celestial Body*, but it is doubtless the timeless. There seems to be a reversed attribution in the *Faculties*. In the *Faculties' Mask* (the forms "created by passion to unite us to ourselves", in the *antithetical* phases beauty) is apparently the timeless, *Will* the future, *Body of Fate*, or Fact, the present, *Creative Mind* the past. The past of the *Faculties* is abstract, a series of judgments. "When did Julius Caesar die?" "What are the chemical constituents of water?" Memory is a series of judgments and such judgments imply a reference to something that is not memory, that something is the *Daimon*, which contains within it, co-existing in its eternal moment, all the events of our life, all that we have known of other lives, or that it can discover within itself of other *Daimons*. Seeing that object and judgment imply space, we may call *Husk* and *Creative Mind* by that name, for in both Time spatialises.

In the wheel of the *Faculties, Will* predominates during the first quarter, *Mask* during the second, *Creative Mind* during the third, *Body of Fate* during the fourth. In the wheel of the *Principles, Husk* (the new still unopened *Husk*) predominates during the first quarter, *Passionate Body* during the second, *Spirit* during the third, and *Celestial Body* during the fourth. If we put future,

---

[1] Dante describes the spirits in *The Inferno* as having no present, as they approach the present all grows dim. Their future is not, however, the future of spiritual freedom.

present, past and the timeless in the four quarters of each wheel according to their attribution to *Faculty* or *Principle*, we find that the present and the timeless, past and future, are opposite.

IV

The ultimate reality because neither one nor many, concord nor discord, is symbolised as a phaseless sphere, but as all things fall into a series of antinomies in human experience it becomes, the moment it is thought of, what I shall presently describe as the thirteenth cone. All things are present as an eternal instant to our *Daimon* (or *Ghostly Self* as it is called, when it inhabits the sphere), but that instant is of necessity unintelligible to all bound to the antinomies. My instructors have therefore followed tradition by substituting for it a *Record* where the images of all past events remain for ever "thinking the thought and doing the deed". They are in popular mysticism called "the pictures in the astral light", a term that became current in the middle of the nineteenth century, and what Blake called "the bright sculptures of Los's Hall". We may describe them as the *Passionate Body* lifted out of time.

V

My instructors, keeping as far as possible to the phenomenal world, have spent little time upon the sphere, which can be symbolised but cannot be known, though certain chance phrases show that they have all the necessary symbols. When I try to imagine the *Four Principles* in the sphere, with some hesitation I identify the *Celestial Body* with the First Authentic Existant of Plotinus, *Spirit* with his Second Authentic Existant, which holds the First in its moveless circle; the discarnate *Daimons*, or *Ghostly Selves*, with his Third Authentic Existant or soul of the world (the Holy Ghost of Christianity), which holds the Second in its moving circle. Plotinus has a fourth condition which is the Third Authentic Existant reflected first as sensation and its object (our *Husk* and *Passionate Body*), then as discursive reason (almost our *Faculties*). The *Husk* as part of the sphere merges in *The Ghostly Self*.

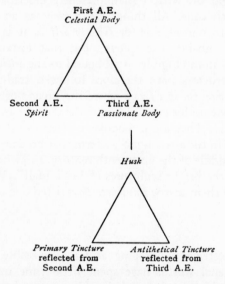

First A.E.
Celestial Body

Second A.E.   Third A.E.
Spirit   *Passionate Body*

Husk

Primary Tincture   Antithetical Tincture
reflected from   reflected from
Second A.E.   Third A.E.

But this diagram implies a descent from *Principle* to *Principle*, a fall of water from ledge to ledge, whereas a system symbolising the phenomenal world as irrational because a series of unresolved antinomies, must find its representation in a perpetual return to the starting-point. The resolved antinomy appears not in a lofty source but in the whirlpool's motionless centre, or beyond its edge.[1]

I must now enumerate certain interactions of *Faculties* and *Principles* which are not defined by diagrams.

The emotions are formed by *Will*, acted upon by *Mask* and *Celestial Body*, or by *Mask* and *Passionate Body*. When *Will*, *Passionate Body* and *Mask* act together there is pleasure and pain in the act itself, but when *Will* acts alone all is abstract utility, economics, a mechanism to prolong existence. When *Passionate Body* and *Celestial Body* give way to *Mask* we dwell in aesthetic process, so much skill in bronze or paint, or on some symbol that rouses emotion for emotion's sake. When *Mask* and *Passionate Body* are in unison we desire emotion that excites the senses. When *Mask* and *Celestial Body* are in unison we are possessed by love *antithetical* to our normal self. When *Creative Mind* is added to either combination love or desire is unified or objectified whether in action or in a work of art. When *Creative Mind* is separated from *Spirit* there is abstract thought, classification, syllogism, number, everything whereby the fact is established, and the sum of such facts is the world of science and common sense. *Creative Mind* united to *Spirit* brings not fact but truth, not science but philosophy. The *Principles* alone cannot distinguish between fact and hallucination. Ruskin, according to Frank Harris, saw a phantom cat at the end of the room and stooped to fling it out of the window. That cat may have had more significant form than the house cat; displayed all cat nature as if it were the work of some

[1] The whirlpool is an *antithetical* symbol, the descending water a *primary*.

great artist; symbolised with every movement *Spirit* and *Celestial Body*; been visible to others—there are houses haunted by animals—but it was never littered, could not overset the jug, had no settled place in that continuity of images, that sum of facts that has yet no value in itself. Spurious art is the conquest of *Mask* by *Husk* and *Passionate Body*, and commercial art its conquest by *Will*. Common realism is conquest by *Body of Fate*, and so on.

VI

I am told to give Phases 1, 8, 15, 22 a month apiece, the other phases the third of a month, and begin the year like the early Roman year in the lunar month corresponding to March, when days begin to grow longer than nights:

March	.	.	Phase 15
April	.	.	Phases 16, 17, 18
May	.	.	Phases 19, 20, 21
June	.	.	Phase 22

and so on. There is no reason why March, June, etc., should have one Phase, all others three; it is classification not symbolism. The relation between the wheel of twenty-eight Phases and that of twelve months has turned out as insoluble to the symbolist as was that between the solar and lunar year to the ancient astronomers. I must keep myself at liberty to consider any period, whether between signs or enclosed in a lunar Phase, as a simple microcosm containing days, months, years. At the Ides of March, at the full moon in March, is the Vernal Equinox, symbolical of the first degree of Aries, the first day of our symbolical or ideal year, and at the middle of each month the sign changes. Aries changes to Taurus at the middle of the second month, the middle of Phase 17, and so on. The *Will* marks its course by the lunar months, the *Creative Mind* by the signs. When the Great Wheel is a month the symbolism seems simpler, for the lunar periods are the natural phases of such a month, each solar period beginning and ending in the middle of a phase.

A solar period is a day from sunrise to sunrise, or a year from March to March, a month from full moon to full moon. On the other hand a lunar period is a day from sunset to sunset, a year from September to September, a month from moonless night to moonless night. In other words every month or phase when we take it as a whole is a double vortex moving from Phase 1 to Phase 28, or two periods, one solar and one lunar, which in the words of Heraclitus "live each other's death, die each other's life".

If we consider East as symbolical of the head, as in Astrology, a diagonal line drawn from East in a solar wheel will cross at right angles a similar line drawn from East in a lunar. My instructors fixed this upon my mind by saying that the man of a solar wheel stood upright whereas the man of a lunar lay horizontal like a sleeping man. That the small wheels and vortexes that run from birth to birth may be part of the symbolism of the wheel of the twenty-eight incarnations without confusing it in the mind's eye, my instructors have preferred to give to the *Principles* of these small wheels cones that cannot be confused with that of the *Faculties*. The dominant thought is to show *Husk* starting on its journey from the centre of the wheel, the incarnate *Daimon*, and *Spirit* from the circumference as though it received its impulse from beyond the *Daimon*. These cones are drawn across the centre of the wheel from *Faculty* to *Faculty*, two with bases joined between *Creative Mind* and *Body of Fate*, and two with apexes joined between *Will* and *Mask*.

Within these figures move the *Principles*; *Spirit* and *Celestial Body* in the figure shaped like an ace of diamonds, *Husk* and *Passionate Body* in that shaped like an hour-glass. The first figure is divided according to the signs of the Zodiac, though it can be divided as readily according to the points of the compass, the East or sunrise taking the place of the Vernal Equinox, the second divided into the twenty-eight lunar phases. In the cones of the *Spirit* and the *Celestial Body* there is only one gyre, that of *Spirit*, *Celestial Body* being represented by the whole diamond. The union of *Spirit* and *Celestial Body* has a long approach and is complete when the gyre reaches its widest expansion. There is only one gyre because, whereas *Husk* faces an object alien to itself, *Spirit's* object is of like nature to itself. The gyre of the *Husk* starts at the centre (its Phase 1), reaches its Phase 8, where the circumference can be marked *Mask*, and returns to its centre for Phase 15, passes from its centre to its Phase 22, where the circumference can be marked *Will*, and finishes at the centre. One records these movements upon the edges of the figures, phases for *Husk*, Zodiacal signs for *Spirit*,[1] *Husk*

---

[1] My instructors sometimes give *Husk* and *Will* Zodiacs of their own; these lunar Zodiacs are counted from right to left, a line joining Cancer and Capricorn in a lunar Zodiac cuts a line joining Cancer and Capricorn in a solar Zodiac at right angles. "Lunar South is Solar East." I have left them out for the sake of simplicity, but will return to them later.

and *Passionate Body* moving from right to left and the single gyre of *Spirit* from left to right. *Husk* and *Passionate Body* remain always opposite, *Passionate Body* at Phase 15 when *Husk* is at Phase 1 and so on. When *Husk* is at Phase 15, *Spirit* sets out from Aries. It reaches Cancer when *Husk* is at Phase 22 and Libra when *Husk* is at Phase 1. When *Spirit* is at edge of Wheel *Husk* is at centre.

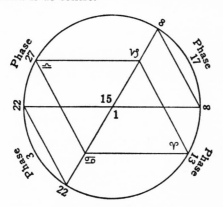

When cone and diamond are superimposed (see p. 200) we get a simple figure corresponding to the double cone (p. 79 and elsewhere). Diamond and hour-glass revolve on one another like the sails of a windmill. As the diamond represents a sphere, at its gyre's greatest expansion *Spirit* contains the whole Wheel. Though for convenience we make the diamond narrow, like the diamond of a playing-card, its widest expansion must be considered to touch the circumference of the wheel where the wheel meets the gyre of the *Thirteenth Cone*. Indeed, its gyre touches that circumference throughout. The diamond is a convenient substitute for a sphere, the hour-glass for two meeting spheres. Taken in relation to the wheel, the diamond and the hour-glass are two pulsations, one expanding, one contracting. I can see them like jelly fish in clear water.

The foregoing figure shows the position of diamond and hour-glass when *Will* on the wheel is passing Phase 17. The following diagram shows such cones when *Will* on the wheel of the twenty-eight phases is at Phase 15.

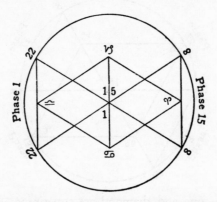

At Phases 15, 22, 1 and 8 of the wheel of the incarnations the cones are superimposed. These gyres complete their movement, whether of twelve months or twenty-eight days, while *Will* as marked upon the circumference completes its phase, their *Husk* starting at the centre when the phase begins and returning there at its end. Sometimes the automatic script substitutes this figure for the wheel itself, the revolving cones drawn without any containing circle, roughly indicating the phase by their position in relation to one another. The Communicators often scribbled it on margins, or on scraps of paper, without relation to the text as if to remind themselves of some Phase they would speak of later.

VII

The *Four Faculties* have a movement also within the cones of the *Principles*. Their double vortex is super-imposed upon the half of the cone of *Husk* and *Passionate Body* which lies between *Will* (the *Will* on the circumference of the wheel) and the centre of the wheel.

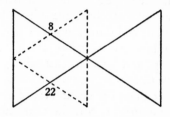

When *Husk* has reached Phase 8 they are at Phase 15; when *Husk* has reached its Phase 15 they are at Phase 1. While *Will* (*Will* on circumference) is passing through half a phase, *Husk* passing from Phase 1 to Phase 15, the *Faculties* complete their full movement, Phase 1 to Phase 28, and when their movement represents an in-carnation disappear at its completion. The *Principles* thereupon take their place defining the state between death and birth. Death which comes when the *Spirit* gyre is at Aries is symbolised as spring or dawn; and birth which comes when the *Spirit* gyre is at Libra, as autumn or sunset. Incarnate life is night or winter, discarnate life is day or summer.

VIII

A Great Wheel of twenty-eight incarnations is considered to take, if no failure compels repetition of a phase, some two thousand odd years, and twelve such wheels or gyres constitute a single great cone or year of some twenty-six thousand years. But these twenty-six thousand years [1] are but a norm, a convenient measure, much may shorten or lengthen the whole or some part of the whole. All men, it is assumed, once passed through their year at the same pace; all were at the same moment, at the same phase, but gradually some fell behind, and some ran ahead, and now there is a year that ends when the life-period of the individual winds itself up, and a Great Year which is a norm or average struck among the individual years. I shall, when I come to write upon the Great Year of antiquity, refer to the fact that Proclus had the same conception and gave to the smallest living creature its individual year.

IX

Hegel identifies Asia with Nature; he sees the whole process of civilisation as an escape from Nature; partly achieved by Greece, fully achieved by Christianity. Oedipus—Greece—solved the riddle of the Sphinx—

[1] My instructors are playing with the period necessary to complete the precession of the Equinox from Aries to Aries. It has been a part of literary tradition since Edmund Spenser described it in *The Faerie Queene*, Book V, Introd. stanzas I-II. They have, however, adopted the twenty-six thousand years of modern astronomy instead of the thirty-six thousand years Spenser took from the Platonic Year.

Nature—compelled her to plunge from the precipice, though man himself remained ignorant and blundering. I accept his definition. When my great diagram of the wheel was first drawn for me, all from Phase 1 to Phase 15 had the word Nature written beside it; all from Phase 15 to Phase 1 the word God. I reject, however, his description of Nature in the *Philosophy of History*, a description that seems applicable to the first eight phases alone. Nor do I see Asia as he sees it. Asia is *primary, solar*, and only becomes Nature at Phase 1. A wheel of the Great Year must be thought of as the marriage of symbolic Europe and symbolic Asia, the one begetting upon the other.[1] When it commenced at its symbolic full moon in March—Christ or Christendom was begotten by the West upon the East. This begetting has been followed by a spiritual predominance of Asia. After it must come an age begotten by the East upon the West that will take after its Mother in turn. The Lunar Months of 2200 years apiece, in a year of 26,000 years, are years of civilisation, while the Solar Months of a similar symbolical length[2] correspond to periods of religion.

---

[1] Flinders Petrie in *The Revolutions of Civilisation* says that the Eastern phase is five hundred years ahead of Europe, and draws attention to the coincidence between the rise of Arabian civilisation and the fall of that of Europe. My system seems to imply that the rise of Arabian civilisation and that of Christianity are the same phenomena. European art did not cast off the influence of Eastern art, as the Japanese interpreter of Botticelli has shown, until the establishment of "tonal values" after the Renaissance as a principal vehicle of expression. They have been accompanied by the decline of Christianity. It is not, however, easy to say how far I should interpret my symbols according to the letter.

[2] We may compare these equal periods to the incarnations of equal length attributed by Plato to his man of Ur, his ideal man, whose individual year of 36,000 years or of 360 incarnations later

Each solar month may be called a revolution of *Creative Mind* and *Body of Fate* beginning and ending with *Creative Mind* in Aries, each lunar month a revolution of *Will* and *Mask* beginning and ending with *Will* at Phase 1. When, however, one wants to show, as the automatic script generally does, that each civilisation and religious dispensation is the opposite of its predecessor, a single revolution constitutes two solar or lunar months. For instance, classical civilisation—1000 B.C. to A.D. 1000 let us say—is represented by the movement of *Will* from Phase 1, the place of birth, to Phase 15, the place of death, and our own civilisation is· now almost midway in the movement of the *Will* from Phase 15 to Phase 1. The student of ancient symbolism discovers the darkening and brightening fortnights of Brahminical symbolism, the fortnight during which the moon increases in light and represents an *antithetical* civilisation, and that during which it decreases and represents a *primary* civilisation. At or near the central point of a lunar month of classical civilisation—the first degree of Aries on the Great Wheel—came the Christian *primary* dispensation, the child born in the Cavern. At or near the central point of our civilisation must come *antithetical* revelation, the turbulent child of the Altar.[1] The antithesis between lunar and solar is emphasised by the correspondence of summer to the darkening fortnight and of winter to the brightening.

generations identified with the Platonic Year. The Platonic Year is an average or norm fixed by many individual years, but the year of an ideal man would conform to it.

[1] I am thinking of the two symbols discovered by Frobenius in Africa, the Cavern, symbol of the nations moving westward, the Altar at the centre of radiating roads, symbol of the nations moving eastward.

X

When I relate this symbol to reality various fancies pass before the mind. The Great Wheel revolved innumerable times before the beast changed into man and many times before the man learned to till the ground. Perhaps the hunting age gave way to agriculture when our present revolution brought round Phase 4 or 5. At Phase 4 or 5 or perhaps a little later may have emerged the Sacred Legend of the sun's annual journey, symbol of all history and of individual life, foundation of all the earliest civilisations; and at the phases where Unity of Being became possible began perhaps those civilisations, Egypt or Sumer, which had made a progressive, conscious, intellectual life possible by the discovery of writing.

Is that marriage of Europe and Asia a geographical reality? Perhaps, yet the symbolic wheel is timeless and spaceless.

When I look in history for the conflict or union of *antithetical* and *primary* I seem to discover that conflict or union of races stated by Petrie and Schneider as universal law. A people who have lived apart and so acquired unity of custom and purity of breed unite with some other people through migration, immigration or conquest. A race (the new *antithetical*) emerges that is neither the one nor the other, after somewhere about 500 years it produces, or so it seems, its particular culture or civilisation. This culture lives only in certain victorious classes; then comes a period of revolution (Phase 22) terminated by a civilisation of policemen, schoolmasters, manufacturers, philanthropists, a second

soon exhausted blossoming of the race. Schneider [1] finds
three such race cultures, each with its double blossoming, in China and India, four in Egypt, though doubt-
ful whether the final imitative period can be called a
distinct culture, two among the Greeks, one and part
of another among the Romans, and I forget how many
in Persia, Babylon, Judea. All these cultures, as I am
directed to see them, having attained some Achilles in
the first blossoming, find pious Aeneas in their second,
and that second is preceded by Utopian dreams that
come to little because no civilisation can spend what it
has not earned. The Saint suffers a like impediment;
the love he brings to God at his twenty-seventh phase
was found in some past life upon a woman's breast, his
loyalty and wisdom were prepared perhaps a thousand
years before in serving a bad master, and that is why
the Indian minstrel sings God as woman, husband,
lover and child.

The historian thinks of Greece as an advance on
Persia, of Rome as in something or other an advance
of Greece, and thinks it impossible that any man could
prefer the hunter's age to the agricultural. I, upon the
other hand, must think all civilisations equal at their
best; every phase returns, therefore in some sense every
civilisation. I think of the hunter's age and that which
followed immediately as a time when man's waking
consciousness had not reached its present complexity
and stability. There was little fear of death, sometimes
men lay down and died at will, the world of the gods
could be explored easily whether through some orgiastic
ceremony or in the trance of the ascetic. Apparitions

---

[1] *The History of World Civilisation*, by Hermann Schneider, translated by Margaret M. Green.

came and went, bringing comfort in the midst of
tragedy.

XI

I shall write little of the *Principles* except when
writing of the life after death. They inform the *Faculties* and it is the *Faculties* alone that are apparent and
conscious in human history. Vico said that we know
history because we create it, but as nature was created
by God only God can know it.

I must now explain a detail of the symbolism which
has come into my poetry and, in ways I am not yet ready
to discuss, into my life. When *Will* is passing through
Phases 16, 17 and 18 the *Creative Mind* is passing through
the Phases 14, 13 and 12, or from the sign Aries to the
sign Taurus, that is to say, it is under the conjunction of
Mars and Venus.[1] When *Will* upon the other hand is
passing through Phases 12, 13 and 14 the *Creative Mind*
is passing through the Phases 18, 17 and 16, or from
the sign Pisces to the sign Aquarius, it is, as it were,
under the conjunction of Jupiter and Saturn. These two
conjunctions which express so many things are certainly, upon occasion, the outward-looking mind, love
and its lure, contrasted with introspective knowledge of
the mind's self-begotten unity, an intellectual excitement. They stand, so to speak, like heraldic supporters
guarding the mystery of the fifteenth phase. In certain
lines written years ago in the first excitement of discovery I compared one to the Sphinx and one to

---

[1] I set down what follows less for present use than because at
some later date I may return to the theme and wake these dry
astrological bones into breathing life.

Buddha. I should have put Christ instead of Buddha,
for according to my instructors Buddha was a Jupiter-
Saturn influence.

> Although I saw it all in the mind's eye
> There can be nothing solider till I die;
> I saw by the moon's light
> Now at its fifteenth night.

> One lashed her tail; her eyes lit by the moon
> Gazed upon all things known, all things unknown,
> In triumph of intellect
> With motionless head erect.

> The other's moonlit eyeballs never moved,
> Being fixed on all things loved, all things unloved,
> Yet little peace he had,
> For those that love are sad.

XII

As a religious dispensation begins and ends at Phase
15, a Mars-Venus conjunction presides over its beginning and a Saturn-Jupiter over its close. The group of
phases so dominated are those where Unity of Being is
possible. The influx that dominates a *primary* dispensation comes a little after the start of the dispensation
itself, at its Phase 16 perhaps, and that which dominates an *antithetical* dispensation a considerable time
before the close of the preceding *primary* dispensation,
its Phase 26 let us say; it is, as it were, not so much a
breaking out of new life as the vivification of old
intellect. A *primary* revelation begins therefore under
Mars-Venus, an *antithetical* under Saturn-Jupiter.

XIII

Nations, cultures, schools of thought may have their
Daimons. These *Daimons* may move through the Great
Year like individual men and women and are said to
use men and women as their bodies, to gather and disperse those bodies at will. Leibnitz, whose logical
monads resemble somewhat my perceptive *Daimons,*
thought there must be many monads much greater than
those of individual men and women. Lionel Johnson
was fond of quoting from Dionysius the Areopagite,
"He has set the borders of his nations according to his
angels", but Swedenborg thought that all angels had
once been men.

XIV

The twelve months or twelve cycles can be considered
not as a wheel but as an expanding cone, and to this is
opposed another cone which may also be considered as
divided into twelve cycles or months. As the base of
each cone has at its centre the apex of the other cone
the double vortex is once more established. The twelve
cycles or months of the second cone are so numbered
that its first month is the last of the first cone, the
summer of the one the winter of the other. It resembles
exactly every other double cone in the system. The
passage from Phase 1 to Phase 15 is always, whether
we call it a month or six months or twelve months, or
an individual life, set over against a passage from Phase
15 to Phase 1; and whether we consider the cone that
of incarnate or that of discarnate life, the gyre of *Husk*
or *Will* cuts the gyre of *Spirit* or *Creative Mind* with the

same conflict of seasons,[1] a being racing into the future
passes a being racing into the past, two footprints perpetually obliterating one another, toe to heel, heel to
toe.

I shall consider the gyre in the present expanding
cone for the sake of simplicity as the whole of human
life, without waiting to portion out the *Faculties* and
Principles, and the contrasting cone as the other half of
the antinomy, the "spiritual objective". Although when
we are in the first month of this expanding cone we are
in the twelfth of the other, when we are in the second
in the eleventh of the other, and so on, that month of
the other cone which corresponds to ours is always called
by my instructors the Thirteenth Cycle or *Thirteenth
Cone*, for every month is a cone. It is that cycle which
may deliver us from the twelve cycles of time and space.
The cone which intersects ours is a cone in so far as we
think of it as the antithesis to our thesis, but if the time
has come for our deliverance it is the phaseless sphere,
sometimes called the Thirteenth Sphere, for every lesser
cycle contains within itself a sphere that is, as it were,
the reflection or messenger of the final deliverance.
Within it live all souls that have been set free and

---

[1] I thought I discovered this antithesis of the seasons when some
countryman told me that he heard the lambs of Faery bleating in
November, and, read in some heroic tale of supernatural flowers
in midwinter. I may have deceived myself, but if I did I got out
of the deception the opening passage in my play *The Hour-Glass*:
"Where is the passage I am to explain to my pupils to-day? Here it
is, and the book says that it was written by a beggar on the walls
of Babylon: 'There are two living countries, the one visible and
the other invisible; and when it is winter with us it is summer
in that country, and when the November winds are up among us
it is lambing-time there'."

every *Daimon* and *Ghostly Self*; our expanding cone seems to cut through its gyre; spiritual influx is from its circumference, animate life from its centre. "Eternity also", says Hermes in the Aeslepius dialogue, "though motionless itself, appears to be in motion." When Shelley's Demogorgon — eternity — comes from the centre of the earth it may so come because Shelley substituted the earth for such a sphere.[1]

XV

All these symbols can be thought of as the symbols of the relations of men and women and of the birth of children. We can think of the *antithetical* and *primary* cones, or wheels, as the domination, now by the man, now by the woman, and of a child born at Phase 15 or East as acquiring a *primary* character from its father who is at Phase 1, or West, and of a child born at Phase 1 or West as acquiring an *antithetical* character from its father at Phase 15, or East, and so on, man and woman being alternately Western and Eastern. Such symbolical children, sealed as it were by Saturn and Jupiter or Mars and Venus, cast off the mother and display their true characters as their cycle enters its last quarter. We may think of the wheel as an expression of alternations of passion, and think of the power of the woman beginning at symbolical East or Aries and seated in *Creative Mind*, and of the power of the man as seated in *Will* and

---

[1] Shelley, who had more philosophy than men thought when I was young, probably knew that Parmenides represented reality as a motionless sphere. Mrs. Shelley speaks of the "mystic meanings" of *Prometheus Unbound* as only intelligible to a "mind as subtle as his own".

beginning at symbolical West when *Creative Mind* is in Libra, or half-way through its course, and *Will* at Phase 1 (Blake's *Mental Traveller*), or think of the Wheel as an expression of the birth of symbolical children bound together by a single fate. When we so think of it we recreate the lives of Christ and St. John as they are symbolised in the Christian year, Christ begotten in spring and brought forth in midwinter, begotten in joy and brought forth in sorrow, and St. John begotten in autumn and brought forth in midsummer, begotten in sorrow and brought forth in joy. Coventry Patmore claimed the Church's authority for calling Christ supernatural love and St. John natural love, and took pleasure in noticing that Leonardo painted a Dionysius like a St. John, a St. John like a Dionysius. But I need not go further, for all the symbolism of this book applies to begetting and birth, for all things are a single form which has divided and multiplied in time and space.

There are certain numbers, certain obscure calculations in Plato's *Republic* meant to suggest and hide the methods adopted by the ruling philosophers to secure that the right parents shall beget the right children, and it is foretold that when these numbers and calculations are forgotten the Republic must decay. The latest authoritative work, Taylor's *Plato*, thinks it probable that the "Golden Number", on which these calculations are based, is 36,000 years or a lunar year of 360 days, each day 100 years. If I may think of those days or incarnations as periods wherein symbolic man grows old and young alternately, as he does in certain other Platonic periods, I have, but for a different length and enumeration, my Great Wheel of twelve cycles. Plato may have brought such an ideal year into the story, its periods all of exactly the same length, to remind us that he dealt in myth. My instructors, however, insist that a man of, let us say, the seventh cycle married to a woman of, let us say, the sixth cycle will have a certain type of child, that this type is further modified by the phases and by the child's position in time and place at birth, a position which is itself but an expression of the interaction of cycles and phases. Will some mathematician some day question and understand, as I cannot, and confirm all, or have I also dealt in myth?

XVI

When my instructors see woman as man's goal and limit, rather than as mother, they symbolise her as *Mask* and *Body of Fate*, object of desire and object of thought, the one a perpetual rediscovery of what the other destroys; the seventh house of the horoscope where one finds friend and enemy; and they set this double opposite in perpetual opposition to *Will* and *Creative Mind*. In Book III I shall return to this symbolism, which perhaps explains, better than any I have used, Blake's *Mental Traveller*.

XVII

I have now described many symbols which seem mechanical because united in a single structure, and of which the greater number, precisely because they tell always the same story, may seem unnecessary. Yet every symbol, except where it lies in vast periods of time and so beyond our experience, has evoked for me some form of human destiny, and that form, once evoked, has appeared everywhere, as if there were but one destiny,

as my own form might appear in a room full of mirrors.
When one discovers, as will be seen presently, at a certain moment between life and death, what ancient
legends have called the Shape-Changers, one illustrates
a moment of European history, of every mind that
passes from premise to judgment, of every love that
runs its whole course. The present Pope has said in his
last Encyclical that the natural union of man and woman
has a kind of sacredness. He thought doubtless of the
marriage of Christ and the Church, whereas I see in it
a symbol of that eternal instant where the antinomy
is resolved. It is not the resolution itself. There is a
passage in Lucretius translated by Dryden, to the great
scandal of his enemy Collier, which is quite conclusive.

XVIII

My instructors identify consciousness with conflict,
not with knowledge, substitute for subject and object
and their attendant logic a struggle towards harmony,
towards Unity of Being. Logical and emotional conflict
alike lead towards a reality which is concrete, sensuous,
bodily. My imagination was for a time haunted by
figures that, muttering "The great systems", held out
to me the sun-dried skeletons of birds, and it seemed
to me that this image was meant to turn my thoughts to
the living bird. That bird signifies truth when it eats,
evacuates, builds its nest, engenders, feeds its young;
do not all intelligible truths lie in its passage from egg
to dust? Passages written by Japanese monks on attain-
ing Nirvana, and one by an Indian, run in my head. "I
sit upon the side of the mountain and look at a little
farm. I say to the old farmer, 'How many times have

you mortgaged your farm and paid off the mortgage?'
I take pleasure in the sound of the rushes." "No more
does the young man come from behind the embroidered
curtain amid the sweet clouds of incense; he goes among
his friends, he goes among the flute-players; something
very nice has happened to the young man, but he can
only tell it to his sweetheart." "You ask me what is
my religion and I hit you upon the mouth." "Ah!
Ah! The lightning crosses the heavens, it passes from
end to end of the heavens. Ah! Ah!"[1]

[1] I have compared these memories with their source in Zazuki's
Zen Buddhism, an admirable and exciting book, and find that they
are accurate except that I have substituted here and there better-
sounding words.

THE SOUL IN JUDGMENT

BOOK III: THE SOUL IN JUDGMENT

I

PAUL VALÉRY in the *Cimetière Marin* describes a seaside cemetery, a recollection, some commentator explains, of a spot known in childhood. The midday light is the changeless absolute and its reflection in the sea "les œuvres purs d'une cause éternelle". The sea breaks into the ephemeral foam of life; the monuments of the dead take sides as it were with the light and would with their inscriptions and their sculptured angels persuade the poet that he is the light, but he is not persuaded. The worm devours not only the dead, but as self-love, self-hate, or whatever one calls it, devours the living also. Then after certain poignant stanzas and just when I am deeply moved he chills me. This metropolitan, who has met so many reformers, who has learnt as a part of good manners to deny what has no remedy, cries out "Cruel Zénon! Zénon d'Elée!", condemning that problem of a tortoise and Achilles because it suggested that all things only seemed to pass; and in a passage of great eloquence rejoices that human life must pass.[1] I was about to put his poem among my sacred books, but I cannot now, for I do not believe him. My imagination goes some

[1] Professor Bradley believed also that he could stand by the death-bed of wife or mistress and not long for an immortality of body and soul. He found it difficult to reconcile personal immortality with his form of Absolute idealism, and besides he hated the common heart; an arrogant, sapless man.

219

years backward, and I remember a beautiful young girl singing at the edge of the sea in Normandy words and music of her own composition. She thought herself alone, stood barefooted between sea and sand; sang with lifted head of the civilisations that there had come and gone, ending every verse with the cry: "O Lord, let something remain".

II

I cannot imagine an age without metropolitan poet and singing girl, though I am convinced that the Upanishads—somebody had already given her the Pyramids—were addressed to the girl.

Certain Upanishads describe three states of the soul, that of waking, that of dreaming, that of dreamless sleep, and say man passes from waking through dreaming to dreamless sleep every night and when he dies. Dreamless sleep is a state of pure light, or of utter darkness according to our liking, and in dreams "the spirit serves as light for itself". "There are no carts, horses, roads, but he makes them for himself."

III

The *Spirit* is not those changing images—sometimes in ancient thought as in the *Cimetière Marin* symbolised by the sea [1]—but the light,[2] and at last draws backward into itself, into its own changeless purity, all it has felt

---

[1] I think it was Porphyry who wrote that the generation of images in the mind is from water.

[2] In my symbolism solar light, intellectual light; not the lunar light, perception.

or known. I am convinced that this ancient generalisation, in so far as it saw analogy between a "separated spirit", or phantom and a dream of the night, once was a universal belief, for I find it, or some practice founded upon it, everywhere. Certainly I find it in old Irish literature, in modern Irish folk-lore, in Japanese plays, in Swedenborg, in the phenomena of spiritualism, accompanied as often as not by the belief that the living can assist the imaginations of the dead. A farmer near Doneraile once told me that an aunt of his own appeared stark naked after her death and complained that she could not go about with the other spirits unless somebody cut a dress to her measure and gave it to a poor woman in her name. This done she appeared wearing the dress and gave thanks for it. Once an old woman came to Coole Park, when I was there, to tell Lady Gregory that Sir William Gregory's ghost had a tattered sleeve and that a coat must be given to some beggar in his name. A man, returned after many years spent in the West Indies, once told me and others of the apparition of a woman he had known in a dress that he had not known, copied, he discovered, from her portrait made after he had left England. May I not use such tales to interpret all those model houses, boats, weapons, slaves, all those portraits and statues buried in ancient tombs?

Certain London Spiritualists for some years past have decked out a Christmas tree with presents that have each the names of some dead child upon it, and sitting in the dark on Christmas night they hear the voice of some grown-up person, who seems to take the presents from the tree, and the clamorous voices of the children as they are distributed. Yet the presents still hang there and are given next day to an hospital. Could anything be

more Egyptian, more Assyrian? It was essential that the
clothes should be given in the name of the dead, that
the portrait should be the ghost's own portrait, that the
presents for the children should be dedicated or given,
not merely hung there; in dreams we finish what we
began awake or what the waking suggest. I think of two
ghost lovers in a Japanese play asking a wandering
Buddhist priest to marry them, of two that appeared to
a Catholic priest in Aran, according to an Aran tale,
with a like object, of a young spirit medium who
promised that she would marry a certain old man after
death but was compelled by her controls to withdraw
the promise because, though she had not meant it, she
might have had to fulfil it, of an Indian who told Florence Farr that he hated acting, for if a man died playing
Hamlet he would be Hamlet after death. Upon the
other hand a spirit may meet some spirit in the séance-
room to ask forgiveness for something done in life, a
forgiveness not always granted, and once at the request
of a certain dead Sister of Mercy I discovered where the
Mother Superior she had served under in the Crimea
lived and died, and she came again to thank me. Because
I had connected their lives here she had found her there,
though not to share her state, being less holy. I had
suggested away the nightmare as though sitting by the
bedside of a somnambulist.

IV

The Mandookya Upanishad describes a fourth state, which
is reached not in dreamless sleep but in contemplation and in wakefulness. This fourth state, pure light
to those that reach it, is that state wherein the soul,

as much ancient symbolism testifies, is united to the blessed dead.

Because we no longer discover the still unpurified dead through our own and others' dreams, and those in freedom through contemplation, religion cannot answer the atheist, and philosophy talks about a first cause or a final purpose, when we would know what we were a little before conception, what we shall be a little after burial.

V

The period between death and birth is divided into states analogous to the six solar months between Aries and Libra.[1] The first state is called *The Vision of the Blood Kindred*, a vision of all those bound to us through *Husk* and *Passionate Body*. Apparitions seen at the moment of death are part of the vision, a synthesis, before *disappearance*, of all the impulses and images which constitute the *Husk*. It is followed by the *Meditation*, which corresponds to what is called the "emotion of sanctity" on the Great Wheel; the *Spirit* and *Celestial Body appear*. The *Spirit* has its first vision and understanding of the *Celestial Body*, but that it may do so, it requires the help of the incarnate, for without them it is without language and without will. During the *Meditation* [2] *Husk*

---

[1] They correspond roughly to Phase 22, Phases 23, 24, 25, Phases 26, 27, 28, etc., upon the wheel of the *Faculties* which is at right angles to that of the *Principles*.

[2] An automatic script describes this *Meditation* as lasting until burial and as strengthened by the burial service and by the thoughts of friends and mourners. I left this statement out of the text because it did not so much seem a necessary deduction from the symbol as an unverifiable statement of experience. The meaning is doubtless

and *Passionate Body disappear*, but may persist in some
simulacrum of themselves as do the *Mask* and *Will*
in *primary* phases. If the *Husk* so persist, the *Spirit*
still continues to feel pleasure and pain, remains a
fading distortion of living man, perhaps a dangerous
succuba or incubus, living through the senses and
nerves of others. If there has been great animal egotism,
heightened by some moment of tragedy, the *Husk* may
persist for centuries, recalled into a sort of life, and
united to its *Spirit*, at some anniversary, or by some
unusually susceptible person or persons connected with
its past life.

In the third discarnate state, a state I shall presently
describe, it may renounce the form of a man and take
some shape from the social or religious tradition of
its past life, symbolical of its condition. Leap Castle,
though burnt down during our Civil War and still
a ruin, is haunted by what is called an evil spirit
which appears as a sheep with short legs and decaying
human head. I suggest that some man with the *Husk*
exaggerated and familiar with religious symbolism, torn
at the moment of death between two passions, terror of
the body's decay with which he identified himself, and
an abject religious humility, projected himself in this
image. If the *Passionate Body* does not *disappear*, the
Spirit finds the *Celestial Body*, only after long and perhaps
painful dreams of the past, and it is because of such

that the ceremonial obliteration of the body symbolises the *Spirit's*
separation from the *Husk*. Another automatic script describes the
Spirit as rising from the head at death, *Celestial Body* from the feet,
the *Passionate Body* from the genitals, while the *Husk* remains prone
in the body (the *Husk* itself seen objectively) and shares its form.
The *Spirit* is described as awakened from its sleep in the dead body.

dreams that the second state is sometimes called the
Dreaming Back. If death has been violent or tragic the
Spirit may cling to the *Passionate Body* for generations.
A gambler killed in a brawl may demand his money,[1]
a man who has believed that death ends all may see
himself as a decaying corpse,[2] nor is there any reason
why some living man might not see reflected in a
mirror or otherwise some beloved ghost, thinking herself unobserved, powdering her face as in Mr. Davies'
poem.[3]

> The first night she was in her grave,
> As I looked in the glass
> I saw her sit upright in bed;
> Without a sound it was;
> I saw her hand feel in the cloth
> To fetch a box of powder forth.
>
> She sat and watched me all the while
> For fear I looked her way;
> I saw her powder cheek and chin,
> Her fast corrupting clay.
> Then down my lady lay and smiled,
> She thought her beauty saved, poor child.

VI

The true name of the second state,[4] that of Taurus, is

[1] The late Dr. Abraham Wallace told me that he brought a
medium to a haunted house and had a conversation with just such
a ghost. He afterwards found, in an *Annual Register* for somewhere
about 1770, a record of just such a brawl at that very house.

[2] I came on this example years ago; it seemed well authenticated.

[3] This would be one of the most poignant poems in the language
had not Mr. Davies in a verse I have not quoted made an inexplic-
able transition from "thou" to "you".

[4] Roughly Phases 23, 24, 25 on the wheel of the *Faculties*.

the *Return* and it has for its object the *Spirit's* separation from the *Passionate Body,* considered as nature, and from the *Husk* considered as pleasure and pain. In the *Dreaming Back,* the *Spirit* is compelled to live over and over again the events that had most moved it; there can be nothing new, but the old events stand forth in a light which is dim or bright according to the intensity of the passion that accompanied them. They occur in the order of their intensity or luminosity, the more intense first, and the painful are commonly the more intense, and repeat themselves again and again. In the *Return,* upon the other hand, the *Spirit* must live through past events in the order of their occurrence, because it is compelled by the *Celestial Body* to trace every passionate event to its cause until all are related and understood, turned into know-ledge, made a part of itself. All that keeps the *Spirit* from its freedom may be compared to a knot that has to be untied or to an oscillation or a violence that must end in a return to equilibrium. I think of the Homeric contrast between Heracles passing through the night, bow in hand, and Heracles, the freed spirit, a happy god among the gods. I think of it in William Morris' translation:

And Heracles the mighty I saw when these went by;
His image indeed: for himself mid the gods that never die
Sits glad at the feast, and Hebe fair-ankled there doth hold,
The daughter of Zeus the mighty and Hera shod with gold.

After its imprisonment by some event in the *Dreaming Back,* the *Spirit* relives that event in the *Return* and turns it into knowledge, and then falls into the *Dreaming Back* once more. The *Spirit* finds the concrete events in the *Passionate Body,* but the names and words of the drama it must obtain, the *Faculties* having gone when the *Husk* and *Passionate Body disappeared*, from some incarnate Mind, and this it is able to do because all spirits inhabit our unconsciousness or, as Swedenborg said, are the Dramatis Personae of our dreams.[1] One thinks of those apparitions haunting the places where they have lived that fill the literature [2] of all countries and are the theme of the Japanese Nō drama. Though only visible to the seer when *Spirit* and *Passionate Body* are joined, they are constantly repeated until, at last forgotten by the *Spirit*, they fade into the *Thirteenth Cone*. The more complete the *Dreaming Back* the more complete the *Return* and the more happy or fortunate the next incarnation.[3] After each event of the *Dreaming Back* the *Spirit*

[1] My instructors said once that under certain circumstances a *Spirit* can draw knowledge of such things as language from the *Husks* of the other dead, but only if those *Husks* are separated from their *Spirits*. It seems that a mind must, as it were, release a thought before it becomes general property. Somebody years ago, at, I think, a meeting of the Society of Psychical Research, suggested that we transferred thought at some moment when we ceased to think of it.

[2] See *An Adventure* (Faber & Faber). This anonymous book was the work of two women, one the Head of St. Hugh's College, Oxford, the other her predecessor. It describes with minute detail a vision of Marie Antoinette and her Court, and of the gardens of the Petit Trianon as they were before the Revolution, and the research that proved the vision's accuracy. The two ladies walking in the garden of the Petit Trianon shared the same vision. I have confirmed, as far as the meagre records permitted, a similar vision in my own family, and Sligo pilots and Galway farmers have told me of visions that seem to reproduce the costumes of past times.

[3] Compare the account of the *Dreaming Back* in Swedenborg's *Heaven and Hell*. My account differs from his mainly because he denied or ignored rebirth. Somebody has suggested that he kept silent deliberately, that it was amongst those subjects that he thought forbidden. It is more likely that his instructors were silent. They spoke to the Christian Churches, explaining the "linen

explores not merely the causes but the consequences of
that event.

Where the soul has great intensity and where those
consequences affected great numbers, the *Dreaming Back*
and the *Return* may last with diminishing pain and joy
for centuries. The *Spirit*,[1] that it may make the *Passionate
Body* intelligible, can not only tap the minds of the living
but examine letters and books, once they come before
the eyes of the living, although it can see nothing that
does not concern the dream, for it is without reflection
or the knowledge that it is dead. If the event was shared
by many, those many may seem present and yet be but
the figures of the dream. Each must dream the event
alone. Sometimes the *Spirit* under the influence of the
Celestial Body and what are called *Teaching Spirits—Spirits*
of the *Thirteenth Cone*—may not merely dream through
the consequences of its acts but amend them, bringing
this or that to the attention of the living. I have found
a belief among Irish country people that the death of
father or mother may sometimes bring good luck to
child or family. Upon the other hand our actions affect
the dead. Some years ago there were various small inex-
plicable noises and movements in my house, and I was
told that a certain *Spirit* wanted to discover certain facts

clothes folded up", and even what they said or sought to say was
half-transformed into an opium dream by the faith of those
Churches in the literal inspiration of the Bible.

[1] A Robinson Crusoe who died upon his island and had not even
a Man Friday for witness could, I am told, get the necessary information from his own *Husk*, but his *Dreaming Back* would be imperfect. He would lack not only physical but spiritual burial. The
contents of his *Husk* being, as I suppose, too much himself, he would
continue to look through a window-pane upon which he had
breathed.

necessary to her *Dreaming Back* by creating discussion, or that *Teaching Spirits* wished to assist her by creating that discussion. It is from the *Dreaming Back* of the dead, though not from that of persons associated with our past, that we get the imagery of ordinary sleep. Much of a dream's confusion comes from the fact that the image belongs to some unknown person, whereas emotion, names, language, belong to us alone. Having kept a steady watch upon my dreams for years I know that so long as I dream in words I know that my father, let us say, was tall and bearded. If, on the other hand, I dream in images and examine the dream immediately upon waking I may discover him there represented by a stool or the eyepiece of a telescope, but never in his natural shape, for we cast off the concrete memory (lose contact with the *Record* as it affects ourselves) but not the abstract memory when we sleep.

Teaching Spirits are *Spirits* of the *Thirteenth Cone*, or their representatives who may be chosen from any state, and are those who substitute for *Husk* and *Passionate Body* supersensual emotion and imagery; the "unconscious" or unapparent for that which has *disappeared*; the *Spirit* itself being capable of knowledge only. They conduct the *Spirit* through its past acts; should the code that *Spirit* accepted during life permit, they may conduct it through those in past lives, especially those that fell where the *Four Faculties*[1] of its Phase fall upon

[1] The past incarnations corresponding to his *Four Faculties* seem to accompany a living man. Once when a child was born in the house, the doctor, the mother and I smelt roses everywhere. Years afterwards I read in a book called *Nursery Life Three Hundred Years Ago* (I forget the author's name) of a custom that lasted into the seventeenth century of washing new-born children in a bath "made wholesome . . . with red roses", of rolling them in

the wheel of the cycle, seeking always the source of its action. We must, however, avoid attributing to them the pure benevolence our exhausted Platonism and Christianity attribute to an angelical being. Our actions, lived in life, or remembered in death, are the food and drink of the *Spirits* of the *Thirteenth Cone*, that which gives them separation and solidity.

But knowledge of the past is not sufficient. The second stage contains in addition to the *Dreaming Back* and the *Return* what is called the *Phantasmagoria*, which exists to exhaust, not nature, not pain and pleasure, but emotion, and is the work of *Teaching Spirits*. The physical and moral life is completed, without the addition of any new element that the objects of hope may be completed, for only that which is completed can be known and dismissed. Houses appear built by thought in a moment, the spirit seems to eat, drink and smoke, the child appears to grow to maturity, or perhaps with the help of *Teaching Spirits* a Christmas Tree is created, Christ or some saint or angel descends, dressed as in statue or picture; if the life was evil, then the *Phantasmagoria* is evil, the criminal completes his crime. It is indeed a necessary act of the human soul that has cut off the incarnate and discarnate from one another, plunging the discarnate into our "unconsciousness". The *Phantasmagoria* completes not only life but imagination. Cornelius Agrippa speaks of those among the dead

salt and roses, and of sprinkling them, when the parents could afford it, with oil of roses. If I assume that the *Thirteenth Cone* can send the forms from any incarnation which correspond to the place of *Faculty* or *Principle*, whether in the present or an earlier cycle, I have an explanation of that emergence during vision of an old Cretan myth described in my book *Autobiographies*.

who imagine themselves "surrounded by flames and persecuted by demons" and, according to his seventeenth-
century translator, confers upon them the name "Hob-
goblin". The various legends of spirits that appear
under the impulse of moral and emotional suffering
must be attributed to this state and not to the *Dreaming
Back*, where the constraint is physical. I think of a girl
in a Japanese play whose ghost tells a priest of a slight
sin, if indeed it was sin, which seems great because of
her exaggerated conscience. She is surrounded by flames,
and though the priest explains that if she but ceased to
believe in those flames they would cease to exist, believe she must, and the play ends in an elaborate dance,
the dance of her agony. I think of those stories which I
have already summarised where some ghost seeks not
to perfect an event that concerns the living, but its own
emotional or moral peace.

VII

At the end of the second state, the events of the past
life are a whole and can be dismissed; the emotional and
moral life, however, is but a whole according to the
code accepted during life. The *Spirit* is still unsatisfied,
until after the third state, which corresponds to Gemini,[1]
called the *Shiftings*, where the *Spirit* is purified of good
and evil. In so far as the man did good without knowing
evil, or evil without knowing good, his nature is reversed
until that knowledge is obtained. The *Spirit* lives—I
quote the automatic script—"The best possible life in

---

[1] My instructors do not seem to use the astrological character of
this, or indeed of any sign except Taurus, Pisces and the Cardinal
signs.

the worst possible surroundings" or the contrary of this; yet there is no suffering: "For in a state of equilibrium there is neither emotion nor sensation". In the limits of the good and evil of the previous life . . . the soul is brought to a contemplation of good and evil; "neither its utmost good nor its utmost evil can force sensation or emotion". I remember MacKenna's translation of the most beautiful of the *Enneads*, "The Impassivity of the Dis-Embodied". This state is described as a true life, as distinguished from the preceding states; the soul is free in the sense that it is subject to necessary truth alone, the *Celestial Body* is described as present in person instead of through "Messengers".

It is followed by a state corresponding to Cancer which is said to pass in unconsciousness, or in a moment of consciousness called the *Marriage* or the *Beatitude*. It is complete equilibrium after the conflict of the *Shiftings*; good and evil vanish into the whole. It is followed by an oscillation, a reversal of the old life; this lasts until birth and death bring the *Shiftings* and the *Marriage* once more, a reversal not in knowledge but in life, or until the *Spirit* is free from good and evil.[1] My instructors have described the *Marriage* as follows: "The *Celestial Body* is the Divine Cloak lent to all, it falls away at the consummation and Christ is revealed", words which seem to echo Bardesan's *Hymn of the Soul*, where a King's son asleep in Egypt (physical life) is sent a cloak

---

[1] The reversals of *The Shiftings* and the *Purification* are reflected in the alternation between *Sage* and *Victim*. Solar South (Cancer) is Lunar East. Lunar East is Phase 22. The interchange of *Sage* and *Victim* is comparable to the exchange of the *Tinctures*, but there is no reversal at the opposite point because the wheel of the *Faculties* completes itself while that of the *Principles* goes but half its distance (Book II, section VII).

which is also an image of his body.[1] He sets out to his
father's kingdom wrapped in the cloak.

VIII

In the *Purification* (corresponding to the sign Leo) a new
Husk and *Passionate Body* take the place of the old; made
from the old, yet, as it were, pure. All memory has
vanished, the *Spirit* no longer knows what its name has
been, it is at last free and in relation to *Spirits* free like
itself. Though the new *Husk* and *Mask* have been born,
they do not *appear*, they are subordinate to the *Celestial
Body*. The *Spirit* must substitute for the *Celestial Body*,
seen as a Whole, its own particular aim. Having substituted this aim it becomes self-shaping, self-moving,
plastic to itself, as that self has been shaped by past
lives. If its nature is unique it must find circumstances
not less unique before rebirth is possible. It may stay
in the *Purification* for centuries—become, if it died
amidst some primitive community, the guardian of
well or temple or be called by the *Thirteenth Cone* to
the care of the newly dead. I think of those phantoms
in ancient costumes seen by some peasant seers exercising such authority. "We have no power", said an in-
habitant of the state, "except to purify our intention",
and when I asked of what, replied: "Of complexity".
But that *Purification* may require the completion of some
syntheses left unfinished in its past life. Because only

[1] A living man sees the *Celestial Body* through the *Mask*. I
awoke one night when a young man to find my body rigid and to
hear a voice that came from my lips and yet did not seem my voice
saying, "We make an image of him who sleeps, and it is not he who
sleeps and we call it Emmanuel".

the living create it may seek the assistance of those
living men into whose "unconsciousness" or incarnate
Daimon, some affinity of aim, or the command of the
Thirteenth Cone, permits it to enter. Those who taught
me this system did so, not for my sake, but their own.[1]
The *Spirit's* aim, however, appears before it as a form of
perfection, for during the *Purification* those forms copied
in the Arts and Sciences are present as the *Celestial Body*.
In piecing together detached statements, I remember
that some spirit once said to me: "We do nothing
singly, every act is done by a number at the same
instant." Their perfection is a shared purpose or idea.
I connect them in my imagination with an early conviction of mine, that the creative power of the lyric
poet depends upon his accepting some one of a few
traditional attitudes, lover, sage, hero, scorner of life.
They bring us back to the spiritual norm. They may,
however, if permitted by the *Thirteenth Cone*, so act
upon the events of our lives as to compel us to attend
to that perfection which, though it seems theirs, is the
work of our own *Daimon*.

IX

The sixth and final state (corresponding to Scorpio)
called the *Foreknowledge* must substitute the next incarnation, as fate has decreed it, for that form of perfection. The *Spirit* cannot be reborn until the vision
of that life is completed and accepted. The *Spirit*, now

[1] They say that only the words spoken in trance or written in
the automatic script assist them. They belong to the "unconscious"
and what comes from them alone serves. My interpretations do not
concern them. In the mediumistic condition it sometimes seems
as if dreams awoke and yet remained dreams.

almost united to *Husk* and *Passionate Body*, may know
the most violent love and hatred possible, for it can see
the remote consequences of the most trivial acts of the
living, provided those consequences are part of its future
life. In trying to prevent them it may become one of
those frustrators dreaded by certain spirit mediums.
It cannot, however, without the assistance of the *Thirteenth Cone* affect life in any way except to delay its
own rebirth. With that assistance it can so shape circumstances as to make possible the rebirth of a unique
nature. One must suppose such spirits gathered into
bands—for as yet they are without individuality—
and with the consent of the *Thirteenth Cone* playing a
part resembling that of the "censor" in modern psychology. During its sleep in the womb the *Spirit* accepts
its future life, declares it just.

X

The *Spirits* before the *Marriage* are spoken of as the
dead. After that they are spirits, using that word as it
is used in common speech. During the *Dreaming Back*
the *Spirit* is alone with its dream; during the *Return* in
the presence of those who had a part in the events explored in the *Dreaming Back*; in the *Phantasmagoria* and in
the *Shiftings* of those summoned by the *Thirteenth Cone*
and the *Celestial Body* respectively; in the *Purification*, of
those chosen by itself.

In the *Meditation* it wears the form it had immediately
before death; in the *Dreaming Back* and the *Phantasmagoria*, should it appear to the living, it has the form
of the dream, in the *Return* the form worn during the
event explored, in the *Shiftings* whatever form was most

familiar to others during its life; in the *Purification* whatever form it fancies, for it is now the Shape-changer of legend:

> 'Twas said that she all shapes could wear;
> And oftentimes before him stood,
> Amid the trees of some thick wood,
> In semblance of a lady fair;
> And taught him signs, and showed him sights
> In Craven's dens, on Cumbrian heights.

The *Dreaming Back* is represented upon the cone or wheel by a periodical stoppage of movement.

Indian Buddhists cease to offer sacrifice for a particular dead person after three generations, for after that time he must, they believe, have found a new body. A typical series of lives described by my instructors suggest that as an average limit, but in some cases rebirth comes very soon. If a *Spirit* cannot escape from its *Dreaming Back* to complete its expiation, a new life may come soon and be, as it were, a part of its *Dreaming Back* and so repeat the incidents of the past life. There are stories Asiatic and European of those who die in childhood being reborn almost at once.

The more complete the expiation, or the less the need for it, the more fortunate the succeeding life. The more fully a life is lived, the less the need for—or the more complete is—the expiation. Neither the *Phantasmagoria*, nor the *Purification*, nor any other state between death and birth should be considered as a reward or paradise. Neither between death and birth nor between birth and death can the soul find more than momentary happiness; its object is to pass rapidly round its circle and find freedom from that circle.

Those who inhabit the "unconscious mind" are the complement or opposite of that mind's consciousness and are there, unless as messengers of the *Thirteenth Cone*, because of spiritual affinity or bonds created during past lives.

XI

All the involuntary acts and facts of life are the effect of the whirring and interlocking of the gyres; but gyres may be interrupted or twisted by greater gyres, divide into two lesser gyres or multiply into four and so on. The uniformity of nature depends upon the constant return of gyres to the same point. Sometimes individuals are *primary* and *antithetical* to one another and joined by a bond so powerful that they form a common gyre or series of gyres. This gyre or these gyres no greater gyre may be able to break till exhaustion comes. We all to some extent meet again and again the same people and certainly in some cases form a kind of family of two or three or more persons who come together life after life until all passionate relations are exhausted, the child of one life the husband, wife, brother or sister of the next. Sometimes, however, a single relationship will repeat itself, turning its revolving wheel again and again, especially, my instructors say, where there has been strong sexual passion. All such passions, they say, contain "cruelty and deceit"—I think of similar statements in D. H. Lawrence's *Rainbow* and in his *Women in Love*—and this *antithetical* cruelty and deceit must be expiated in *primary* suffering and submission, or the old tragedy will be repeated.

They are expiated between birth and death because they are actions, but their victim must expiate between

death and birth the ignorance that made them possible.
The victim must, in the *Shiftings*, live the act of
cruelty, not as victim but as tyrant; whereas the tyrant
must by a necessity of his or her nature become the
victim. But if one is dead and the other living they
find each other in thought and symbol, the one that
has been passive and is now active may from within
control the other, once tyrant now victim. If the
act is associated with the *Return* or the *Purification* the
one that controls from within, reliving as a form of
knowledge what once was tyranny, gives not pain but
ecstasy. The one whose expiation is an act needs for the
act some surrogate [1] or symbol of the other and offers
to some other man or woman submission or service,
but because the unconscious mind knows that this act
is fated no new gyre is started. The expiation, because
offered to the living for the dead, is called "expiation
for the dead" but is in reality expiation for the *Daimon*,
for passionate love is from the *Daimon* which seeks by
union with some other *Daimon* to reconstruct above the
antinomies its own true nature. The souls of victim and
tyrant are bound together and, unless there is a redemp-
tion through the intercommunication of the living and
the dead, that bond may continue life after life, and this
is just, for there had been no need of expiation had they
seen in one another that other and not something else.
The expiation is completed and the oscillation brought
to an end for each at the same moment. There are other

---

[1] A Bombay friend of mine once saw an Indian peasant standing
by the road with many flowers beside her. She gave a flower to each
passer-by with the words "I give this to my Lord". Her Lord was
the god Krishna, but the passionate may offer to their own dead a
similar worship.

bonds, master and servant, benefactor and beneficiary, any relation that is deeper than the intellect may become such a bond. We get happiness, my instructors say, from those we have served, ecstasy from those we have wronged.

XII

Sometimes the bond is between an incarnate *Daimon* and a *Spirit of the Thirteenth Cone.* This bond created by the fixed attention of the *Daimon* will pass through the same stages as if it were between man and some ordinary discarnate spirit. *Victimage for the Dead* arises through such act as prevents the union of two incarnate *Daimons* and is therefore the prevention or refusal of a particular experience, but *Victimage* for a *Spirit of the Thirteenth Cone* results from the prevention or refusal of experience itself. This refusal may arise from pride, from the fear of injuring another or oneself, from something which we call asceticism; it may have any cause, but the *Spirit of the Thirteenth Cone* is starved. Such *Spirit* may itself create the events that incited the man to refuse experience, St. Simon may be driven to his pillar. In the whirling of the gyres the incarnate *Daimon* is starved in its turn, but starved not of natural experience, but of supernatural; for, compelled to take the place of the *Spirit*, it transforms its natural craving—*Eli! Eli! Lama Sabacthani!?*— and this state is called *Victimage for the Ghostly Self*, and is described as the sole means for acquiring a supernatural guide. So closely do all the bonds resemble each other that in the most ascetic schools of India the novice tortured by his passion will pray to the God to come to him as a woman and have with him sexual intercourse; nor is the symbol subjective, for in the morning his pillow

will be saturated with temple incense, his breast yellow
with the saffron dust of some temple offering. Such
experience is said, however, to wear itself out swiftly
giving place to the supernatural union. Sometimes the
God may select some living symbol of himself. If
the ascetic is a woman, some wandering priest perhaps, if a man, some wandering priestess, but such
loves are brief. Sometimes, however, *Victimage for the
Ghostly Self* and *Victimage for the Dead* coincide and
produce lives tortured throughout by spirituality and
passion. Cruelty and ignorance, which echo the *Sage*
and *Victim* of Book I, constitute evil as my instructors
see it, and are that which makes possible the conscious
union of the *Daimons* of Man and Woman or that of
the *Daimon* of the Living and a *Spirit of the Thirteenth
Cone*, which is the deliverance from birth and death.

The *Thirteenth Cone* is a sphere because sufficient to
itself; but as seen by Man it is a cone. It becomes
even conscious of itself as so seen, like some great
dancer, the perfect flower of modern culture, dancing
some primitive dance and conscious of his or her
own life and of the dance. There is a mediaeval story of
a man persecuted by his Guardian Angel because it was
jealous of his sweetheart, and such stories seem closer to
reality than our abstract theology. All imaginable relations may arise between a man and his God. I only speak
of the *Thirteenth Cone* as a sphere and yet I might say
that the gyre or cone of the *Principles* is in reality a
sphere, though to Man, bound to birth and death, it
can never seem so, and that it is the antinomies that
force us to find it a cone. Only one symbol exists,
though the reflecting mirrors make many appear and
all different.

THE GREAT YEAR OF THE ANCIENTS

BOOK IV: THE GREAT YEAR
OF THE ANCIENTS

I

WHEN a religious-minded Roman of the first century before Christ thought of the first month of a new Great Year, did he think of some ideal king such as Virgil foretold, or think of Attis who died and rose again at the beginning of their old lunar year? Which did he prefer of those incompatible ideas, Triumph or Sacrifice, Sage or Victim? When did he expect the one or the other?

To the time when Marius sat at home planning a sedition that began the Roman civil wars, popular imagination attributed many prodigies; the wooden support of the eagles burst into flames; three ravens brought their young into the open field, picked their bones and carried the bones back into the nest; a mouse gnawed the consecrated corn in the temple and when caught brought forth five young and devoured them; and, greatest marvel of all, out of the calm and clear sky came the sound of a trumpet. The Etruscans declared that this trumpet meant "the mutation of the age and a general revolution of the world". A generation later Virgil sang his song: "the latest age of the Cumaean song is at hand; the cycles in their vast array begin anew; Virgin Astraea comes, the reign of Saturn comes, and from the heights of Heaven a new generation of man-

kind descends. . . . Apollo now is king and in your
Consulship, in yours, Pollio, the age of glory shall com-
mence and the mighty months begin their course."

II

Caesar and Christ always stand face to face in our
imagination. Did not Dante put Judas and Brutus into
the mouth of Satan? Some nine months before the
assassination of Caesar his image was carried among the
images of the gods in a procession at the Ludi Circenses,
and a rumour, afterwards disproved, reached Cicero that
Cotta, the official exponent of the Oracles, proposed
announcing to the Senate "That he whom we really had
as King should be given the title of King if we desired
to remain safe". If this was really in the Sibylline Books,
to what man and to what time did it refer? [1] Cicero
thought such books were so written that they could fit
any time or man, and adds: "Let us ask their Priests to
produce anything out of those books rather than a King".
He was writing after the assassination. Had what
Cicero calls elsewhere "the religious party of the Sibyl"
found that prophecy Virgil was to sing in the next
generation? Did they expect a mystic king to restore
justice, "the girl Astraea"? What did the Roman slums
hope for when their half-oriental population under the
influence of a fanatical cow-doctor, horse-doctor or eye-
doctor, for scholars differ as to his occupation—the
Clare and Galway of my youth had such men—burnt
the body of Caesar on the Capitol, and with, it may be,
some traditional ceremony of apotheosis set up his
statue and worshipped him? They drove the tyranni-

[1] See Cicero's letter to Atticus, XIII. 44, and his *De Divinatione*.

cides from Rome, and when Dolabella, Cicero's son-
in-law, dispersed and punished them Cicero thanked
him for a deed equal in courage and importance to the
assassination of Caesar. Did the Julian House inherit
from that apotheosis and those prayers the Cumaean
song? Caesar was killed on the 15th day of March, the
month of victims and of saviours. Two years before he
had instituted our solar Julian Year, and in a few generations the discovery of the body of Attis among the
reeds would be commemorated upon that day, though,
before "Ides" lost its first meaning, the ceremony
needed a full moon or the fifteenth day of a lunar
March. Even Easter, which the rest of Christendom
commemorated on the first full moon after the Vernal
Equinox, would sometimes be commemorated by
Christians living under the influence of the Julian Year
upon the day before the fifteenth day of the solar
March.[1] It seemed as if the magical character of the full
moon was transferred to a day and night where the moon
had as it were a merely legal or official existence. One
thinks of Mommsen's conviction that though Caesar
chose the lesser of two evils the Roman State was from
his day to the end a dead thing, a mere mechanism.

III

"By common consent men measure the year", wrote
Cicero, "by the return of the sun, or in other words by
the revolution of one star. But when the whole of the
constellations shall return to the positions from which
they once set forth, thus after a long interval re-making

[1] The sacrifice of the Passover took place upon the fourteenth
lunar day and night which were counted full moon.

the first map of the heavens, that may indeed be called
the Great Year wherein I scarce dare say how many are
the generations of men." But that Great or Greatest
Year was sometimes divided into lesser periods by the
return of the sun and moon to some original position,
by the return of a planet or of all the planets to some
original position, or by their making an astrological
aspect with that position; and sometimes it was dis-
sociated from the actual position of the stars and divided
into twelve months, each month a brightening and a
darkening fortnight, and at the same time perhaps a
year with its four seasons. I do not remember the
brightening and darkening fortnights in any classical
author, but they are in the Upanishads and in the Laws
of Manu for the Great Year and its Months pervaded
the ancient world. Perhaps at the start a mere magni-
fication of the natural year, it grew more complicated
with the spread of Greek astronomy, but it is always
the simpler, more symbolic form, with its conflict of
light and dark, heat and cold, that concerns me most.

IV [1]

Anaximander, a pre-Socratic philosopher, thought
there were two infinities, one of co-existence where
nothing ages, the other of succession and mortality,
world coming after world and lasting always the same
number of years. Empedocles and Heraclitus thought
that the universe had first one form and then its opposite in perpetual alternation, meaning, as it seems, that

[1] Most of the quotations and summaries in this section are
from Pierre Duhem's *Le Système du monde*, vol. i, chap. v, sections
VI and VII.

all things were consumed with fire when all the planets
so stood in the sign Cancer that a line could be drawn
through all their centres and the centre of the earth,
destroyed by water when all stood in Capricorn; a fire
that is not what we call fire but "the fire of heaven",
"the fire where all the universe returns to its seed", a
water that is not what we call water but a "lunar water"
that is nature. Love and Discord, Fire and Water, dominate in turn, Love making all things One, Discord
separating all, but Love no more than Discord the
changeless eternity. Here originated perhaps the symbol expounded in this book of a phaseless sphere that
becomes phasal in our thought, Nicholas of Cusa's
undivided reality which human experience divides into
opposites, and here too, as Pierre Duhem points out, we
discover for the first time the Platonic doctrine of
imitation—the opposing states copy eternity.

But when the age of Fire or that of Water returns,
did the same man return, or a new man who resembled
him, and if the same man, must he have the old wart
upon his nose? Some thought one thing and some another. Was the world completely destroyed at the solstice or did it but acquire a new shape? Philaus thought
the fire and water but destroyed the old shape and
nourished the new. Did one world follow another without a break? Empedocles thought there must be an
intermediate state of rest.

So far the Ideas had been everything, the individual
nothing; beauty and truth alone had mattered to
Plato and Socrates, but Plotinus thought that every
individual had his Idea, his eternal counterpart; the
Greatest Year and the Great Years that were its Months
became a stream of souls. To the next generation it

seemed plain that the Eternal Return, though it remained for the stream as a whole, had ceased for the
wise man, for the wise man could withdraw from the
circuit. Proclus discovered in the Golden Number of
the *Republic* a Greatest Year, that is "the least common
number of all revolutions visible and invisible", and in
the *Timaeus* a much smaller year, "which is the least
common multiple" of the revolutions of the eight
spheres, and thought this smaller year alone calculable
by reason.

Yet Plato's statements are there that scholars may
solve the Golden Number, and they have found
fourteen different solutions. To Taylor they suggest
36,000 years, 360 incarnations of Plato's Man of Ur.
Proclus thought the duration of the world is found
"when we bring into contemplation the numerical
unity, the one self-unfolding power, the sole creation
that completes its work, that which fills all things with
universal life. One must see all things wind up their
careers and come round again to the beginning; one
must see everything return to itself and so complete by
itself the circle allotted to that number; or that unity
which encloses an infinity of numbers, contains within
itself the instability of the Duad and yet determines
the whole movement, its end and its beginning. and is
for that reason called the Number and the Perfect
Number." It is as though innumerable dials, some that
recorded minutes alone, some seconds alone, some hours
alone, some months alone, some years alone, were all to
complete their circles when Big Ben struck twelve upon
the last night of the century. My instructors offer for a
symbol the lesser unities that combine into a work of
art and leave no remainder, but we may substitute if we

will the lesser movements which combine into the
circle that in Hegel's *Logic* unites not summer solstice
to summer solstice but absolute to absolute. "The
Months and Years are also numbered, but they are not
perfect numbers but parts of other numbers. The time
of the development of the universe is perfect, for it is
a part of nothing, it is a whole and for that reason
resembles eternity. It is before all else an integrity, but
only eternity confers upon existence that complete integrity which remains in itself; that of time develops,
development is indeed a temporal image of that which
remains in itself."

V

A doctrine which showed all things returning to the
seed of Fire at the midsummer of the Great Year may
have sounded the more natural to a Greek because
Athenian years began at midsummer. But from somewhere in Asia Minor, Persia perhaps, spread a doctrine
which transferred attention from Cancer and Capricorn
to Aries, from the extremes where the world was
destroyed to the midway point where it was restored,
where Love began to prevail over Discord, Day over
Night. The destroying flood rose in Capricorn but lasted
through the two succeeding signs, only disappearing
when the World-restorer appeared; the creation itself
had been but a restoration. To many Christians and
Jews, though the doctrine soon ceased to be orthodox,
not the Messiah alone but the Spirit that moved upon
the Waters, and Noah on Mount Ararat, seemed such
world-restorers. "Certain Christians", wrote Neme-
sius, Bishop of Emessa, "would have us consider the
Resurrection linked to the restoration of the world, but

they deceive themselves strangely, for it is proved by the words of Christ that the Resurrection could not happen more than once, that it came not from a periodical revolution but from the Will of God." [1] The doctrine, however, reappears in various forms as a recognised heresy until the thirteenth century, though that learned scholar, great poet and devout man, Francis Thompson, did not recognise it as such when he wrote:

> Not only of cyclic Man
> Thou here discern'st the plan,
> Not only of cyclic Man, but of the cyclic Me,
> Not solely of Mortalities great years
>   The reflex just appears,
> But thine own bosom's year, still circling round
> In ample and in ampler gyre
> Towards the far completion, wherewith crowned,
> Love unconsumed shall chant in his own funeral pyre.

VI

Christ rose from the dead at a full moon in the first month of the year, the month that we have named from Mars the ruler of the first of the twelve signs.

I do not know if my instructors were the first to make a new lunar circuit equal in importance with the solar out of that archetypal month. To this month, to

---

[1] Quoted by Pierre Duhem, *Le Système du monde*, vol. ii, part 2, chap. i, section VIII. The section shows the attitude of the Fathers of the Church to the Great Year and is of great interest. Defending the freedom of the will they seem to know the Eternal Return in its most mechanical form. Their argument does not affect the position of Proclus.

touch upon a symbolism I have hitherto avoided for the sake of clarity, they gave a separate zodiac where the full moon falls at Capricorn. The two abstract zodiacs are so imposed the one upon the other that a line drawn between Cancer and Capricorn in the one is at right angles to a similar line in the other. As Capricorn is the most southerly sign—"lunar south is solar east"—a line drawn between east and west in the one is at right angles to a line drawn between east and west in the other. As every period of time is both a month and a year the circles can be superimposed, the signs in the lunar circle running from right to left, those in the solar from left to right. They have much the same character, being respectively particular and universal, as the circles of the Other and the Same in the *Timaeus*. In the first *Will* moves and its opposite, in the second *Creative Mind* and its opposite, or we may consider the first the wheel of the *Faculties*, the second that of the *Principles*.

VII

There was little agreement as to the length of the Great Year, every philosopher had a different calculation, but the majority divided it into 360 days or 365 days according to the prevailing view as to the number of days in the year. The Stoics of Cicero's time thought it was divided into 365 days of 15,000 years apiece. Cicero thought it began with an eclipse at the time of Romulus, or wished men to think so to confound the local Mother Shipton who had gone over to his enemies; and why did Virgil make that prophecy accepted all through the Middle Ages as prophesying Christ? There were similar prophecies elsewhere, for the world felt itself at the beginning of a great change, but I know no book that has studied them and traced them to their origin.

VIII

In the second century before Christ, Hipparchus discovered [1] that the Zodiacal constellations were moving, that in a certain number of years the sun would no longer rise at the Vernal Equinox in the constellation Aries, but his discovery seems to have been little noticed until the third century after Christ when Ptolemy fixed the rate of movement at 100 years [2] for each degree, that Aries might return to its original position every 36,000 years, the 360 incarnations of a man of Ur. He named these 36,000 years the Platonic Year and by that name they were known henceforth. But if the eighth sphere, the sphere of the fixed stars, moved, it was necessary to transfer the diurnal movement to a ninth sphere or abstract zodiac divided into twelve equal parts; the first month of the year must, no matter where the constellations went, retain its martial energy of the Ram, midwinter its goatish cold and wet even if the constellations of Goat had strayed. So too must each individual life retain to the end the seal set upon it at birth.

Ptolemy must have added new weight to the conviction of Plotinus that the stars did not themselves affect

[1] If we judge by written evidence alone we must say that Hipparchus discovered precession, but there are scholars who think that he but introduced into the Graeco-Roman world a very ancient Asiatic discovery.

[2] The rate is about one-third less, and the whole precession takes some 26,000 years.

human destiny but were pointers which enabled us to calculate the condition of the universe at any particular moment and therefore its effect on the individual life.[1] "It is impossible that any single form", said Hermes in a passage from which I have already quoted a few words, "should come into being which is exactly like a second, if they originate at different points and at times differently situated; the forms change at every moment in each hour of the revolution of that celestial circuit . . . thus the type persists unchanged but generates at successive moments copies of itself as numerous and different as the revolutions of the sphere of heaven; for the sphere of heaven changes as it revolves, but the type neither changes nor revolves." But nations also were sealed at birth with a character derived from the whole, and had, like individuals, their periods of increase and decrease. When the trumpet sounded in the sky in Sulla's time the Etruscan sages, according to Plutarch, declared the Etruscan cycle of 11,000 years at an end, and that "another sort of men were coming into the world".

IX

Syncellus said that a new epoch began when the constellation Aries returned to its original position, and that this was the doctrine of "Greeks and Egyptians . . .

[1] This doctrine must have spread widely during the Middle Ages. Lady Gregory was told in County Clare that there was a "woman in the sky" and whatever she did at any particular moment a child born at that moment did throughout life. Mr. Robin Flower found a like story in the Blasket Islands; and has not Mr. Wyndham Lewis accused Mr. Bertrand Russell of turning Mr. Smith into Mr. Four-thirty-in-the-afternoon by his exposition of space-time?

as stated in the *Genetica* of Hermes and in the Cyrannic books".[1] Was Ptolemy the first to give a date to that return? The inventor of the ninth sphere, whether Ptolemy or another, was bound to make that calculation. What was the date? I have not read his *Almagest*, nor am I likely to, and no historian or commentator on his discoveries known to me has given it. It would depend on the day he selected for the equinox (at Rome March 25th), and upon what star seemed to mark the end of Aries and the beginning of Pisces. It was certainly near enough to the assassination of Caesar to make the Roman Empire seem miraculous, near enough to the Crucifixion to confer upon the early Church, had it not been committed to its war with Grecian fatalism, the greatest of its miracles:

> Then did all the Muses sing
> Of Magnus Annus at the spring.

X

On the map of Twenty-eight Incarnations—Book I, part ii, sec. 1—there is the sign of Aries between Phases 18 and 19. Some years passed before I understood the meaning of this sign or of the other cardinal signs in the original automatic map. It is the position that will be occupied by the vernal equinox at the central moment of the next religious era, or at the beginning of the succeeding *antithetical* civilisation, for the position of the equinox marks the phase of *Will* in the wheel of 26,000 years. It is the Aries or solar east of the double cone of its particular era set within the cir-

[1] Quoted in E. M. Plunkett's *Ancient Calendars*.

cuit of the Great Year. At present it approaches the central point of Phase 17 where the next influx must take place. It passed into Phase 16 at the end of the eleventh century when our civilisation began. That position between Phases 18 and 19 is said to define the greatest possible intellectual power because it is the centre of that quarter of the Wheel symbolical of the logical intellect, and because it is one of the four moments where the *Faculties* are at equal distance from one another: conflict, and therefore intensity of consciousness, apportioned out through the whole being.

The corresponding moment in the lesser wheel of our Gothic civilisation came near the close of the seventeenth century just before that first decade of the eighteenth where Oliver thinks the European intellect reached its climax in power and authority. It is a moment of supreme abstraction; nor do I think of Spinoza, Leibnitz, Newton alone, I think of those monks at Port Royal who cut up live dogs to study the circulation of the blood, believing the lower animals but automata constructed to simulate by bellows and whistle the scream of agony. That such a moment echoed the greater period to come gave it importance, a special shaping power. It does not, however, help us to judge what form abstraction may take in a religious era which must move towards an *antithetical* civilisation and the concrete and sensuous unity of Phase 15. An historical symbolism which covers too great a period of time for imagination to grasp or experience to explain may seem too theoretical, too arbitrary, to serve any practical purpose; it is, however, necessary to the myth if we are not to suggest, as Vico did, civilisation perpetually returning to the same point.

XI

At the opening of Book V is a diagram where every date was fixed by my instructors. They have adopted a system of cones not used elsewhere in this exposition. If one ignores the black numbers it is simple enough. It shows the gyre of religion expanding as that of secular life contracts, until at the eleventh century the movements are reversed. *Mask* and *Body of Fate* are religion, *Will* and *Creative Mind* secular life. My instructors have inserted the black numbers because it enables them to bring into a straight line four periods corresponding to the *Four Faculties* that are in Flinders Petrie's sense of the word "contemporaneous". If we push this line of *Faculties* down from its starting-point at the birth of Christ (Year 1, and Phase 1 in the red letters), to the eleventh century, with *Will* on the left red line, *Body of Fate* on the left black line, *Mask* on the next and so on; then push it upward, changing the order of the *Faculties* to that on the diagram, every moment of the era reveals itself as constituted by four interacting periods. If we keep the straight line passing through the *Four Faculties* of the same length as the bases of the triangles we can mark upon it the twenty-eight phases, putting Phase 1 at the left hand, and the line will show what the position of the *Faculties* would be upon an ordinary double cone which completed its movement in the two thousand years of the era. My instructors scrawled a figure with a line so marked once or twice upon the margin of the automatic script while writing of something else, and left me to guess its relevance. When one examines the line so divided one discovers that at the present moment, although we are passing into Phase 23 on the cone of civilisation, we are between Phases 25 and 26 on the cone of the era. I consider that a conflict between religious and secular thought, because it governs all that is most interior and spiritual in myself, must be the projector of the era, and I find it upon this slow-moving cone. Its *Four Faculties* so found are four periods of time eternally co-existent, four co-existent acts; as seen in time we explain their effect by saying that the spirits of the three periods that seem to us past are present among us, though unseen.

When our historical era approaches Phase 1, or the beginning of a new era, the *antithetical* East will beget upon the *primary* West and the child or era so born will be *antithetical*. The *primary* child or era is predominantly western, but because begotten upon the East, eastern in body, and if I am right in thinking that my instructors imply not only the symbolical but the geographical East, Asiatic. Only when that body begins to wither can the Western Church predominate visibly.

XII

That most philosophical of archaeologists Josef Strzygowski haunts my imagination. To him the East, as certainly to my instructors, is not India or China, but the East that has affected European civilisation, Asia Minor, Mesopotamia, Egypt. From the Semitic East he derives all art which associates Christ with the attributes of royalty. It substitutes Christ Pantokrator for the bearded mild Hellenic Christ, makes the Church hierarchical and powerful. The East, in my symbolism, whether in the circle of the *Principles* or the *Faculties*, is always human power, whether *Will* or *Spirit*, stretched to its utmost. In the decorative diagram from the *Stories of*

Michael Robartes and his Friends, printed at the opening of
Book I, the East is marked by a sceptre. From the South,
whether India or Egypt, he derives all representation of
naturalistic human form, and has not Dante compared
Unity of Being, the unity of man not of God, and therefore of the *antithetical tincture,* to a perfectly proportioned
human body? I am not, however, so certain, though more
than half convinced, that his geographical North and my
symbolical North are the same. He finds amid the nomad
Aryans of northern Europe and Asia the source of all
geometrical ornament, of all non-representative art. It is
only when he comes to describe such art as a subordination of all detail to the decoration of some given surface,
and to associate it with domed and arched buildings
where nothing interferes with the effect of the building
as a whole, and with a theology which so exalts the Deity
that every human trait disappears, that I begin to wonder
whether the non-representative art of our own time may
not be but a first symptom of our return to the *primary
tincture.* He does not characterise the West except to
describe it as a mirror where all movements are reflected.
It is symbolised in the diagram in the Robartes stories
as a cup, for it is an emotional or natural intoxication. If I translate his geographical symbolism into
the language of the system I say that South and East
are human form and intellectual authority, whereas
North and West are superhuman form and emotional
freedom.

XIII

The German traveller Frobenius discovered among
the African natives two symbolical forms, one founded
upon the symbol of the Cavern, one upon that of a

central Altar and sixteen roads radiating outward; and
the races of the Cavern seemed of eastern origin while
the races of the roads had moved eastward from the
Atlantic seaboard. These races and their forms had
passed everywhere. He found methods of divination
based upon the symbolism of the roads in the furthest
East, and the symbolism of the Cavern in the West.
One thinks of them as existing side by side as does fair
Northern hair with the dark hair of the South. I do not
know how far he has been supported by other ethno-
logists, but certainly Spengler's vast speculation was
founded in part upon his discovery, and I think that
my instructors,[1] who seemed to know so much of
Spengler, knew something of Frobenius. Spengler con-
tinually refers to the symbol of the Cavern and gives
Frobenius as his authority, but, as I think, inverts his
meaning; he never refers to the Altar and the radiating
roads but shows in all his interpretations of the Faustian
or modern mind that he is thinking of them. The
Cavern is identified in the Hermetic Fragments with
the Heavens, and it is so identified by Spengler, but to
the Hermetic writer the Heavens were the orbit of the
stars and planets, the source of all calendars, the symbol
of the soul's birth and rebirth. The Cavern is Time,
and to call it Space, as Spengler does, is to suffer the
modern conception of a finite space always returning to
itself to obsess one's thought; and nothing but a like
obsession with what somebody has called the "Time

[1] I am amused to notice, though I do not give it great significance, that the Etruscans, who, according to Frobenius, had a
mythology of the central Altar, turned like the *Creative Mind* from
East to West when they prayed, whereas the races of the Cavern
turned like the *Will* from West to East.

philosophy" of our day can have made Spengler identify
the Faustian soul, which, as he points out, has created
the great windows of the cathedrals and is always moving outwards, always seeking the unlimited, with Time.
The radiating roads and that mind, which I too consider
essentially Western, could never suggest anything to
ancient man but Space. Though Spengler inverted the
meaning of his symbols, he has so constantly described
them as if he had not, that I find, putting aside his great
learning, and my lack of any, that our thoughts run
together. He probably kept silent about the Altar and
the radiating roads through the scholar's dread that a
too simplifying metaphor might cast doubt upon the
sincerity of his research.

XIV

Only the later Upanishads, according to certain scholars,
were aware of the soul's rebirth. They substituted the
doctrine of Karma for sacrifice and ritual purgation. At
first the sacrifice was almost the sole source of symbol,
its smoke had such and such a meaning, its ascending
flame such another, and by it stood the Brahmin and
the priest; then came the new doctrine "which no
Brahmin ever knew".[1] Instead of a levelling pantheism
came innumerable souls, no two souls alike, a belief
that nothing else exists or that nothing exists, a doctrine
first taught not by priest but by king, a discipline that
seemed always aristocratic, solitary and *antithetical*. I do
not know what Frobenius has written in German, for I

---

[1] When I wrote this sentence I had not met Shree Purohit Swami,
who considers that the Sanskrit words do not mean that the doctrine is not known, but that it is not innate even in a Brahmin
(*Ten Principal Upanishads*, p. 157).

have not that language, but it seems possible that he found in ancient India also his Altar and Cavern where I have found the first distinction between *primary* and *antithetical* civilisations.

XV

When the automatic script began, neither I nor my wife knew, or knew that we knew, that any man had tried to explain history philosophically. I, at any rate, would have said that all written upon the subject was a paragraph in my own *Per Amica Silentia Lunae,* so ignorant a man is a poet and artist. When I came to summarise on paper or in speech what the scripts contained no other theme made me so timid. Then Mr. Gerald Heard, who has since made his own philosophy of history, told me of Henry Adams' two essays, where I found some of the dates I had been given and much of the same interpretation, of Petrie's *Revolutions of Civilisation,* where I found more, and then a few months after the publication of the first edition of *A Vision* a translation of Spengler's *Decline of the West* was published, and I found there a correspondence too great for coincidence between most of his essential dates and those I had received before the publication of his first German edition. After that I discovered for myself Spengler's main source in Vico, and that half the revolutionary thoughts of Europe are a perversion of Vico's philosophy. Marx and Sorel have taken from Vico's cycle, writes Croce, his "idea of the struggle of classes and the regeneration of society by a return to a primitive state of mind and a new barbarism".[1] Cer-

[1] I have read in an essay of Squire's that Lenin studied *The Philosophy of History* at the British Museum.

tainly my instructors have chosen a theme that has
deeply stirred men's minds though the newspapers are
silent about it; the newspapers have the happy counter-
myth of progress; a theme as important perhaps as
Henry Adams thought when he told the Boston Historical Association that were it turned into a science
powerful interests would prevent its publication.

XVI

My instructors certainly expect neither a "primitive
state" nor a return to barbarism as primitivism and
barbarism are ordinarily understood; *antithetical* revelation is an intellectual influx neither from beyond mankind nor born of a virgin, but begotten from our spirit
and history.

XVII

At the birth of Christ took place, and at the coming
antithetical influx will take place, a change equivalent to
the *interchange of the tinctures.* The cone shaped like an
ace of diamonds—in the historical diagram the cone is
folded upon itself—is Solar, religious and vital; those
shaped like an hour-glass Lunar, political and secular;
but *Body of Fate* and *Mask* are in the Solar cones during
a *primary* dispensation, and in the Lunar during an *antithetical*, while *Will* and *Creative Mind* occupy the opposing cones. *Mask* and *Body of Fate* are symbolic woman,
Will and *Creative Mind* symbolic man; the man and
woman of Blake's *Mental Traveller.* Before the birth of
Christ religion and vitality were polytheistic, *antithetical*, and to this the philosophers opposed their
primary, secular thought. Plato thinks all things into

Unity and is the "First Christian". At the birth of
Christ religious life becomes *primary*, secular life *antithetical*—man gives to Caesar the things that are Caesar's.
A *primary* dispensation looking beyond itself towards a
transcendent power is dogmatic, levelling, unifying,
feminine, humane, peace its means and end; an *antithetical* dispensation obeys imminent power, is express-
ive, hierarchical, multiple, masculine, harsh, surgical.
The approaching *antithetical* influx and that particular
antithetical dispensation for which the intellectual preparation has begun will reach its complete systematisation at that moment when, as I have already shown, the
Great Year comes to its intellectual climax. Something
of what I have said it must be, the myth declares, for it
must reverse our era and resume past eras in itself; what
else it must be no man can say, for always at the critical
moment the *Thirteenth Cone*, the sphere, the unique
intervenes.

> Somewhere in sands of the desert
> A shape with lion body and the head of a man,
> A gaze blank and pitiless as the sun,
> Is moving its slow thighs, while all about it
> Reel shadows of the indignant desert birds.

XVIII

The wheel of the *Four Principles* completes its movement in four thousand years. The life of Christ corresponds to the mid-period between birth and death; A.D.
1050 to death; the approaching influx to the mid-point
between death and birth.

DOVE OR SWAN

THE HISTORICAL CONES

The numbers in brackets refer to phases, and the other numbers to dates A.D. The line cutting the cones a little below 250, 900, 1180 and 1927 shows four historical *Faculties* related to the present moment. May 1925.

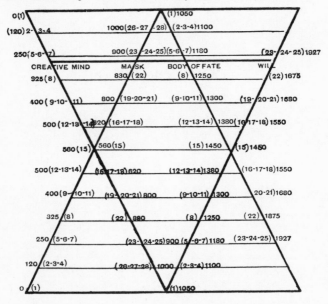

BOOK V: DOVE OR SWAN

I

LEDA

A SUDDEN blow: the great wings beating still
Above the staggering girl, her thighs caressed
By the dark webs, her nape caught in his bill,
He holds her helpless breast upon his breast.

How can those terrified vague fingers push
The feathered glory from her loosening thighs,
And how can body, laid in that white rush,
But feel the strange heart beating where it lies?

A shudder in the loins engenders there
The broken wall, the burning roof and tower
And Agamemnon dead.
                              Being so caught up,
So mastered by the brute blood of the air,
Did she put on his knowledge with his power
Before the indifferent beak could let her drop?

II

STRAY THOUGHTS

One must bear in mind that the Christian Era, like
the two thousand years, let us say, that went before it,
is an entire wheel, and each half of it an entire wheel,
that each half when it comes to its 28th Phase reaches
the 15th Phase or the 1st Phase of the entire era. It
follows therefore that the 15th Phase of each millennium, to keep the symbolic measure of time, is Phase 8
or Phase 22 of the entire era, that Aphrodite rises from

a stormy sea, that Helen could not be Helen but for
beleaguered Troy. The era itself is but half of a greater
era and its Phase 15 comes also at a period of war or
trouble. The greater number is always more *primary*
than the lesser and precisely because it contains it. A
millennium is the symbolic measure of a being that
attains its flexible maturity and then sinks into rigid age.

A civilisation is a struggle to keep self-control, and
in this it is like some great tragic person, some Niobe
who must display an almost superhuman will or the cry
will not touch our sympathy. The loss of control over
thought comes towards the end; first a sinking in upon
the moral being, then the last surrender, the irrational
cry, revelation—the scream of Juno's peacock.

III

2000 B.C. TO A.D. 1

I imagine the annunciation that founded Greece as
made to Leda, remembering that they showed in a
Spartan temple, strung up to the roof as a holy relic,
an unhatched egg of hers; and that from one of her eggs
came Love and from the other War. But all things are
from antithesis, and when in my ignorance I try to
imagine what older civilisation that annunciation rejected
I can but see bird and woman blotting out some corner
of the Babylonian mathematical starlight.[1]

Was it because the older civilisation like the Jewish

[1] Toynbee considers Greece the heir of Crete, and that Greek
religion inherits from the Minoan monotheistic mother goddess
its more mythical conceptions (*A Study of History*, vol. i, p. 92).
'Mathematic Starlight' Babylonian astrology is, however, present
in the friendships and antipathies of the Olympic gods.

thought a long life a proof of Heavenly favour that the Greek races thought those whom the Gods love must die young, hurling upon some age of crowded comedy their tragic sense? Certainly their tribes, after a first multitudinous revelation—dominated each by its *Daimon* and oracle-driven—broke up a great Empire and established in its stead an intellectual anarchy. At some 1000 years before Christ I imagine their religious system complete and they themselves grown barbaric and Asiatic. Then came Homer, civil life, a desire for civil order dependent doubtless on some oracle, and then (Phase 10 of the new millennium) for independent civil life and thought. At, let me say, the sixth century B.C. (Phase 12) personality begins, but there is as yet no intellectual solitude. A man may rule his tribe or town but he cannot separate himself from the general mass. With the first discovery of solitude (Phases 13 and 14) comes, as I think, the visible art that interests us most to-day, for Phidian art, like the art of Raphael, has for the moment exhausted our attention. I recall a Nike at the Ashmolean Museum with a natural unsystematised beauty like that before Raphael, and above all certain pots with strange half-supernatural horses dark on a light ground. Self-realisation attained will bring desire of power—systematisation for its instrument—but as yet clarity, meaning, elegance, all things separated from one another in luminous space, seem to exceed all other virtues. One compares this art with the thought of Greek philosophers before Anaxagoras, where one discovers the same phases, always more concerned with the truth than with its moral or political effects. One longs for the lost dramatists, the plays that were enacted before Aeschylus and Sophocles arose, both Phidian men.

But one must consider not the movement only from the beginning to the end of the ascending cone, but the gyres that touch its sides, the horizontal dance.

> Hands gripped in hands, toes close together,
> Hair spread on the wind they made;
> That lady and that golden king
> Could like a brace of blackbirds sing.

Side by side with Ionic elegance there comes after the Persian wars a Doric vigour, and the light-limbed dandy of the potters, the Parisian-looking young woman of the sculptors, her hair elaborately curled, give place to the athlete. One suspects a deliberate turning away from all that is Eastern, or a moral propaganda like that which turned the poets out of Plato's Republic, and yet it may be that the preparation for the final systematisation had for its apparent cause the destruction, let us say, of Ionic studios by the Persian invaders, and that all came from the resistance of the *Body of Fate* to the growing solitude of the soul. Then in Phidias Ionic and Doric influence unite—one remembers Titian—and all is transformed by the full moon, and all abounds and flows. With Callimachus pure Ionic revives again, as Furtwängler has proved, and upon the only example of his work known to us, a marble chair, a Persian is represented, and may one not discover a Persian symbol in that bronze lamp, shaped like a palm, known to us by a description in Pausanias? But he was an archaistic workman, and those who set him to work brought back public life to an older form. One may see in masters and man a momentary dip into ebbing Asia.

Each age unwinds the thread another age had wound, and it amuses one to remember that before Phidias, and

his westward-moving art, Persia fell, and that when
full moon came round again, amid eastward-moving
thought, and brought Byzantine glory, Rome fell; and
that at the outset of our westward-moving Renaissance
Byzantium fell; all things dying each other's life, living
each other's death.

After Phidias the life of Greece, which being *antithetical* had moved slowly and richly through the *antithetical* phases, comes rapidly to an end. Some Greek or
Roman writer whose name I forget will soon speak of
the declining comeliness of the people, and in the arts
all is systematised more and more, and the antagonist
recedes. Aristophanes' passion-clouded eye falls before
what one must believe, from Roman stage copies, an
idler glance. (Phases 19, 20, 21.) Aristotle and Plato end
creative system—to die into the truth is still to die—and
formula begins. Yet even the truth into which Plato dies
is a form of death, for when he separates the Eternal
Ideas from Nature and shows them self-sustained he
prepares the Christian desert and the Stoic suicide.

I identify the conquest of Alexander and the break-
up of his kingdom, when Greek civilisation, formalised
and codified, loses itself in Asia, with the beginning and
end of the 22nd Phase, and his intention recorded by
some historian to turn his arms westward shows that he
is but a part of the impulse that creates Hellenised
Rome and Asia. There are everywhere statues where
every muscle has been measured, every position debated,
and these statues represent man with nothing more to
achieve, physical man finished and complacent, the
women slightly tinted, but the men, it may be, who
exercise naked in the open air, the colour of mahogany.
Every discovery after the epoch of victory and defeat

(Phase 22) which substitutes mechanics for power is an elimination of intellect by delight in technical skill (Phase 23), by a sense of the past (Phase 24), by some dominant belief (Phase 25). After Plato and Aristotle, the mind is as exhausted as were the armies of Alexander at his death, but the Stoics can discover morals and turn philosophy into a rule of life. Among them doubtless—the first beneficiaries of Plato's hatred of imitation —we may discover the first benefactors of our modern individuality, sincerity of the trivial face, the mask torn away. Then, a Greece that Rome has conquered, and a Rome conquered by Greece, must, in the last three phases of the wheel, adore, desire being dead, physical or spiritual force.

This adoration which begins in the second century before Christ creates a world-wide religious movement as the world was then known, which, being swallowed up in what came after, has left no adequate record. One knows not into how great extravagance Asia, accustomed to abase itself, may have carried what soon sent Greeks and Romans to stand naked in a Mithraic pit, moving their bodies as under a shower-bath that those bodies might receive the blood of the bull even to the last drop. The adored image took everywhere the only form possible as the *antithetical* age died into its last violence—a human or animal form. Even before Plato that collective image of man dear to Stoic and Epicurean alike, the moral double of bronze or marble athlete, had been invoked by Anaxagoras when he declared that thought and not the warring opposites created the world. At that sentence the heroic life, passionate fragmentary man, all that had been imagined by great poets and sculptors began to pass away, and instead of seeking noble antagonists, imagination moved towards divine man and the ridiculous devil. Now must sages lure men away from the arms of women because in those arms man becomes a fragment; and all is ready for revelation.

When revelation comes athlete and sage are merged; the earliest sculptured image of Christ is copied from that of the Apotheosis of Alexander the Great; the tradition is founded which declares even to our own day that Christ alone was exactly six feet high, perfect physical man. Yet as perfect physical man He must die, for only so can *primary* power reach *antithetical* mankind shut within the circle of its senses, touching outward things alone in that which seems most personal and physical. When I think of the moment before revelation I think of Salome—she, too, delicately tinted or maybe mahogany dark—dancing before Herod and receiving the Prophet's head in her indifferent hands, and wonder if what seems to us decadence was not in reality the exaltation of the muscular flesh and of civilisation perfectly achieved. Seeking images, I see her anoint her bare limbs according to a medical prescription of that time, with lion's fat, for lack of the sun's ray, that she may gain the favour of a king, and remember that the same impulse will create the Galilean revelation and deify Roman Emperors whose sculptured heads will be surrounded by the solar disk. Upon the throne and upon the cross alike the myth becomes a biography.

IV

A.D. 1 TO A.D. 1050

God is now conceived of as something outside man and man's handiwork, and it follows that it must be idolatry to worship that which Phidias and Scopas made, and seeing that He is a Father in Heaven, that Heaven will be found presently in the Thebaid, where the world is changed into a featureless dust and can be run through the fingers; and these things are testified to from books that are outside human genius, being miraculous, and by a miraculous Church, and this Church, as the gyre sweeps wider, will make man also featureless as clay or dust. Night will fall upon man's wisdom now that man has been taught that he is nothing. He had discovered, or half-discovered, that the world is round and one of many like it, but now he must believe that the sky is but a tent spread above a level floor, and that he may be stirred into a frenzy of anxiety and so to moral transformation, blot out the knowledge or half-knowledge that he has lived many times, and think that all eternity depends upon a moment's decision. Heaven itself, transformation finished, must appear so vague and motionless that it seems but a concession to human weakness. It is even essential to this faith to declare that God's messengers, those beings who show His will in dreams or announce it in visionary speech, were never men. The Greeks thought them great men of the past, but now that concession to mankind is forbidden. All must be narrowed into the sun's image cast out of a burning-glass and man be ignorant of all but the image.

The mind that brought the change, if considered as man only, is a climax of whatever Greek and Roman thought was most a contradiction to its age; but considered as more than man He controlled what Neo-Pythagorean and Stoic could not—irrational force. He could announce the new age, all that had not been thought of, or touched, or seen, because He could substitute for reason, miracle.

We say of Him because His sacrifice was voluntary that He was love itself, and yet that part of Him which made Christendom was not love but pity, and not pity for intellectual despair, though the man in Him, being *antithetical* like His age, knew it in the Garden, but *primary* pity, that for the common lot, man's death, seeing that He raised Lazarus, sickness, seeing that He healed many, sin, seeing that He died.

Love is created and preserved by intellectual analysis, for we love only that which is unique, and it belongs to contemplation, not to action, for we would not change that which we love. A lover will admit a greater beauty than that of his mistress but not its like, and surrenders his days to a delighted laborious study of all her ways and looks, and he pities only if something threatens that which has never been before and can never be again. Fragment delights in fragment and seeks possession, not service; whereas the Good Samaritan discovers himself in the likeness of another, covered with sores and abandoned by thieves upon the roadside, and in that other serves himself. The opposites are gone; he does not need his Lazarus; they do not each die the other's life, live the other's death.

It is impossible to do more than select an arbitrary general date for the beginning of Roman decay (Phases 2 to 7, A.D. 1 to A.D. 250). Roman sculpture—sculpture made under Roman influence whatever the sculptor's blood—did not, for instance, reach its full vigour, if we consider what it had of Roman as distinct from Greek, until the Christian Era. It even made a discovery which affected all sculpture to come. The Greeks painted the eyes of marble statues and made out of enamel or glass or precious stones those of their bronze statues, but the Roman was the first to drill a round hole to represent the pupil, and because, as I think, of a preoccupation with the glance characteristic of a civilisation in its final phase. The colours must have already faded from the marbles of the great period, and a shadow and a spot of light, especially where there is much sunlight, are more vivid than paint, enamel, coloured glass or precious stone. They could now express in stone a perfect composure. The administrative mind, alert attention had driven out rhythm, exaltation of the body, uncommitted energy. May it not have been precisely a talent for this alert attention that had enabled Rome and not Greece to express those final *primary* phases? One sees on the pediments troops of marble Senators, officials serene and watchful as befits men who know that all the power of the world moves before their eyes, and needs, that it may not dash itself to pieces, their unhurried, unanxious, never-ceasing care. Those riders upon the Parthenon had all the world's power in their moving bodies, and in a movement that seemed, so were the hearts of man and beast set upon it, that of a dance; but presently all would change and measurement succeed to pleasure, the dancing-master outlive the dance. What need had those young lads for careful eyes? But in Rome of the first and second centuries, where the dancing-master himself has died, the delineation of character as shown in face and head, as with us of recent years, is all in all, and sculptors, seeking the custom of occupied officials, stock in their workshops toga'd marble bodies upon which can be screwed with the least possible delay heads modelled from the sitters with the most scrupulous realism. When I think of Rome I see always those heads with their world-considering eyes, and those bodies as conventional as the metaphors in a leading article, and compare in my imagination vague Grecian eyes gazing at nothing, Byzantine eyes of drilled ivory staring upon a vision, and those eyelids of China and of India, those veiled or half-veiled eyes weary of world and vision alike.

Meanwhile the irrational force that would create confusion and uproar as with the cry "The Babe, the Babe is born"—the women speaking unknown tongues, the barbers and weavers expounding Divine revelation with all the vulgarity of their servitude, the tables that move or resound with raps—but creates a negligible sect.

All about it is an *antithetical* aristocratic civilisation in its completed form, every detail of life hierarchical, every great man's door crowded at dawn by petitioners, great wealth everywhere in few men's hands, all dependent upon a few, up to the Emperor himself who is a God dependent upon a greater God, and everywhere in court, in the family, an inequality made law, and floating over all the Romanised Gods of Greece in their physical superiority. All is rigid and stationary, men fight for centuries with the same sword and spear, and though in naval warfare there is some change of tactics to avoid those single combats of ship with ship that needed the seamanship of a more skilful age, the speed of a sailing ship remains unchanged from the time of Pericles to that of Constantine. Though sculpture grows more and more realistic and so renews its vigour, this realism is without curiosity. The athlete becomes the boxer that he may show lips and nose beaten out of shape, the individual hairs show at the navel of the bronze centaur, but the theme has not changed. Philosophy alone, where in contact with irrational force—holding to Egyptian thaumaturgy and the Judean miracle but at arm's length—can startle and create. Yet Plotinus is as *primary*, as much a contradiction of all that created Roman civilisation, as St. Peter, and his thought has its roots almost as deep among the *primary* masses. The founder of his school was Ammonius Sacca, an Alexandrine porter. His thought and that of Origen, which I skimmed in my youth, seem to me to express the abstract synthesis of a quality like that of race, and so to display a character which must always precede Phase 8. Origen, because the Judean miracle has a stronger hold upon the masses than Alexandrian thaumaturgy, triumphs when Constantine (Phase 8) puts the Cross upon the shields of his soldiers and makes the bit of his war-horse from a nail of the True Cross, an act equivalent to man's cry for strength amid the animal chaos at the close of the first lunar quarter. Seeing that Constantine was not converted till upon his deathbed, I see him as half statesman, half thaumaturgist, accepting in blind obedience to a dream the new fashionable talisman, two sticks nailed together. The Christians were but six millions of the sixty or seventy of the Roman Empire, but, spending nothing upon pleasure, exceedingly rich like some Nonconformist sect of the eighteenth century. The world became Christian, "that fabulous formless darkness" as it seemed to a philosopher of the fourth century, blotted out "every beautiful thing", not through the conversion of crowds or general change of opinion, or through any pressure from below, for civilization was *antithetical* still, but by an act of power.

I have not the knowledge (it may be that no man has the knowledge) to trace the rise of the Byzantine State through Phases 9, 10 and 11. My diagram tells me that a hundred and sixty years brought that State to its 15th Phase, but I that know nothing but the arts and of these little, cannot revise the series of dates "approximately correct" but given, it may be, for suggestion only. With a desire for simplicity of statement I would have preferred to find in the middle, not at the end, of the fifth century Phase 12, for that was, so far as the known evidence carries us, the moment when Byzantium became Byzantine and substituted for formal Roman magnificence, with its glorification of physical power, an architecture that suggests the Sacred City in the Apocalypse of St. John. I think if I could be given a month of Antiquity and leave to spend it where I chose, I would spend it in Byzantium a little before Justinian opened St. Sophia and closed the Academy of Plato. I think I could find in some little wine-shop some philosophical worker in mosaic who could answer all my questions, the supernatural descending nearer to him than to Plotinus even, for the pride of his delicate skill would make what was an instrument of power to princes and clerics, a murderous madness in the mob, show as a lovely flexible presence like that of a perfect human body.

I think that in early Byzantium, maybe never before or since in recorded history, religious, aesthetic and practical life were one, that architect and artificers —though not, it may be, poets, for language had been the instrument of controversy and must have grown abstract—spoke to the multitude and the few alike. The painter, the mosaic worker, the worker in gold and silver, the illuminator of sacred books, were almost impersonal, almost perhaps without the consciousness of individual design, absorbed in their subject-matter and that the vision of a whole people. They could copy out of old Gospel books those pictures that seemed as sacred as the text, and yet weave all into a vast design, the work of many that seemed the work of one, that made building, picture, pattern, metal-work of rail and lamp, seem but a single image; and this vision, this proclamation of their invisible master, had the Greek nobility, Satan always the still half-divine Serpent, never the horned scarecrow of the didactic Middle Ages.

The ascetic, called in Alexandria "God's Athlete", has taken the place of those Greek athletes whose statues have been melted or broken up or stand deserted in the midst of cornfields, but all about him is an incredible splendour like that which we see pass under our closed eyelids as we lie between sleep and waking, no representation of a living world but the dream of a somnambulist. Even the drilled pupil of the eye, when the drill is in the hand of some Byzantine worker in ivory, undergoes a somnambulistic change, for its deep shadow among the faint lines of the tablet, its mechanical circle, where all else is rhythmical and flowing, give to Saint or Angel a look of some great bird staring at miracle. Could any visionary of those days, passing through the Church named with so un-theological a grace "The Holy Wisdom", can even a visionary of to-day wandering among the mosaics at Ravenne or in Sicily, fail to recognise some one image seen under his closed eyelids? To me it seems that He, who among the first Christian communities was little but a ghostly exorcist,

had in His assent to a full Divinity made possible this
sinking-in upon a supernatural splendour, these walls
with their little glimmering cubes of blue and green
and gold.

I think that I might discover an oscillation, a revolution of the horizontal gyre like that between Doric and
Ionic art, between the two principal characters of
Byzantine art. Recent criticism distinguishes between
Greco-Roman figures, their stern faces suggesting Greek
wall-painting at Palmyra, Greco-Egyptian painting upon
the cases of mummies, where character delineations are
exaggerated as in much work of our time, and that decoration which seems to undermine our self-control, and is,
it seems, of Persian origin, and has for its appropriate
symbol a vine whose tendrils climb everywhere and
display among their leaves all those strange images of
bird and beast, those forms that represent no creature
eye has ever seen, yet are begotten one upon the other
as if they were themselves living creatures. May I consider the domination of the first *antithetical* and that of
the second *primary*, and see in their alternation the work
of the horizontal gyre? Strzygowski thinks that the
church decorations where there are visible representa-
tions of holy persons were especially dear to those who
believed in Christ's double nature, and that wherever
Christ is represented by a bare Cross and all the rest is
bird and beast and tree, we may discover an Asiatic art
dear to those who thought Christ contained nothing
human.

If I were left to myself I would make Phase 15 coincide with Justinian's reign, that great age of building
in which one may conclude Byzantine art was perfected;
but the meaning of the diagram may be that a building

like St. Sophia, where all, to judge by the contemporary
description, pictured ecstasy, must unlike the declamatory St. Peter's precede the moment of climax. Of the
moment of climax itself I can say nothing, and of what
followed from Phase 17 to Phase 21 almost nothing, for
I have no knowledge of the time; and no analogy from
the age after Phidias, or after our own Renaissance, can
help. We and the Greeks moved towards intellect, but
Byzantium and the Western Europe of that day moved
from it. If Strzygowski is right we may see in the
destruction of images but a destruction of what was
Greek in decoration accompanied perhaps by a renewed
splendour in all that came down from the ancient
Persian Paradise, an episode in some attempt to make
theology more ascetic, spiritual and abstract. Destruction was apparently suggested to the first iconoclastic
Emperor by followers of a Monophysite Bishop,
Xenaias, who had his see in that part of the Empire
where Persian influence had been strongest. The return
of the images may, as I see things, have been the failure
of synthesis (Phase 22) and the first sinking-in and
dying-down of Christendom into the heterogeneous
loam. Did Europe grow animal and literal? Did the
strength of the victorious party come from zealots as
ready as their opponents to destroy an image if permitted to grind it into powder, mix it with some
liquid and swallow it as a medicine? Did mankind
for a season do, not what it would, or should, but what
it could, accept the past and the current belief because
they prevented thought? In Western Europe I think I
may see in Johannes Scotus Erigena the last intellectual
synthesis before the death of philosophy, but I know
little of him except that he is founded upon a Greek

book of the sixth century, put into circulation by a last
iconoclastic Emperor, though its Angelic Orders gave
a theme to the image-makers. I notice too that my
diagram makes Phase 22 coincide with the break-up
of Charlemagne's Empire and so clearly likens him to
Alexander, but I do not want to concern myself, except
where I must, with political events.

Then follows, as always must in the last quarter,
heterogeneous art; hesitation amid architectural forms,
some book tells me; an interest in Greek and Roman
literature; much copying out and gathering together;
yet outside a few courts and monasteries another book
tells me an Asiatic and anarchic Europe. The intellectual cone has so narrowed that secular intellect
has gone, and the strong man rules with the aid of
local custom; everywhere the supernatural is sudden,
violent, and as dark to the intellect as a stroke or St.
Vitus' dance. Men under the Caesars, my own docu-
ments tell me, were physically one but intellectually
many, but that is now reversed, for there is one common
thought or doctrine, town is shut off from town, village
from village, clan from clan. The spiritual life is alone
overflowing, its cone expanded, and yet this life—
secular intellect extinguished—has little effect upon
men's conduct, is perhaps a dream which passes beyond
the reach of conscious mind but for some rare miracle or
vision. I think of it as like that profound reverie of the
somnambulist which may be accompanied by a sensuous
dream—a Romanesque stream perhaps of bird and beast
images—and yet neither affect the dream nor be affected
by it.

It is indeed precisely because this double mind is
created at full moon that the *antithetical* phases are but,

at the best, phases of a momentary illumination like
that of a lightning flash. But the full moon that now
concerns us is not only Phase 15 of its greater era, but
the final phase, Phase 28, of its millennium, and in its
physical form, human life grown once more automatic.
I knew a man once who, seeking for an image of the
Absolute, saw one persistent image, a slug, as though
it were suggested to him that Being which is beyond
human comprehension is mirrored in the least organised
forms of life. Intellectual creation has ceased, but men
have come to terms with the supernatural and are agreed
that, if you make the usual offerings, it will remember
to live and let live; even Saint or Angel does not seem
very different from themselves: a man thinks his
guardian Angel jealous of his mistress; a King, dragging a Saint's body to a new church, meets some
difficulty upon the road, assumes a miracle, and de-
nounces the Saint as a churl. Three Roman courtesans
who have one after another got their favourite lovers
chosen Pope have, it pleases one's mockery to think,
confessed their sins, with full belief in the supernatural
efficacy of the act, to ears that have heard their cries of
love, or received the Body of God from hands that have
played with their own bodies. Interest has narrowed to
what is near and personal and, seeing that all abstract
secular thought has faded, those interests have taken the
most physical forms. In monasteries and in hermit cells
men freed from the intellect at last can seek their God
upon all fours like beasts or children. Ecclesiastical
Law, in so far as that law is concerned not with government, Church or State, but with the individual soul, is
complete; all that is necessary to salvation is known, yet
there is apathy everywhere. Man awaits death and

judgment with nothing to occupy the worldly faculties
and helpless before the world's disorder, drags out of
the subconscious the conviction that the world is about
to end. Hidden, except at rare moments of excitement
or revelation, even then shown but in symbol, the stream
set in motion by the Galilean Symbol has filled its
basin, and seems motionless for an instant before it falls
over the rim. In the midst of the basin stands, in
motionless contemplation, blood that is not His blood
upon His Hands and Feet, One that feels but for the
common lot, and mourns over the length of years and
the inadequacy of man's fate to man. Two thousand
years before, His predecessor, careful of heroic men
alone, had so stood and mourned over the shortness of
time, and man's inadequacy to his fate.

Full moon over, that last Embodiment shall grow
more like ourselves, putting off that stern majesty,
borrowed, it may be, from the Phidian Zeus—if we can
trust Cefalù and Monreale; and His Mother—putting
off her harsh Byzantine image—stand at His side.

V

A.D. 1050 TO THE PRESENT DAY

When the tide changed and faith no longer sufficed,
something must have happened in the courts and castles
of which history has perhaps no record, for with the
first vague dawn of the ultimate *antithetical* revelation
man, under the eyes of the Virgin, or upon the breast
of his mistress, became but a fragment. Instead of that
old alternation, brute or ascetic, came something obscure or uncertain that could not find its full explanation
for a thousand years. A certain Byzantine Bishop had

said upon seeing a singer of Antioch, "I looked long upon her beauty, knowing that I would behold it upon the day of judgment, and I wept to remember that I had taken less care of my soul than she of her body", but when in the *Arabian Nights* Harun Al-Rashid looked at the singer Heart's Miracle, and on the instant loved her, he covered her head with a little silk veil to show that her beauty "had already retreated into the mystery of our faith". The Bishop saw a beauty that would be sanctified, but the Caliph that which was its own sanctity, and it was this latter sanctity, come back from the first Crusade or up from Arabian Spain or half Asiatic Provence and Sicily, that created romance. What forgotten reverie, what initiation, it may be, separated wisdom from the monastery and, creating Merlin, joined it to passion? When Merlin in Chrestien de Troyes loved Ninian he showed her a cavern adorned with gold mosaics and made by a prince for his beloved, and told her that those lovers died upon the same day and were laid "in the chamber where they found delight". He thereupon lifted a slab of red marble that his art alone could lift and showed them wrapped in winding-sheets of white samite. The tomb remained open, for Ninian asked that she and Merlin might return to the cavern and spend their night near those dead lovers, but before night came Merlin grew sad and fell asleep, and she and her attendants took him "by head and foot" and laid him "in the tomb and replaced the stone", for Merlin had taught her the magic words, and "from that hour none beheld Merlin dead or alive". Throughout the German *Parsifal* there is no ceremony of the Church, neither Marriage nor Mass nor Baptism, but instead we discover that strangest creation of romance or of life, "the love trance". Parsifal in such a trance, seeing nothing before his eyes but the image of his absent love, overcame knight after knight, and awakening at last looked amazed upon his dinted sword and shield; and it is to his lady and not to God or the Virgin that Parsifal prayed upon the day of battle, and it was his lady's soul, separated from her entranced or sleeping body, that went beside him and gave him victory.

The period from 1005 to 1180 is attributed in the diagram to the first two gyres of our millennium, and what interests me in this period, which corresponds to the Homeric period some two thousand years before, is the creation of the Arthurian Tales and Romanesque architecture. I see in Romanesque the first movement to a secular Europe, but a movement so instinctive that as yet there is no antagonism to the old condition. Every architect, every man who lifts a chisel, may be a cleric of some kind, yet in the overflowing ornament where the human form has all but disappeared and where no bird or beast is copied from nature, where all is more Asiatic than Byzantium itself, one discovers the same impulse that created Merlin and his jugglery.

I do not see in Gothic architecture, which is a character of the next gyre, that of Phases 5, 6 and 7, as did the nineteenth-century historians, ever looking for the image of their own age, the creation of a new communal freedom, but a creation of authority, a suppression of that freedom though with its consent, and certainly St. Bernard when he denounced the extravagance of Romanesque saw it in that light. I think of that curious sketchbook of Villars de Honecourt with its insistence upon mathematical form, and I see that form in Mont St. Michel—Church, Abbey, Fort and town, all that dark

geometry that makes Byzantium seem a sunlit cloud—
and it seems to me that the Church grows secular that
it may fight a new-born secular world. Its avowed appeal
is to religion alone: nobles and great ladies join the
crowds that drag the Cathedral stones, not out of love
for beauty but because the stones as they are trundled
down the road cure the halt and the blind; yet the
stones once set up traffic with the enemy. The mosaic
pictures grown transparent fill the windows, quarrel
one with the other like pretty women, and draw all
eyes, and upon the faces of the statues flits once more
the smile that disappeared with archaic Greece. That
smile is physical, *primary* joy, the escape from supernatural terror, a moment of irresponsible common life
before *antithetical* sadness begins. It is as though the
pretty worshippers, while the Dominican was preaching
with a new and perhaps incredible sternness, let their
imaginations stray, as though the observant sculptor,
or worker in ivory, in modelling his holy women has
remembered their smiling lips.

Are not the cathedrals and the philosophy of St.
Thomas the product of the abstraction that comes
before Phase 8 as before Phase 22, and of the moral synthesis that at the end of the first quarter seeks to control
the general anarchy? That anarchy must have been exceedingly great, or man must have found a hitherto unknown sensitiveness, for it was the shock that created
modern civilisation. The diagram makes the period from
1250 to 1300 correspond to Phase 8, certainly because in
or near that period, chivalry and Christendom having
proved insufficient, the King mastered the one, the
Church the other, reversing the achievement of Constantine, for it was now the mitre and the crown that protected

the Cross. I prefer, however, to find my example of the first victory of personality where I have more knowledge. Dante in the *Convito* mourns for solitude, lost through poverty, and writes the first sentence of modern autobiography, and in the *Divina Commedia* imposes his own personality upon a system and a phantasmagoria hitherto impersonal; the King everywhere has found his kingdom.

The period from 1300 to 1380 is attributed to the fourth gyre, that of Phases 9, 10 and 11, which finds its character in painting from Giotto to Fra Angelico, in the Chronicles of Froissart and in the elaborate canopy upon the stained glass of the windows. Every old tale is alive, Christendom still unbroken; painter and poet alike find new ornament for the tale, they feel the charm of everything but the more poignantly because that charm is archaistic; they smell a pot of dried roses. The practical men, face to face with rebellion and heresy, are violent as they have not been for generations, but the artists separated from life by the tradition of Byzantium can even exaggerate their gentleness, and gentleness and violence alike express the gyre's hesitation. The public certainty that sufficed for Dante and St. Thomas has disappeared, and there is yet no private certainty. Is it that the human mind now longs for solitude, for escape from all that hereditary splendour, and does not know what ails it; or is it that the Image itself encouraged by the new technical method, the flexible brush-stroke instead of the unchanging cube of glass, and wearied of its part in a crowded ghostly dance, longs for a solitary human body? That body comes in the period from 1380 to 1450 and is discovered by Masaccio, and by Chaucer who is partly of the old gyre, and by Villon who is wholly of the new.

Masaccio, a precocious and abundant man, dying

like Aubrey Beardsley in his six-and-twentieth year,
cannot move us, as he did his immediate successors,
for he discovered a naturalism that begins to weary
us a little; making the naked young man awaiting
baptism shiver with the cold, St. Peter grow red with
the exertion of dragging the money out of the miraculous fish's mouth, while Adam and Eve, flying before
the sword of the Angel, show faces disfigured by their
suffering. It is very likely because I am a poet and not a
painter that I feel so much more keenly that suffering
of Villon—of the 13th Phase as man, and of it or near it
in epoch—in whom the human soul for the first time
stands alone before a death ever present to imagination,
without help from a Church that is fading away; or is it
that I remember Aubrey Beardsley, a man of like phase
though so different epoch, and so read into Villon's
suffering our modern conscience which gathers intensity
as we approach the close of an era? Intensity that has
seemed to me pitiless self-judgment may have been but
heroic gaiety. With the approach of solitude bringing
with it an ever-increasing struggle with that which
opposes solitude—sensuality, greed, ambition, physical
curiosity in all its species—philosophy has returned
driving dogma out. Even amongst the most pious the
worshipper is preoccupied with himself, and when I
look for the drilled eyeball, which reveals so much, I
notice that its edge is no longer so mechanically perfect,
nor, if I can judge by casts at the Victoria and Albert
Museum, is the hollow so deep. Angel and Florentine
noble must look upward with an eye that seems dim
and abashed as though to recognise duties to Heaven,
an example to be set before men, and finding both difficult seem a little giddy. There are no miracles to stare

at, for man descends the hill he once climbed with so
great toil, and all grows but natural again.

As we approach the 15th Phase, as the general movement grows more and more westward in character, we
notice the oscillation of the horizontal gyres, as though
what no Unity of Being, yet possible, can completely
fuse displays itself in triumph.

Donatello, as later Michael Angelo, reflects the hard-
ness and astringency of Myron, and foretells what must
follow the Renaissance; while Jacopo della Guercia and
most of the painters seem by contrast, as Raphael later
on, Ionic and Asiatic. The period from 1450 to 1550 is
allotted to the gyre of Phase 15, and these dates are no
doubt intended to mark somewhat vaguely a period that
begins in one country earlier and in another later. I do
not myself find it possible to make more than the first
half coincide with the central moment, Phase 15 of the
Italian Renaissance—Phase 22 of the cone of the entire
era—the breaking of the Christian synthesis as the corresponding period before Christ, the age of Phidias, was
the breaking of Greek traditional faith. The first half
covers the principal activity of the Academy of Florence
which formulated the reconciliation of Paganism and
Christianity. This reconciliation, which to Pope Julius
meant that Greek and Roman Antiquity were as sacred
as that of Judea, and like it "a vestibule of Christianity",
meant to the mind of Dürer—a visitor to Venice during
the movement of the gyre—that the human norm,
discovered from the measurement of ancient statues,
was God's first handiwork, that "perfectly proportioned
human body" which had seemed to Dante Unity of
Being symbolised. The ascetic, who had a thousand years
before attained his transfiguration upon the golden

ground of Byzantine mosaic, had turned not into an
athlete but into that unlabouring form the athlete
dreamed of: the second Adam had become the first.

Because the 15th Phase can never find direct human
expression, being a supernatural incarnation, it im-
pressed upon work and thought an element of strain
and artifice, a desire to combine elements which may be
incompatible, or which suggest by their combination
something supernatural. Had some Florentine Platonist
read to Botticelli Porphyry upon the Cave of the
Nymphs? for I seem to recognise it in that curious cave,
with a thatched roof over the nearer entrance to make it
resemble the conventional manger, in his "Nativity"[1]
in the National Gallery. Certainly the glimpse of forest
trees, dim in the evening light, through the far entrance,
and the deliberate strangeness everywhere, gives one an
emotion of mystery which is new to painting.

Botticelli, Crivelli, Mantegna, Da Vinci, who fall
within the period, make Masaccio and his school seem
heavy and common by something we may call intellectual beauty or compare perhaps to that kind of bodily

[1] There is a Greek inscription at the top of the picture which says
that Botticelli's world is in the "second woe" of the Apocalypse,
and that after certain other Apocalyptic events the Christ of the
picture will appear. He had found, maybe in some utterance of
Savonarola's, a promise of an ultimate Marriage of Heaven and Earth,
of sacred and profane, and pictures it by the Angels and shepherds
embracing, and as I suggest by Cave and Manger. When I saw the
Cave of Mithras at Capri I wondered if that were Porphyry's Cave.
The two entrances are there, one reached by a stair of a hundred
feet or so from the sea and once trodden by devout sailors, and one
reached from above by some hundred and fifty steps and used, my
guide-book tells me, by priests. If he knew that cave, which may have
had its recognised symbolism, he would have been the more ready
to discover symbols in the cave where Odysseus landed in Ithaca.

beauty which Castiglione called "the spoil or monu-
ment of the victory of the soul". Intellect and emotion,
primary curiosity and the *antithetical* dream, are for the
moment one. Since the rebirth of the secular intellect
in the eleventh century, faculty has been separating from
faculty, poetry from music, the worshipper from the
worshipped, but all have remained within a common
fading circle—Christendom—and so within the human
soul. Image has been separated from image but always
as an exploration of the soul itself; forms have been displayed in an always clear light, have been perfected by
separation from one another till their link with one
another and with common associations has been broken;
but, Phase 15 past, these forms begin to jostle and fall
into confusion, there is as it were a sudden rush and
storm. In the mind of the artist a desire for power
succeeds to that for knowledge, and this desire is com-
municated to the forms and to the onlooker.

The eighth gyre, which corresponds to Phases 16,
17 and 18 and completes itself say between 1550 and
1650, begins with Raphael, Michael Angelo and Titian,
and the forms, as in Titian, awaken sexual desire—we
had not desired to touch the forms of Botticelli or even
of Da Vinci—or they threaten us like those of Michael
Angelo, and the painter himself handles his brush with
a conscious facility or exultation. The subject-matter
may arise out of some propaganda as when Raphael in
the Camera della Segnatura, and Michael Angelo in the
Sistine Chapel, put, by direction of the Pope, Greek Sages
and Doctors of the Church, Roman Sibyls and Hebrew
Prophets, opposite one another in apparent equality.
From this on, all is changed, and where the Mother of
God sat enthroned, now that the Soul's unity has been

found and lost, Nature seats herself, and the painter can paint only what he desires in the flesh, and soon, asking less and less for himself, will make it a matter of pride to paint what he does not at all desire. I think Raphael almost of the earlier gyre — perhaps a transitional figure—but Michael Angelo, Rabelais, Aretino, Shakespeare, Titian—Titian is so markedly of the 14th Phase as a man that he seems less characteristic—I associate with the mythopoeic and ungovernable beginning of the eighth gyre. I see in Shakespeare a man in whom human personality, hitherto restrained by its dependence upon Christendom or by its own need for self-control, burst like a shell. Perhaps secular intellect, setting itself free after five hundred years of struggle, has made him the greatest of dramatists, and yet because an *antithetical* age alone could confer upon an art like his the unity of a painting or of a temple pediment, we might, had the total works of Sophocles survived—they too born of a like struggle though with a different enemy—not think him greatest. Do we not feel an unrest like that of travel itself when we watch those personages, more living than ourselves, amid so much that is irrelevant and heterogeneous, amid so much *primary* curiosity, when we are carried from Rome to Venice, from Egypt to Saxon England, or in the one play from Roman to Christian mythology?

Were he not himself of a later phase, were he of the 16th Phase like his age and so drunk with his own wine, he had not written plays at all, but as it is he finds his opportunity among a crowd of men and women who are still shaken by thought that passes from man to man in psychological contagion. I see in Milton, who is characteristic of the moment when the first violence of the gyre has begun to sink, an attempted return to the synthesis of the Camera della Segnatura and the Sistine Chapel. It is this attempt made too late that, amid all the music and magnificence of the still violent gyre, gives him his unreality and his cold rhetoric. The two elements have fallen apart in the hymn "On the Morning of Christ's Nativity", the one is sacred, the other profane; his classical mythology is an artificial ornament; whereas no great Italian artist from 1450 to the sack of Rome saw any difference between them, and when difference came, as it did with Titian, it was God and the Angels that seemed artificial.

The gyre ebbs out in order and reason, the Jacobean poets succeed the Elizabethan, Cowley and Dryden the Jacobean as belief dies out. Elsewhere Christendom keeps a kind of spectral unity for a while, now with one, now with the other element of the synthesis dominant; a declamatory holiness defaces old churches, innumerable Tritons and Neptunes pour water from their mouths. What had been a beauty like the burning sun fades out in Vandyke's noble ineffectual faces, and the Low Countries, which have reached the new gyre long before the rest of Europe, convert the world to a still limited curiosity, to certain recognised forms of the picturesque constantly repeated, chance travellers at an inn door, men about a fire, men skating, the same pose or grouping, where the subject is different, passing from picture to picture. The world begins to long for the arbitrary and accidental, for the grotesque, the repulsive and the terrible, that it may be cured of desire. The moment has come for the ninth gyre, Phases 19, 20 and 21, for the period that begins for the greater part of Europe with 1650 and lasts, it may be, to 1875.

The beginning of the gyre like that of its forerunner
is violent, a breaking of the soul and world into fragments, and has for a chief character the materialistic
movement at the end of the seventeenth century, all
that comes out of Bacon perhaps, the foundation of our
modern inductive reasoning, the declamatory religious
sects and controversies that.first in England and then in
France destroy the sense of form, all that has its very
image and idol in Bernini's big Altar in St. Peter's
with its figures contorted and convulsed by religion as
though by the devil. Men change rapidly from deduction
to deduction, opinion to opinion, have but one impression at a time and utter it always, no matter how often
they change, with the same emphasis. Then the gyre
develops a new coherence in the external scene; and
violent men, each master of some generalisation, arise
one after another: Napoleon, a man of the 20th Phase
in the historical 21st—personality in its hard final
generalisation—typical of all. The artistic life, where
most characteristic of the general movement, shows the
effect of the closing of the *tinctures*. It is external, sentimental and logical—the poetry of Pope and Gray, the
philosophy of Johnson and of Rousseau—equally simple
in emotion or in thought, the old oscillation in a new
form. Personality is everywhere spreading out its fingers
in vain, or grasping with an always more convulsive
grasp a world where the predominance of physical
science, of finance and economics in all their forms, of
democratic politics, of vast populations, of architecture
where styles jostle one another, of newspapers where all
is heterogeneous, show that mechanical force will in a
moment become supreme.

That art discovered by Dante of marshalling into a

vast *antithetical* structure *antithetical* material became
through Milton Latinised and artificial—the Shades, as
Sir Thomas Browne said, "steal or contrive a body"—
and now it changes that it may marshal into a still
antithetical structure *primary* material, and the modern
novel is created, but even before the gyre is drawn
to its end the happy ending, the admired hero, the
preoccupation with desirable things, all that is un-
disguisedly *antithetical* disappears.

All the art of the gyre that is not derived from the
external scene is a Renaissance echo growing always
more conventional or more shadowy, but since the
Renaissance — Phase 22 of the cone of the era —
the "Emotion of Sanctity", that first relation to the
spiritual primary, has been possible in those things that are
most intimate and personal, though not until Phase 22
of the millennium cone will general thought be ready
for its expression. A mysterious contact is perceptible
first in painting and then in poetry and last in prose.
In painting it comes where the influence of the Low
Countries and that of Italy mingle, but always rarely
and faintly. I do not find it in Watteau, but there is a
preparation for it, a sense of exhaustion of old interests
—"they do not believe even in their own happiness",
Verlaine said—and then suddenly it is present in the
faces of Gainsborough's women as it has been in no face
since the Egyptian sculptor buried in a tomb that image
of a princess carved in wood. Reynolds had nothing of
it, an ostentatious fashionable man fresh from Rome,
he stayed content with fading Renaissance emotion and
modern curiosity. In frail women's faces the soul
awakes—all its prepossessions, the accumulated learning
of centuries swept away—and looks out upon us wise

and foolish like the dawn. Then it is everywhere, it
finds the village Providence of the eighteenth century
and turns him into Goethe, who for all that comes to
no conclusion, his Faust after his hundred years but
reclaiming land like some Sir Charles Grandison or
Voltaire in his old age. It makes the heroines of Jane
Austen seek, not as their grandfathers and grandmothers
would have done, theological or political truth, but
simply good breeding, as though to increase it were
more than any practical accomplishment. In poetry
alone it finds its full expression, for it is a quality of the
emotional nature (*Celestial Body* acting through *Mask*);
and creates all that is most beautiful in modern English
poetry from Blake to Arnold, all that is not a fading
echo. One discovers it in those symbolist writers who
like Verhaeren substitute an entirely personal wisdom
for the physical beauty or passionate emotion of the
fifteenth and sixteenth centuries. In painting it shows
most often where the aim has been archaistic, as though
it were an accompaniment of what the popular writers
call decadence, as though old emotions had first to
be exhausted. I think of the French portrait-painter
Ricard, to whom it was more a vision of the mind than
a research, for he would say to his sitter, "You are so
fortunate as to resemble your picture", and of Charles
Ricketts, my education in so many things. How often
his imagination moves stiffly as though in fancy dress,
and then there is something—Sphinx, Danaides—that
makes me remember Callimachus' return to Ionic
elaboration and shudder as though I stared into an
abyss full of eagles. Everywhere this vision, or rather
this contact, is faint or intermittent and it is always
fragile; Dickens was able with a single book, *Pickwick*,

to substitute for Jane Austen's privileged and perilous research the camaraderie of the inn parlour, qualities that every man might hope to possess, and it did not return till Henry James began to write.

Certain men have sought to express the new emotion through the *Creative Mind*, though fit instruments of expression do not yet exist, and so to establish, in the midst of our ever more abundant *primary* information, *antithetical* wisdom; but such men, Blake, Coventry Patmore at moments, Nietzsche, are full of morbid excitement and few in number, unlike those who, from Richardson to Tolstoi, from Hobbes down to Spencer, have grown in number and serenity. They were begotten in the Sistine Chapel and still dream that all can be transformed if they be but emphatic; yet Nietzsche, when the doctrine of the Eternal Recurrence drifts before his eyes, knows for an instant that nothing can be so transformed and is almost of the next gyre.

The period from 1875 to 1927 (Phase 22—in some countries and in some forms of thought the phase runs from 1815 to 1927) is like that from 1250 to 1300 (Phase 8) a period of abstraction, and like it also in that it is preceded and followed by abstraction. Phase 8 was preceded by the Schoolmen and followed by legalists and inquisitors, and Phase 22 was preceded by the great popularisers of physical science and economic science, and will be followed by social movements and applied science. Abstraction which began at Phase 19 will end at Phase 25, for these movements and this science will have for their object or result the elimination of intellect. Our generation has witnessed a first weariness, has stood at the climax, at what in *The Trembling of the Veil* I call *Hodos Chameliontos*, and when the climax passes will recognise that there common secular thought began to break and disperse. Tolstoi in *War and Peace* had still preference, could argue about this thing or that other, had a belief in Providence and a disbelief in Napoleon, but Flaubert in his *St. Anthony* had neither belief nor preference, and so it is that, even before the general surrender of the will, there came synthesis for its own sake, organisation where there is no masterful director, books where the author has disappeared, painting where some accomplished brush paints with an equal pleasure, or with a bored impartiality, the human form or an old bottle, dirty weather and clean sunshine. I too think of famous works where synthesis has been carried to the utmost limit possible, where there are elements of inconsequence or discovery of hitherto ignored ugliness, and I notice that when the limit is approached or past, when the moment of surrender is reached, when the new gyre begins to stir, I am filled with excitement. I think of recent mathematical research; even the ignorant can compare it with that of Newton—so plainly of the 19th Phase—with its objective world intelligible to intellect; I can recognise that the limit itself has become a new dimension, that this ever-hidden thing which makes us fold our hands has begun to press down upon multitudes. Having bruised their hands upon that limit, men, for the first time since the seventeenth century, see the world as an object of contemplation, not as something to be remade, and some few, meeting the limit in their special study, even doubt if there is any common experience, doubt the possibility of science.

.   .   .   .   .

Written at Capri, February 1925

THE END OF THE CYCLE

I

DAY after day I have sat in my chair turning a symbol over in my mind, exploring all its details, defining and again defining its elements, testing my convictions and those of others by its unity, attempting to substitute particulars for an abstraction like that of algebra. I have felt the convictions of a lifetime melt though at an age when the mind should be rigid, and others take their place, and these in turn give way to others. How far can I accept socialistic or communistic prophecies? I remember the decadence Balzac foretold to the Duchess de Castries. I remember debates in the little coach-house at Hammersmith or at Morris' supper-table afterwards. I remember the Apocalyptic dreams of the Japanese Saint and labour leader Kagawa, whose books were lent me by a Galway clergyman. I remember a Communist described by Captain White in his memoirs ploughing on the Cotswold Hills, nothing on his great hairy body but sandals and a pair of drawers, nothing in his head but Hegel's *Logic*. Then I draw myself up into the symbol and it seems as if I should know all if I could but banish such memories and find everything in the symbol.

II

But nothing comes—though this moment was to reward me for all my toil. Perhaps I am too old. Surely something would have come when I meditated under the direction of the Cabalists. What discords will drive

Europe to that artificial unity—only dry or drying sticks can be tied into a bundle—which is the decadence of every civilisation? How work out upon the phases the gradual coming and increase of the counter movement, the *antithetical* multiform influx:

> Should Jupiter and Saturn meet,
> O what a crop of mummy wheat!

Then I understand. I have already said all that can be said. The particulars are the work of the *thirteenth sphere* or cycle which is in every man and called by every man his freedom. Doubtless, for it can do all things and knows all things, it knows what it will do with its own freedom but it has kept the secret.

III

Shall we follow the image of Heracles that walks through the darkness bow in hand, or mount to that other Heracles, man, not image, he that has for his bride Hebe, "The daughter of Zeus, the mighty, and Hera, shod with gold"?

1934–1936

ALL SOULS' NIGHT

AN EPILOGUE

MIDNIGHT has come and the great Christ Church bell
And many a lesser bell sound through the room;
And it is All Souls' Night.
And two long glasses brimmed with muscatel
Bubble upon the table. A ghost may come;
For it is a ghost's right,
His element is so fine
Being sharpened by his death,
To drink from the wine-breath
While our gross palates drink from the whole wine.

I need some mind that, if the cannon sound
From every quarter of the world, can stay
Wound in mind's pondering,
As mummies in the mummy-cloth are wound;
Because I have a marvellous thing to say,
A certain marvellous thing
None but the living mock,
Though not for sober ear;
It may be all that hear
Should laugh and weep an hour upon the clock.

Horton's the first I call. He loved strange thought
And knew that sweet extremity of pride
That's called platonic love,
And that to such a pitch of passion wrought
Nothing could bring him, when his lady died,
Anodyne for his love.
Words were but wasted breath;
One dear hope had he:
The inclemency
Of that or the next winter would be death.

Two thoughts were so mixed up I could not tell
Whether of her or God he thought the most,
But think that his mind's eye,
When upward turned, on one sole image fell;
And that a slight companionable ghost,
Wild with divinity,
Had so lit up the whole
Immense miraculous house
The Bible promised us,
It seemed a gold-fish swimming in a bowl.

On Florence Emery I call the next,
Who finding the first wrinkles on a face
Admired and beautiful,
And by foreknowledge of the future vexed;
Diminished beauty, multiplied commonplace;
Preferred to teach a school
Away from neighbour or friend,
Among dark skins, and there
Permit foul years to wear
Hidden from eyesight to the unnoticed end.

Before that end much had she ravelled out
From a discourse in figurative speech
By some learned Indian
On the soul's journey. How it is whirled about
Wherever the orbit of the moon can reach,
Until it plunge into the sun;
And there, free and yet fast,
Being both Chance and Choice,
Forget its broken toys
And sink into its own delight at last.

I call MacGregor Mathers from his grave,
For in my first hard spring-time we were friends,
Although of late estranged.
I thought him half a lunatic, half knave,
And told him so, but friendship never ends;
And what if mind seem changed,

And it seem changed with the mind,
When thoughts rise up unbid
On generous things that he did
And I grow half contented to be blind!

He had much industry at setting out,
Much boisterous courage, before loneliness
Had driven him crazed ;
For meditations upon unknown thought
Make human intercourse grow less and less;
They are neither paid nor praised.
But he'd object to the host,
The glass because my glass;
A ghost-lover he was
And may have grown more arrogant being a ghost.

But names are nothing. What matter who it be,
So that his elements have grown so fine
The fume of muscatel
Can give his sharpened palate ecstasy
No living man can drink from the whole wine.
I have mummy truths to tell
Whereat the living mock,
Though not for sober ear,
For maybe all that hear
Should laugh and weep an hour upon the clock.

Such thought—such thought have I that hold it tight
Till meditation master all its parts,
Nothing can stay my glance
Until that glance run in the world's despite
To where the damned have howled away their hearts,
And where the blessed dance;
Such thought, that in it bound
I need no other thing,
Wound in mind's wandering
As mummies in the mummy-cloth are wound.

Oxford, Autumn 1920